AUTOBIOGRAPHY OF JAMES SILK BUCKINGHAM; (VOLUME 1)

AUTOBIOGRAPHY OF JAMES SILK BUCKINGHAM; (VOLUME 1)

James Silk Buckingham

www.General-Books.net

Publication Data:

Title: Autobiography of James Silk Buckingham;
Volume: 1
Author: Buckingham, James Silk, 1786-1855
Publisher: London : Longman, Brown, Green, and Longmans
Publication date: 1855

How We Made This Book for You
We made this book exclusively for you using patented Print on Demand technology.
First we scanned the original rare book using a robot which automatically flipped and photographed each page.
We automated the typing, proof reading and design of this book using Optical Character Recognition (OCR) software on the scanned copy. That let us keep your cost as low as possible.
If a book is very old, worn and the type is faded, this can result in typos or missing text. This is also why our books don't have illustrations; the OCR software can't distinguish between an illustration and a smudge.
We understand how annoying typos, missing text or illustrations, foot notes in the text or an index that doesn't work, can be. That's why we provide a free digital copy of most books exactly as they were originally published. Simply go to our website (www.general-books.net) to check availability. And we provide a free trial membership in our book club so you can get free copies of other editions or related books.
OCR is not a perfect solution but we feel it's more important to make books available for a low price than not at all. So we warn readers on our website and in the descriptions we provide to book sellers that our books don't have illustrations and may have typos or missing text. We also provide excerpts from each book to book sellers and on our website so you can preview the quality of the book before buying it.
If you would prefer that we manually type, proof read and design your book so that it's perfect, simply contact us for the cost. We would be happy to do as much work as you would be like to pay for.

Limit of Liability/Disclaimer of Warranty:
The publisher and author make no representations or warranties with respect to the accuracy or completeness of the book. The advice and strategies in the book may not be suitable for your situation. You should consult with a professional where appropriate. The publisher is not liable for any damages resulting from the book.
Please keep in mind that the book was written long ago; the information is not current. Furthermore, there may be typos, missing text or illustration and explained above.

AUTOBIOGRAPHY OF JAMES SILK BUCKINGHAM; (VOLUME 1)

-' I(mddrl, Langnian. C
   Ex Libris. K. OGDEN
   AUTOBIOGRAPHY
   JMES SILK BUCKINGHAM; INCLUDING HIS
   VOYAGES, TRAVELS, ADVENTURES, SPECULATIONS,
   SUCCESSES AND FAILURES,
   FAITHFULLY AND FEANKLT NABBATED; INTERSPERSED WITH
   CHARACTEEISTIC SKETCHES OF PUBLIC MEN
   WITH WHOM HE HAS HAD INTERCOURSE, DURING A PERIOD OF MORE THAN FIFTY YEARS.
   WITH A PORTRAIT.
   VOL. I.
   LONDON: LONGMAN, BROWN, GREEN, AND LONGMANS.
   1855.
   The Author of thix Work notifies that he reserves the right of translating it.
   ?8A3
   TT1=? TAT? Y
   UNIVER TTv OF ' TFORNIA

SANTA BARBARA
PREFACE.

This Book will surprise many, and entertain, it is hoped, not a few; but, above all, it will help to instruct the humblest of its readers in one of the most important lessons adapted to their condition namely, that there is no obscurity of birth, no privation of property, and no opposition either of powerful individuals, or still more powerful public bodies and governments, that may not be overcome, by industry, integrity, zeal, and perseverance; no depth of misfortune, from which the victim may not hope to emerge, by labour, economy, temperance, and that single-mindedness which regards the faithful discharge of duty as the great object to which all others must be made subordinate.

In illustration of this truth, these pages will contain a full, frank, and impartial detail of the prin- cipal events of my life, in all its varied vicissitudes of extreme want and abundant wealth; of original obscurity and subsequent popularity; of perilous adventures by sea and land, over a range of some of the most interesting countries of the globe; of enterprises and speculations, successes and failures; of projects still regarded as Utopian, and of others happily realised; of personal intercourse with some of the very lowest classes of mankind, and of interviews, banquets, and entertainments in the palaces of kings, princes, and potentates. The work will also be interspersed with delineations of the characters of a host of public men, in our own and other countries, with whom, in the long course of half a century, it has been my lot to become acquainted; accompanied by an exposition of some of the secret springs of conduct, in striking contrast with the public motives avowed by many of the most prominent actors in the great drama of political life, in clubs, senates, and cabinets. I dedicate the work to no patron, but offer it to the consideration and judgment of my countrymen at large; and shall be amply rewarded for the labour of its composition, if its wide diffusion shall bring it within the reach of the classes most likely to need its teachings, and to profit by its example. May it help to rouse them from the apathy which is the usual accompaniment of hopeless toil, and inspire them with an ambition to elevate themselves by their own efforts, so as to end their lives with a pleasing retrospect of progress made, and a well founded belief that they will leave the world something better than they found it, by their labours to promote improvement in the health, wealth, knowledge, and virtue of their contemporaries, as the best legacy that can be left to those who are to come after them.

J. S. BUCKINGHAM.
Stanhope Lodge,
St. John's Wood.
VIII
CONTENTS.
CHAP. ni.
Page
My going to sea at length determined on- 45
Sent accordingly to a Naval Academy at Falmouth 46
Contemporaries at this school, and characteristic portraits 48
Early victim of love. Eomantic display of passion 50

First conception of religious feelings and views 54
Attractions of a sea-life absorbing all others- 57
Appointed to the Lady Harriett, at nine years old 58
Fu'st outfit for sea: pride and delight in the costume-. 61
Ambition to excel in all boat evolutions 61
Preparations for departm-e on my first voyage to Lisbon 62
Mercantile adventure for trading with the Portuguese 63
CHAP. IV.

Sailing from Falmouth, after adieus and struggles First impressions of the grandeur of the Ocean Coasting along the shores of Spain and Portugal Enti-ance to Lisbon, bar of the Tagus Escort of Guarda-Costas, or revenue vessels-Magnificent aspect of the Portuguese capital-Singular scene of official smuggling-Peculiarities of th Portuguese Population Public edifices and other objects of interest Opportunities for reading afforded at sea

CHAP. V.

Second voyage to Lisbon in the same ship- ' Anecdote of a celebrated Portuguese wrestler Encounter with this hero, and his triumph Singular mode of enforcing payment of debt-Efficiency of this maritime machinery of justice Splendid barge of the Queen of Portugal Bathing parties of ladies and gentlemen of the court Reminiscence of Cleopatra's voyage on the Cydnus Free manners of the Court and general society Sacred names of wine-shops and ships of war-Anecdote of a smuggler and revenue searcher Enthusiastic enjoyments of seamen on shore-

CHAP. VI.

Page
Disastrous issue of my third voyage to Lisbon 91
Ludicrous anecdote of a pretended interpreter 92
Capture by a French corvette. English mutineers 93
Seamen from the English frigate Hermione among the crew 95
Confinement of prisoners in the ship's hold. Suffocation 96
Short supply of water, and increased difficulties of drinking 97
Arrival at the Spanish port of Corunna, at ten years old 100 Imprisonment there, and scanty supplies of food 102
Love adventure with the daughter of the Superintendant 103
Orders for our release, to march to Oporto and Lisbon 105
General joy at the prospect of regaining our liberty 105
CHAP. vn.

Setting out on our march through Galicia- io7
Description of oxir party. Scanty travelling allowance 109
Scenery of the way. Benevolence of Spanish women 109
Lodging in stables. Costiune and manners of muleteers 111
Fires lighted to defend us fi"om wolves on the snowy mountains 112
Kindness of the seamen towards ladies and children 114
Arrival at the city of Santiago di Compostella 115
Midnight serenade of a Sijanish lover- 116
Journey to Vigo, Fraternisation of Spanish and English sailors 118

March to Oporto. Frontiers of Spain and Portugal 121
Descrijition of Oporto, Coimbra, and Abrantes 126
Descent of the Tagus from Santarem to Lisbon 130
CHAP. VHL
The English fleet of Sir John Jervis entering the Tagus 131
Followed by the prizes taken by him off Cape St. Vincent 131 Impressment of our own party by the ships of war 132
Embark in the Prince of Wales packet for England 133
Reluctance of my mother to permit me to go to sea again 134
Happy stay at home after my captivity- 134
Placed with a Bookseller at Plymouth Dock 135
Life led there. Association with naval ofiicers 135
Page
Extravagant expenditure. Story of a Negro cook 138
Visits to the Theatre. Composition of a five act Drama 140
Keasons for its not being presented for representation 141
CHAP. IX.
Complete change in the cun-ent of my life- 143
Sincere repentance. Strong religions impressions 143 Intense study of controversial divinity. 145
Conviction of the truth of Calvinistic doctrines 145
Public baptism in the meeting-house of Devonport 146
Practical illustration of Infant Baptism- 147
Public preaching in the pulpit at fifteen years of age 149 Intimacy with the Kev, Dr. Hawker, of Plymouth 150
Gradual relaxation and relapse into woi'ldliness 151
Revival of my passion for a sea-life again- 152
Entry as a volunteer on board a ship of war- 152
Severe discipline. Prequent and capricious punishments 153
Horrid sjiectacle of a deserter flogged round the fleet 154
Eisked a similar fate, by running from the ship 159
Successful concealment and disguise, and final escape 160
Safe arrival once more in the bosom of my family 162
Attempt to induce me to follow the profession of the Law 163
CHAP. X.
Life of ease and pleasure passed on shore- 165
Cultivation of music, and passion for the art- 165
Remarkable history of a Negro musician- 166
Liberality of London composers and artists towards him 170
Voyage of recreation and amusement to the Scilly Islands 172
Singularly primitive state of society there- 174
Voyage from Scilly to Milford Haven- 177
Agreeable associations, and gay life and manners 178
Death of my dear mother while absent here. Speedy return home 179 Property left in trust. Love at first sight. Marriage at nineteen 180

Establislmient of a Bookselling and Nautical Depot at Falmouth 185
Sudden destruction of all our promising prospects 187
CONTENTS. XI CHAP, XI.
Page
Determination to resume my original Sea-life 190
First visit to London to seek for a berth- 190
Landing at Dover. Exorbitant charges. Ship Hotel 191
Journey on foot to London. First impressions 191
Cheap lodging in a humble garret, at 2s. 6c. a week 192
Accidental visit to the British Forum in Piccadilly 192
Speech there. Introduction to John Gale Jones 195
Visit to an Amateur Theatre. Eidiculous scene there 197
An evening passed in the Fleet Prison Mock Election 199
Profligate manners, and demoralizing effects- 201
CHAP. XIL
Delay in the arrival of an expected ship. 203
Procure employment in a London printing office 204
Disgust at London life and dissipated associates 204
"Went into the country to escape from the contagion 205
Peach Oxford, and get lodgings at Is. 6f. per week 205
Obtain employment in the Clarendon Printing Office 206
Anecdote of students altering the marriage service 206
Return to London, and joined there by my family 208
Privations suffered. Acquaintance with Captain Horsburgh 209
Correcting the press for his East India Navigators' Directory 210
Arrival of the long-expected ship from the West Indies 210
Appointed chief officer of the William Ferming, for Port an Prince 211
Lines addressed to my wife on parting- 212
Sudden change in our destination– 215
Transferred to the Titus, bound for Trinidad 215
CHAP. XIII.
First voyage to the West Indies in the Titus- 216
Early captui-e by La Josephine, French privateer 216
Release, after being plundered and stripped- 216
Leisure at sea, and books read in the watches below 218
Recollections of Trinidad. Agreeable French society 220
Deplorable condition of most of the Negro Slaves 221
Advocate their Emancipation at some risk- 221 xn CONTENTS.
Paffc
Sir "Walter Scott's poetical description of the Orinoco 223
Departure on the homeward voyage to England 224
Squally weather in beating up the windwai-d passage 224
Mesmeric trance, and unconscious writing of poetry 225
"Starboard Watch! ahoy! " set to music- 226
Tremendous hurricane on the banks of Newfoundland 228

Wreck and devastation in the fleet— 231
Severe suffering. Circular theory of storms- 233
Safe arrival in the Thames—- 234
CHAP. XIV.
Portuguese merchants from Lisbon and Oporto 236 Instance of tyranny and cruelty in Impressment 237 Impossibility of obtaining redress for such wrongs 239
Visit to the church of the celebrated Joanna Southcott 240
Pictures and Peculiarities seen and learnt there 241
Pregnancy on the expected Shiloh. Passports for heaven 242
Exhibition of Guuy the prize-fighter as champion of England 244
Visit to the Plough public-house kept by him 244
Striking contrast in his condition in after life- 245
Meeting with him at the seat of Earl Eitzwilliam 245
Himself and his daughters " the observed of all observers " 246
Entered as a member of the Koyal Naval Lodge of Freemasons 248
Enthusiastic attention to the duties of the craft 249
CHAP. XV.
Voyage to Virginia, in America, in the ship Rising States 250
Long and stormy passage in the autumn of the year 252
Entry of the Chesapeake and arrival at Norfolk 253
Acquaintance with American naval ofiicers-. 254
Comparison between the naval services of England and America 254
Agreeable society in some of the families on shore 256
Many drawbacks from slavery and its accompaniments 257
Excursion to the Dismal Swamp. Poetic legend 258 Impressions of Moore's poems just then published 259
Detention at Norfolk. Non-intercourse with England 261
Amateur theatrical performance for the benefit of seamen 261
Page
Crew of the Jiising States. Old Testament names 264
Escape of a Virginia Nightingale. Lines to its companion 206
Safe arrival in England, and happy reception 268
CHAP. XVI.
First appointment as Captain of a West Indiaman, at twenty-one 269
Departure for the Island of Ncav Providence- 270
Feeling of responsibility greatly increased- 270
Regulations of discipline for officers and crew 271
Sailed with a fleet of 300 sail from the Downs 273
Anecdote of a passenger's notions of geography 274
Circular whuiwind or white squall encountered 276
Midnight alarm, "The Devil is in the main-top " 277
Capture of a magnificent Osprey, or Sea Eagle 278
Escape of the prize, and deep regret at our loss 279
Safe arrival in the beautiful harbour of Nassau 282
CHAP. XVII.

First entertainment at a military mess-room-. 283
Agreeable society among the civil authorities 284
Dinners, balls, and suppers in constant succession 285
Singular septennial celebi'ation of a marriage 286
Trade of the Bahamas with the Spanish Main 287
Manner of conducting the smuggling or contraband 288
Description of the parties engaged in this trafse 288
Division of profits between smugglers, priests, and revenue officers 29 0
Reminiscences of the old English buccaneers- 291
Portrait of one of the last remaining specimens 291
Wreckers, their character, occupation, and gains 292
CHAP. XVIII.
Homeward voyage fi-om the Bahama Islands- 294
Rapid sailing. American models. Clipper ships 295
Absurdity of the ancient rules for measuring tonnage 295
Cause of the general ugliness of old Enghsh vessels 296
Anecdote of a slow-sailing ship of Bristol- 296
Entry into the British Channel in mid-winter- 298
Running fight with a French privateer off Dungeness 299
Page
Drifted on the French coast. Fired at from the batteries 301
Lost a cable and anchor on a wreck at the Goodwin Sands 303
Driven into the North Sea. Heai gales and long nights 304
Deliberation as to running into the Texel and becoming prisoners 304
Breaking of the gale, and safe run for England 305
Lines written on the occasion to the air " All's Well," 306
Hazardous passage through the Swin Channel 308
CHAP. XIX.
Association with captains, merchants, and ship-owners 312
State of society and manners among these classes 313
Softening and refining influences of female society 314
Practices of ship-owners versfs underwriters- 315 Interest of both parties in increase of shipwrecks 317 Illustrations of the working of this in practice 318
Resignation of my command of the Surrey, and reasons why 321
Appointment to the command of a new ship, the TFi78a? 321
Preparations for a voyage to the Mediterranean 321
French society in London contrasted with English 321
Dinner-party Habit of a learned Oiientalist 322
First dinner with lawyers in chambers at Gray's Inn 324
Shipment of the crew Crimps and their odious practices 326
Procurement of a Mediterranean pass. Humiliating policy 329
Anecdote of suimnary justice on a Wapping lawyer 333
CHAP. XX.
Anticipations and preparations for the Mediterranean 337
Departure from Portsmouth. Farewell lines- 333

Voyage along the coasts of Spain and Portugal 340
Cape St. Vincent. Victory of Sir John Jervis 341
Sagres, the early seat of Portuguese enterprise 342
The Lusiad of Camoens, and his romantic history 343
Straits of Gibraltar. Tariffa and Trafalgar- 346
Description of the bay and town of Gibraltar 348 Immense strength of its rock-hewn batteries- 349
Variety of character and costume in its inhabitants 350
Brief sketch of the sieges of Gibraltar- 354
CONTENTS.
Redeeming traits of humanity to prisoners Lady Mary "Wortley Montague on War Franklin's Apologue on the same subject
Page 357
CHAP. XXI.
Departure from Gibraltar for Malta-
Mountains of Europe and Africa. Ancient lake Constant currents inward from the Atlantic-Equal supply from the Euxine and from large rivers-Theories of evaporation and under currents Opposite coasts of Spain and Numidia Classical reminiscences Hippo Regius. Carthage-Anecdote of a naval captain's caprices Impress of officers and seamen, and their restitution-Arrival at Malta. Harbour of St. Paul Imposing entrance of the port of La Valetta-Stay at Malta. Brief notices of the island Remarkable instance of cruelty and siiperstition Bi'itish influence on native character and society Manners of private life and entertainments

CHAP. XXII.
Departure from Malta for the Archipelago. 353
First sight of the shores of Greece. The Morea 384 Island of Cerigo or Cythera. The birth of Venus 386
Pirates of Greeks and renegades of all nations 386 Islands of Falconera and IMilo. Surrounding scenery 388
The "Shipwreck" of Falconer. Similarity of feeling 389
Enter the harbour of Milo for a Greek pilot 389
Greek visitors. Hatred of Turks Attachment to Russia 390
Excursion to the town of Milo on the mountain 391
Patriarchal state of society and manners. 393 Incident between an English lady and a Greek mother 394
Expensivcness of female costume. Family garments 396
First acquisition for forming an antiquarian taste 398
Voyage through the Mgean Sea Crowded impressions 399
AUTOBIOGRAPHY
JAMES SILK BUCKINGHAM.
CHAPTER I.
Reasons for writing this Autobiography. Outline sketch of its proposed character and contents. Birth, Parentage, and Family Portraits. Earliest aspirations after a sea life. Squadrons of Sir Edward Pellew and Sir John Warren. Gaiety of the harbour of Falmouth and village of Flushing. Boat-racing, and sailing of frigates and packets.

Efforts to check my fondness for the sea. Description of a village school in Devonshire. Death of my father, and return from school. Rising of the Cornish mlnei's for cheap bread. Striking incident in suppressing a riot. Early Intimacy with Quakers, retained through life. Rural sports, and farmhouse manners in early days.

Seveeal reasons induce me to write my own biography, the most prominent of which are the following: Istj a conviction that few public men have been more misrepresented than myself; sometimes from ignorance, but more frequently from political and party motives, by those to whose interests my views

VOL. I. B were thought to be opposed 2d 3 a belief that there are few persons now living who have seen more of the various countries and inhabitants of the globe, and few who have experienced greater vicissitudes of fortune than I have done; having passed through the phases of prosperity and adversity in both their extremes 3rdlj, a desire to encourage others about to begin life, by showing the beneficial results of industry, temperance, and perseverance, in surmounting the greatest difficulties and, 4thly, a wish to leave behind me, for the consideration of posterity, my deliberate views as to many of the evils which still impede the progress of improvement in society; to indicate their causes, suggest their remedies, and thus assist, to the extent at least of my limited power, towards that social reform for which so many hearts are yearning in all ranks and among all classes of my fellow countrymen.

Having commenced active life at the early age of nine years, and being now nearly seventy, the retrospect will present a long series of varied events. But though garrulity is tliought to be an invariable accompaniment of age, I shall endeavour to place a check on this disposition, and select from among the incidents of my life those only which may be considered essential to the completeness of the narrative, explanatory of some undertaking to be described, or illustrative of some opinions wliicli would not be so intelligible without them.

My voyages by sea and travels by land will necessarily form a part of the whole; though these will be given in a more abridged form than when they were first issued to the world, and others will be added that have never yet been published. My projects, speculations, and adventures, which have been more numerous than those of most men, and the varied fortunes of success or failure which attended them, will be succinctly and faithfully recorded. My aim, indeed, will be to place the readers of these memoirs as much as possible in the position of personal friends or companions, making them the depositories of all my own information, and the confidants of my most friendly intercourse, so that at the end of our mutual journey through life, if they accompany me so far, they may have as complete a knowledge of my history, character, and opinions as I have myself; and thus be enabled to participate in whatever benefit mv long and varied experience has brought to me, by adding it to their own. With this brief explanation of my motives and designs, I commence at once tho story of my life.

I was born on the 25tli of August, 1786, in the pretty little marine village of Flushing, within the harbour, and just opposite to the town of Falmouth. My parents had neither high birth, great wealth, nor local influence to give them importance; though they were possessed of a moderate competency, and lived in friendly communication with the principal inhabitants of the place. My father, whose name was Christopher, was a native of Barnstaple in Devonshire, and both he and all his ancestors, as far as they could be traced back to the days of Elizabeth, were sailors or seafarincr men: one havins been an officer in the fleet that discomfited the great Spanish Armada, another having been drowned in the Thunderer, man-of-war, and others having been either in the naval or merchant service, from which last my father had retired with what he deemed a moderate sufficiency. He passed the remainder of his days in the enjoyment of his sailing, rowing, and fishing boats, in which he took great pride, as well as in his fields and orchards, of which he had several; and the improvement of his farm and live stock, with the pleasures of his dogs and guns, of which he was passionately fond, formed a union of summer and winter pastime which agreeably filled up the year.

My mother, whose name was Thomazine, was a native of Bodmin in Cornwall; and as Miss Hambly, of that ancient parliamentary borough, was regarded as a belle in her youth, which may well be credited, as she w as, unquestionably, the handsomest old lady in Flushing, in her declining years.

Both of these were decidedly of the old school, in politics, sentiments, and manners. My father wore a cocked hat, then worn by persons in private life, though since confined to naval, military, or official ranks; a long square-tailed coat, with large buttons on the pockets and sleeves; square-toed shoes, with massive silver buckles, and a tall gold-headed cane: in short, such a costume as one now sees only on the stage, as characterising the reigns of Queen Anne and the first Georges. My mother, too, wore the large stiff" quilted satin petticoat, with the dress open in front, to display, on a lighter ground, the rich pattern of a lace apron, with a stately stomacher, and high cap, enclosing the oval face in a close frame, and strikingly becoming her fine features.

My father died when I was between seven and eight years old; my mother so grieved for his loss, that her health was never good afterwards, and in a few years she followed him to the grave, leaving a family of three sons and four daughters to mourn their loss. Of all these I was the youngest, and as was generally believed, the favourite; and as my two eldei' brothers were grown up men, and eaeli engaged in mercantile business on their own account, while my two elder sisters were comfortably married and settled, the property left by our deceased parents, consisting of mines, lands, houses, and some shares in the fisheries of the county, was divided equally amoncr the three vouno; er children.

All the recollections of my youth, from the earliest period to which I can carry them back, up to the time of my first going to sea, are agreeable. The village of Flushing was then inhabited by a remarkable collection of persons and families. The port of Falmouth being the nearest to the entrance of the British Channel, there were permanently stationed here two squadrons of frigates, one under the command of Sir Edward Pellew (afterwards Lord Ex-mouth), the other under the command of Sir John Borlase Warren. The former, as commodore, hoisted his broad pennant in the Indefatigable, the latter in the Revolutionnaire. Each squadron consisted of five frigates, of 32 and 44 guns each; and, in addition to these, there were continually arriving and departing from Carrick roads, the outer anchorage of Falmouth, line-of-battle ships, and smaller vessels of war: while prizes taken from the French some, after hard-fought battles, as it was during the most enthusiastic period of the first revolutionary war, were constantly brought into the port for adjudication and sale. There were two large prisons, with open courts, for the reception of the French prisoners, thus taken; one at Tregel-lick, the other at Roscrow, both near the borough of Penryn, at the head of Falmouth harbour, and every month added many to their inmates.

Both the naval commodores, as well as such captains of the frigates belonging to the squadrons as were married, had their families residing at Flushing, and the numerous officers of different grades, from the youngest midshipman to the first lieutenant, were continually coming and going to and fro; so that there would be sometimes a dozen men of wars' boats at the quay at the same time, including the barges for the commanding officers, and the cutters, gigs, launches, and jolly boats on duty; the boats' crews mostly dressed in dashing marine trim, with blue jackets and trowsers, and bright scarlet waistcoats, overlaid with gilt buttons, in winter; and striped Guernsey frocks and white flowing trowsers in summer; while the streets of the little village literally sparkled with gold epaulets, gold lace hats, and brilliant uniforms.

In addition to these squadrons of the navy, Falmouth was also then enriched and enlivened by the presence of a fleet of handsome mail packets, in the service of the Post Office, including from thirty to forty full rigged three-masted ships, small in size, but of the most elegant models built, indeed, exclusively for speed and passage accommodation, carrying the royal pennant, as the ships of war; the officers all wearing handsome uniforms, and the crews being picked men, well-dressed and generally young and handsome, the service being so popular that it was a matter of great difficulty to get into it. Both officers and men often made large fortunes by the private contraband trade which they carried on, under the protection of their being in Government ships, and therefore free from the search of the Customs-and Excise, both in the export of British manufactures, which they smuggled into Spain and Portugal, America, and the Spanish possessions of the West Indies, and in the imports into England of wine, spirits, and tobacco, in large quantities, every voyage, which they also smuggled ashore, and on which they made immense gains, from thus avoiding the payment of duty.

The greater number of the captains and officers of these packets, as well as most of their crews, lived also at Flushing; and so added to the wealth and elegance of the place, that, at the period adverted to, between 1790 and 1795, thei e was probably no spot in England, in which, on so limited a siirface and among so small a number in the aggregate, were to be seen so much of the gaiety and elegance of life as in this little village. Dinners, balls, and evening-parties were held at some one or other of the captains' houses every evening; and not a night passed in which there was not three or four dances at least at the more humble places of resort for the sailors and their favourite lasses. The ample supplies of wages and prize money furnished all the naval officers and men with abundant means to meet every demand, and the profits of the officers and crews of the Government packets were not at all less abundant. Marriages were events of weekly occurrence, and scarcely a Sunday ever passed without more than one celebration of this always interesting and attractive rite at the parish church of Mylor, distant about a mile and a half from the village; and involving, therefore, either carriages or pedestrian processions, with white ribbons, and a joyous and happy crowd in their train.

Passing, therefore, my infancy and youth amidst such scenes as these, having been born in a house which was literally washed by the sea, and from the windows overhanging which I had often leaped into it from a height of ten or twelve feet at liigli water.

with a rowing or a sailing boat moored within a stone's throw of the steps leading from our dwelling to the sea, and scarcely a day passing without mj being two or three hours rowing or sailing upon it, no one will wonder that I had a strong and unconquerable predilection for a sea life, and that this passion grew Avitli my growth and strengthened with my strength.

One of my earliest recollections is that of having been placed to sit beside my father, as he steered his own boat, an eight-oared cutter, in a contest with about a dozen others: and when we won the race by less than a boat's length, by the almost superhuman efforts of a most enthusiastic crew, I do not think there was a heart in any of their bosoms that beat with more intense enjoyment than my own; so that when they announced their victory by three lusty English cheers, I stood up in the stern-sheets of the boat, Avaved my little cap with all the triumph of a victor, and made the shrill treble of my infant voice distinguishable amid the tenors and hoarse bass of the veterans by whom the race was won.

Another of my early recollections was this. According to the good old fashion of these bygone times, ray mother's female servants had all been with her from the day of her marriage till the hour of her death, with two exceptions only; these two, after living with her, the one fourteen, and the other sixteen years, having married, one the coxswain of Sir Edward Pellew's barge, and the other, one of the seamen of Sir John Borlase Warren's squadron. By one of these, whose special duty it was to take the children out in fine weather, I was carried to the bowling-green, a beautiful field on the platform of a hill that overlooks the whole harbour and extends the view outside of Pendennis Castle, which guards the entrance, as far west as the remotest visible promontory, called the Manacles. One of the packets destined for the West Indies had just fired her gun, and hoisted her signal for sailing, as we reached the summit. She soon quitted her mooring, and with a favourino; breeze stood out of the harbour under full sail. The servant linajered till the vessel had reached the Manacles, when speedily she disappeared behind the promontory and was lost in the distance. The truth is, her lover was among the crew; and, like " black-eyed Susan," she had a tear to drop for his departure, and waved her handkerchief long after it was possible to perceive it from the ship's deck.

I asked her what was beyond the Manacles, where the ship had disappeared? to which she answered, that there was nothing but sea and sky for many long and weary weeks, till the ship should reach the "West Indies. I remember, as distinctly as if it happened only yesterday, that this vague uncertainty kindled in my infant breast an intense desire to go and see for myself, whether this assertion, which seemed to me so strange, were true or not; and by often dwelling on this idea, the spark was soon fanned into a flame, till it kindled in me an irrepressible desire to become a sailor, and traverse this long and watery space to see the distant Indies.

To check this growing fondness for the sea, which manifested itself in various ways, it was determined that I should be sent to some school at a distance from home, and completely inland, in the hope that I might thus be weaned from my maritime propensities. I was accordingly hurried off, when about seven years old, to a small village, called Hubbarton, some ten or twelve miles from Plymouth, and there placed under the care of a Mr. Scott, who kept an academy for boys, of which I was the youngest among some sixty or seventy. This was a source of great misery to me, and during the year I remained here, I think I suffered more real and intense grief than during any similar period of my life. The master was a tymnt, the ushers almost worse, and the big boys tyrannised over the little ones to an insufferable degree, the example of their teachers being not onlv copied by them but exceeded. The food was so scantily supplied, that though in general revolting in its quality and cooking, bands of hungry boys often leagued together, to descend from their beds in the middle of the night, and rob the pantry of whatever it contained, often wranglino; for the division of the spoil, but devouring it all before they resumed their sleep. The beds were hard, the clothing coarse and insufficient, and two and sometimes three boys slept together. TJie tasks imposed as punishments were most irksome; such as repeating from memory some of the hardest chapters in the Bible, which caused the Sacred Book to be regarded with anything but reverence. We made occasional excursions to Ivy Bridge, to Modbury, to Muddicombe Bay, and other places near, but they gave me no pleasure. The most exciting events that occurred were either single fights between the boys of our own school, which were of daily occurrence, though both the combatants were sure to be well flogged by the chief usher when the contest was over, without any inquiry as to who was the aggressor; or else regular pitched battles between all the boys of our own school, and all the boys of a rival establishment: the scene of which was generally the churchyard, or the brow of a hill rising from the lower part of the town. On such occasions, heaps of stones and other missiles were stored up for action, and the great object of each party was to gain the vantage ground of the upper part of the hill just outside the yard, and make a rush like the charge of cavalry, so as to knock down as many of the enemy as possible by the impetus. No interference of masters or constables, as far as I can recollect, ever took place to separate the combatants; and the teachers either took part themselves in the fray, or hallooed on and encouraged their respective pupils: and as the numbers and ages of the combatants were generally pretty equal, the fights were often hard-contested, and many cracked heads, bloody noses, torn garments, and severe bruises were pretty equally divided among the belligerents. Such were some country boarding-schools " sixty years since."

At the end of about a year, this miserable state of exile and suffering was at length terminated by a very painful event the death of my dear father. This took place so suddenly, that I could not be got home to see him before his death; but though I grieved deeply for his loss, I had some compensation in the welcome news that I was to leave school at the termination of the next quarter. Never did poor pi'isoner, whether in the Bastile or the Inquisition, rejoice more sincerely than I did, when tlie day arrived for my leaving Hubbarton for ever, and returning once more to my happy home.

Here I remained again my own master, and enjoyed my freedom with the greater zest because of the privations and restraints under which I had laboured for the last year; I thus became gradually more and more bold and adventurous in all the boyish games of an athletic kind, in wrestling, swimming, and boating especially, in which

I had long enjoyed a sort of supremacy, and was as anxious as any champion in the chivalrous ages to maintain it against all rivals or competitors.

In consequence of the war Yith France, and other causes of scarcity, corn rose to a high price: and the miners of Cornwall, or "tinners" as they are pro-vincially called, a most numerous and determined body, roamed over the country, waging war against all forestallers, regraters, and hoarders of grain, demanding bread at the old peace prices, and demolishing bakers' shops, mills, and grain stores, and being too formidable to be opposed by any civil or military force then at hand. These were the race of men who, according to the old song, when a Trelawney was consigned to the Tower, exclaimed

"And shall Trelawney die? Then twenty thousand Cornish men Will know the reason why."

A body of some three or four hundred of these men visited Flushing, and as they were all dressed in the mud-stained smock-frocks and trowsers in which they worked under ground, all armed with large clubs and sticks of various kinds, and speaking an vmcouth jargon, which none but themselves could understand, they struck terror wherever they went, and seemed like an irruption of barbarians invading some more civilised country than their own. Their numbers were quite equal to the whole adult male population of the little village, so that the men stood aghast, the women retired into their houses and closed their doors, and the children all seemed to be struck dumb with aflpriiiht. The moment of their visit, too, was most inopportune; for on that very day a large party of the captains and officers of the packets, residing at Flushing, were occupied in storing a cargo of grain, that had just been discharged from a coasting vessel at the quay, and locking it up in warehouses, to secure it from general plunder. Among these guardians of the public weal so occupied, I remember particularly Captains Schuyler, Braithwaite, Wauchop, James,

Ker, Kempthorne, and others; the ships of war being all absent on their cruising grounds, so that every one apprehended an attack, resistance, and bloodshed.

Fortunately a very trifling incident so turned the tide of feeling, tliat almost in a few minutes the rising tempest had subsided into calm. A few boys about my own age and myself, taking courage from our companionship, and strongly stimulated by curiosity, went towards the warehouse where these captains were collected, and where the grain was being stored away, a body of the " tinners" being there remonstrating against the act. Captain Kempthorne, an old friend of my father's, and with whom I had always been a great favourite, seeing me in the group of boys, came to me, took me up in his arms, and planting me on one of the sacks of corn then leaninc; against the wall, bade me give out a hymn which he had often heard me do before for I had nearly all Dr. Watts's collection by heart and having an excellent voice, with some ear and great fondness for music, I was equally acquainted with the most popular of the hymn tunes. I asked him, "Which hymn?" He replied, ' Any one will do; but be quick, and also pitch the tune." The captain then called out, "Silence, for a hymn!" and the " tinners," struck with the

VOL. I. C appeal, hushed their murmurs, and took off their hats and cajdS, as if attending worship. The first verse of the hymn was as follows; one of the most popular for its Avords and tune among all classes:

"Salvation! oh! the joyful sound, ' Tis music to our ears: A sovereiffn bahn for every wound, A cordial for our fears."

As almost the whole body of the miners were at this period followers of Wesley, and many extremely devout, they joined in the simple melody of the hymn, verse by verse, as it was given out, and at its close again covered their heads and retired in peace, crossing the ferry to Falmouth in the boats that brought them over, and relieving all the villagers from any further apprehension.

Great was the satisfaction of the captains at the success of this simple but effectual breakwater, thus extemporised on the spot. I was rewarded with a capful of sixpences, shillings, and half crowns, to an amount I had never before possessed, and hastened home with my suddenly acquired treasure, to place it in my dear mother's keeping

Another of mv earliest recollections is that of a pleasant time passed at the farm house of Trevism, between Flushing and Penryn, then occupied by the family of Farmer Elliott. I was sent there when about six years old, for a few weeks, to be inoculated for the small-pox; Dr. Jenner's invaluable discovery of vaccine not having yet spread in practice so far as Cornwall. The operation was performed by a worthy Quaker, Dr. Fox of Falmouth, and I was put to read aloud a chapter In the Bible to prevent my observing the preparation for the puncture, which was so suddenly and unexpectedly made, that I was saved all the pain of apprehension, which is generally greater than that of the wound itself. I may here remark that all the children of my mother, seven In number, had been brought into the world by Dr. Fox, who was the accoucheur and medical adviser of the family for twenty years and more. My eldest brother, who had been educated abroad, and had visited France, Holland, Germany, Sweden, Denmark, Russia, Spain, and Portugal, In a mercantile capacity, and who was therefore well acquainted with the languages of these countries, was for some years attached as Interpreter to the firm of George Croker Fox and Sons, at Falmouth, who were consuls and agents for half a dozen different nations, and nearly all the Quakers In Cornwall were well known to our family. It Is equally remarkable that In after life my acquaintance with the leading men of this worthy and estimable body, the Society of Friends, has been very extensive, as I enjoyed the intimate friendship of Thomas Clarkson, William Allen, Joseph John Gurney, James Cropper, Robert Benson, Isaac Crewdsen, Richard Ball, Jonathan Priestman, Isaac Whitwell, Joseph Pease, Richard Dykes Alexander, Joseph Sturge, Robert Charlton, William Janson, Joseph Eaton, Samuel Gurney, and many others, from their sympathy with those objects to which my subsequent labours were chiefly devoted; such as the abolition of slavery, the opening of free trade with China, the colonisation of India, the substitution of arbitration for the settlement of national quarrels instead of war, the universal education of the poor; and other philanthropic enterprises, to Avhich, as a body, the Quakers devote more time, labour, and money, than double or treble their number in any other class or sect of the community.

My stay at Trevism Farm was rendered the more agreeable from the then existing state of relations between masters and men, which has long since disappeared. At that period, all the married labourers on the farm lived in neat and tidy cottages near the farm-house, and their wives and children were objects of continual solicitude and care to their employers, the wife and daughters generally looking in upon them once in every daj, taking an interest in their health and domestic affairs, sometimes drinking tea with them in the evenings, and always inviting them to the farm-house on every festive occasion., The unmarried labourers lived in the farmer's family, and took their meals regularly with the master and mistress, who sat at the head and foot of the table, and helped them all round as though they had been their children, taking breakfast at six or seven in the morning, dinner at twelve, and tea or supper at the close of the day's labour, when they all passed the evening together in innocent games, and lively and modest conversation. On Sundays they accompanied their masters and mistresses to the parish church, and were always clean and well-dressed. There were then neither beer-shops nor gin-shops anywhere within reach; tobacco smoking and after-dinner drinking were confined to the upper classes; and the general characteristic of a farm labourer was, then, an erect and muscular figure, full and rosy cheeks, bright eyes, and a manly but yet most respectful demeanour: while farmers' wives and children were among the most healthy looking and blooming of the whole community. The war and its high prices of corn turned the farmers into gentlemen, enabled them to keep hunters, to drink port wine, and discard their ancient simplicity of manners: while farmers' wives set up for ladies, and their daughters were sent to boarding schools to learn music and dancing. The farm labourers soon becoming unsuitable companions at the family board, were sent off to live out of the house as they best could; and from that day to this there seems to have been a progressive deterioration in their physical health and appearance, their morals, and their manners, which the late infliction of beer-shops in every village has aggravated in a great degree.

In those early days also, the town population, at least of the neighbourhood of Falmouth, were as great lovers of rural sports as the peasantry themselves. On May-day in every year, large parties of fifty or sixty persons, of all ages and both sexes, would be up at day-light, and having previously prepared all the materials for their visit, would form a procession from riushing, the men in their best trim, and the women and girls all in white, preceded by music and garlands formed of flowers, birds' eggs, gilding, and ribbons, would wend their way for two or three miles to such farm-house as they might have previously bespoken, arrive therein time for an early breakfast, pass the day in perambulating the fields and gardens, dine early in groups or sections, in the afternoon have rustic games, such as dancing round the may- pole, drop the liandkercliief, hunt the slipper, blind man's buff, wrestling, running, leaping, and other athletic sports. After this, they would take tea, with junkets, syllabub, cream, and hot cakes; at four o'clock, wind up the day with country dances in a large barn, finishing with Sir Roger de Cover-ley, and returning home in the same orderly procession as they had 'come out, not an individual having disgraced himself by intemperance, nor an ill-natured word or look having been exchanged throughout the day. The mingling of the higher, the middle, and the lower classes in cheerful sports was also seen in the custom of dancing the Flora dance through the streets of the towns- and villages in the month of May, in which persons of all ranks and ages, and of both sexes, cordially joined.

Again, at harvest-home, all the rustic and agreeable ceremonies of the olden time were gone through with zest and enthusiasm; and the labourers on the farm rejoiced as heartily as their master in the proofs of an abundant harvest, because they were sure to be benefited by it, in better wages, or more ample supply of enjoyments. Easter and Whitsuntide, Lady-day and Michaelmas, Candlemas-day, and the annual fairs and feasts, were looked forward to as periods of rejoicing; and, above all, Shrove Tuesday,

Ash Wednesday, Christmas-eve, Christmas-day, and Twelfth-night were seasons of more than usual festivity, at which the bands between employers and employed were drawn closer and closer, and the kindly feelings of reciprocal duty and protection, service and reward, were kept in wholesome exercise. How different the life of farm labourers now! and how changed their character, as well as condition, all who are acquainted with the agricultural districts must be too painfully cognisant.

Christmas carols, of the oldest versions extant, were familiar to all classes; and church choirs used to make a round of visits to the different towns and villages, to sing them in parts, at the doors of the the principal residents, before daylight, amid tempest, snow, and sleet; while the enjoyment of their own performanee seemed to them a sufficient reward. In my youthful enthusiasm I often joined such parties, and gave the thin treble or soprano of my voice to mingle with their strains, never heeding the severity of the weather, nor seeking or expecting any reward. Among the greatest favourites one began thus:

"Shepherds, rejoice! lift up your eyes, And send your fears away; News from the regions of the skies! Salvation's born to-day."

Another, of a simpler character, and better liked by many, began

"God rest you, merry gentlemen, Let nothing you dismay; Remember Christ our Saviour Was born on Christmas-day."

But that which carried the palm to female ears and hearts especially, and was by them at least always most loudly applauded, was called the " Seven Joys of Mary," a relic probably of the earliest Catholic poetry of this description, namely

"The first good joy our Mary had. It was the joy of one; To see her own son Jesus Sucking at her breast bone."

The remaining stanzas rose no higher in their imagery or phraseology, and in the simplicity of the rustic taste to which they were addressed, they were as welcome as the most sublime strains of Milton or any other bard.

Christmas plays also were then in full vigour, the last I'emains of the mummers and mysteries of mediaeval times. The most popular of these was the history and exploits of the national patron, St. George, and his encounter with the dragon. Companies of from twelve to fifteen or twenty youths, between eight and sixteen years old, would be formed a month before Chi'istmas, to get up the dramatic representation. No scenery was required, as the drawing room, the parlour, or the kitchen formed the only stage, and the costume was easily arranged. Over the ordinary dress was worn a white linen shirt, plaited and profusely frilled, and ornamented wherever practicable with bows and rosettes of gay coloured ribbons; wdiile the head-dress was a sort of mitre, made of white stiff cardboard, adorned with the crest of the wearer, or of the character he represented, blazoned with heraldic and other ornaments, in bright colours and gold, and banners of the heralds. The war trumpet, the javelin, the lance, the two-edged sword, and the oblong shield of the crusading age, were furnished by the performers themselves; in this guise they went from house to house, on every evening between Christmas-day and Twelfth-night, and added greatly to the festivities of the season. I had for three or four years in succession taken part in these now obsolete performances, and rose at last to the dignity of playing the chief character of St. George himself, never dreaming then that I should in after life visit the supposed scene of his encounter with the dragon, near the river

Adonis, in Syria, which it was my lot to do; this being the same St. George that forms the obverse of some of our coins, and the collar of the order of the Knights of the Garter, the patron saint of the Greek church, and of the Red Cross which forms the groundwork of the British flag.

Excitement of the French Revolution, in 1792. Punished for imjjrudence in a loyal demonstration. Description of a Cornish funeral, in 1794. Great prevalence of intemperance in all classes. Boat exploits, and narrow escape from drowning. Desiorn to have me educated for the Church. Sir Edward Pellew takes me on board his frigate. Become a writer of female servants' love letters. Influence of this occupation on my disposition. Ambitious dreams of naval distinction. Dibdin's sea songs feeding this ambition.

About this period, 1794, the feeling of hatred to France and her bloody revolution was at its greatest height. Every male who could bear arms was enrolled in volunteer corps; patriotic songs were heard every night in the streets, with choruses of forty or fifty voices; the women were as violent in their manifestations of feeling as the men, and even children caught the wide-spread infection. A little regiment of boys, from six to twelve years of age, was embodied at Flushing, and mustered nearly one hundred strong. Wooden muskets, halberts, and pikes were provided by each; cross-belts of white linen, or sometimes paper, were substituted for leather; and wooden swords, without scabbards, were worn by the side. Being thought to be one of the most daring, I was appointed colonel by acclamation; and we had majors, captains, lieutenants, ensigns, sergeants, and corporals, in rather more than due proportion to the rank and file. Two drummers and four fifers did their part as well as the rest, and an old union jack from one of the packets served as the regimental colours. There were parades every morning and evening, and the latter was generally closed at dusk by the burning a stuffed figure to represent some obnoxious Jacobin in effigy. Sometimes it w as Tom Paine, few of us knowing whether he was French or English; at another Robespierre, and at another some revolutionary name that happened to be most obnoxious at the time. On one of these burnings in effigy I received a terrible punishment for my imprudence. For the purpose of giving greater eclat to the conflagration, it was arranged to blow up the stuffed figure into the air: and we anticipated seeing the arms and legs flying in fragments and falling on the ground. Several pounds of gunpowder were placed in a heap beneath the figure as it hung on a gallows prepared for it, and to this a train was laid for a distance of some fifty feet. Either the match was imperfectly lighted, or the powder was damp, so that the train could not be fired; when, impatient at the delay, I rushed to the spot, put my face down close to the match and powder, blew with all my might, and in an instant my head was enwrapped in flame, my hair and eyebrows all burnt oflp, and ray face one mass of burning torture. There was a running stream close by, from a public spring near the quay, in which I attempted to wash my face to allay the pain, when the greater portion of the skin peeled off, and I was led home almost blind, and suffering great agony. The only medical man of the village being from home, an old woman's receipt of common ink was applied all over the face, and after this a plaster or poultice of scraped raw potatoes; with this I lay for three or four days in bed, in great suffering, quite cured of my military ardour and anti-Jacobin zeal; and it was many months before the skin was sufficiently restored to bring me back to my usual healthy appearance.

About this time also I was, for the first time in my life, called away from home, to attend the funeral of one of my godfathers, Mr. Freeman, a wealthy and successful merchant and smuggler on a large scale; this latter occupation being thovight quite as honourable as the former, throughout all the sea-coast of Cornwall, at that period. Being a person in very great esteem, his funeral was attended by more than a hundred persons on horseback, who followed the corpse from Falmouth to the parish of Breague in the west, for twenty or thirty miles, all dressed in mourning. There were then no carriages in general use. I remember only one kept in Falmouth and one in Flushing, and their passage through the streets were followed always by a crowd of children, as if it were something wonderful. It was long subsequent to this that the first mail coach reached Falmouth, and its arrival and departure for many months drew a large assembly to witness it. The corpse of Mr. Freeman was, therefore, borne by relays of men, as bearers resting every two or three miles and the female relatives and friends all rode on pillions behind men, as Queen Elizabeth is said to have done behind the Lord High Chancellor, when she went to St. Paul's, to return thanks for the defeat of the Spanish Armada, for the same reason because coaches were not then in use.

When we arrived at Breague, we seemed to have got among a people whose language was as unintelligible to us as that of any African tribe. I was forcibly struck with this, and had the greatest difficulty to hold any communication with the ostlers and servants whose aid was required to take care of our horses for young as I was, I was well mounted and in a full suit of mournino; like the rest. The interment of the body, after a short sermon in the church, then took place in the usual way; but what followed was so new to me and so revolting, that it made a deep impression.

Dinner was ordered at the inn of the village, for the larctCst number that the largest room would con-tain, and nearly a hundred persons sat down to table together, at two o'clock. The dinner was abundant, and the supply of wines and spirits profuse. At the head of the table sat the chief mourner, a relative of the deceased. On his right was the clergyman who had conducted the. burial service, and on his left the widow in her full mourning weeds. Almost every one drank a glass of raw brandy. before commencing dinner, and some even before grace was said, and these drams were repeated almost after every change of dishes, so that both the eating and drinking were more voracious then I had ever witnessed before. On the cloth being removed, pipes and tobacco, with lighted candles, and decanters of brandy, rum, and gin, with hot water and sugar, were freely supplied. Fortunately, my youth, being then about eight years old, saved me from the necessity of joining in this revel; but the female portion of the guests did not retire till almost every man at the table had drunk three or four tumblers of hot spirits and water, or toddy, as it was called, and most of them were already far advanced towards being drunk. It was then proposed to send for the parish choir and sing anthems, which was done, the drinking going on at the same time without abatement, and nearly all present joining in the choruses. From anthems they passed at last to patriotic songs; and this unseemly revel was kept up till midnight, as I heard from some who remained till then; for I had repaired to bed after tea at an early hour, being tired and disgusted; and many of the later sitters, I was assured, were found at daylight drunk and insensible Ijeneath the table. In short, all that I have ever heard of an Irish wake seemed to have had its counterpart in this barbarous Cornish funeral, from which I was too happy to escape and return home on the following morning.

I may add that at this period, no one, as far as I can remember, thought intoxication unbecoming, but rather the mark of a gentleman, as indicative of high breeding; the higher classes, clergy as well as laity, seemed more frequently inebriated than the lower, their means of indulgence being more ample, it being thought a very shabby sort of hospitality to allow any guest at a great house to leave the table perfectly sober; hence the common expres-

VOL. I. D sions of that day " he was drunk as a lord;" or "drunk as a bishop." Marriages, christenings, and funerals were made special occasions for even the poorest to indulge, and in all classes great consumption of intoxicating drinks took place at these celebrations. It was at funerals especially tliat spirits were profusely drank, and chiefly among the poor. The customary mode was this, the corpse was first brought from the dwelling-house, and the coffin placed on a bench, made of chairs reversed, before the door; here a hymn or psalm was sung, and glasses of brandy handed round at its close to every one present, whether assistants or mere spectators. This frequently stimulated the leader to give out a second hymn or psalm, which was sung wntli greater spirit than the first, and another round of brandy Avas served as before. The corpse was then borne by four or six bearers a certain distance, when these were relieved by others, and at each resting place brandy was again served; so that by the time the parties reached the parish church, some two miles distant, they were nearly all muddled and stupid. Sometimes, however, it had the effect of making the expressions of grief more vehement than if they had been perfectly sober; and then again brandy was applied as a soother of sorrow. As near every church there was sure to be a public-houscj a funeral was a great day for the landlord, and few who attended such funerals went perfectly sober to bed.

No wonder therefore that smugghng in spirits was carried on so extensively as it was in Cornwall, the coasts of which had every day some contraband landings effected in one part or another; where large parties of fifty or sixty men, on horseback, with a keg of spirits on each side of the saddle, and armed with pistols and cutlasses, would bid defiance to the revenue officers, and always connnand the sympathy and aid of the community, all classes of which preferred smuggled spirits to duty paid, not only for their comparative cheapness, but their freedom from adulteration.

In the three towns of Falmouth, Penryn, and Flushing, the hotels, inns, and taverns were numerous; and so far from its being thought disreputable to attend them, they were the usual places of rendezvous in the evening for all classes; the gentry and professional persons assembling in the bar of the hotels, the more respectable tradesmen in the second class inns, and the mere labourers in the inferior taverns: and it may be said that every male above fifteen or sixteen, in each of these towns, consumed and spent, on the average, in beer, spirits, wine, and tobacco, not less than 20Z. a year for the labourers, 50. for the master tradesmen and respectable shopkeepers, and 70. or 80.

a year up to 100. for the higher classes, a drain upon the wealth of the community quite sufficient to account for the pauperism, crime, insanity, and other evils resulting directly from such expenditure. Of some fifty young men of my own age and time, whose history I remember, at least thirty either became bankrupt in trade, or ruined in constitution and character, and died a premature death, by the intemperate habits in which they indulged. Whether the same proportion would hold good in other parts of England I am not prepared to say; but I believe that if any man of the present day would carry his recollections back to the period of his youth, and reckon up the number of those whom he had known to begin life with fair prospects, but afterwards to become shipwrecked through intemperance, he would find the catalogue a long and melancholy one, to be thought of only with sorrow.

To return from this digression to the narrative of my life, I may say that my attachment to the sea, and my love of everything connected with ships, went on daily increasing, and manifested itself in all my occupations and amusements. My hazardous enterprises within the harbour were a constant source of alarm to my dear mother, who was as anxious to wean me from all thoughts of a sea life, as I was desirous of embracing it. Besides my father's own boats, which were frequently at my command, there were many others belonging to friends of the family within my reach, so that scarcely a day passed, except Sundays, when I was not on the water for two or three hours at least; sometimes with one or more companions, but as frequently alone. It was a great object of ambition with me to show them that I could handle a boat under sail without the assistance of any one, though then between seven and eight years old only; and many a cruise I thus enjoyed in a fast yawl, with jib, foresail, mainsail, and mizen, the sheets of all leading aft, within my reach, so that I had never occasion to quit the helm on tacking. With a stiff breeze it was my highest delight to beat to windward, on short tacks, through the crowd of shipping anchored in the harbour, and feel myself to be the " observed of all observers," among the veteran tars, who often looked over the bow and quarter under which I hove about, with a mixture of surprise and admiration at such hardihood in so young a boatman.

Such attempts as these were not wholly free from accidents, such as splitting a sail, carrying away a mast, and running foul of some craft in the way; and on one occasion a capsize in a heavy squall, which had well nigh been fatal. The gust was so violent that the boat was turned keel upward, and being thus-covered, I was a considerable time under water, and was ultimately rescued by a boat's crew sent off from one of the nearest packets. I was found to be so completely exhausted, and so cold and pulseless, as to be given over for dead, and in this condition brought on shore, rolled up in the boat's wet sail; but one of the naval surgeons beins; sent for, he thought life was not entirely irrecoverable, though apparently quite suspended; and by the application of hot bricks to the feet, rolling the body in hot dry salt, and the forcible administration of emetics, to bring the sea w ater out of the stomach, I was slowly but gradually restored, though so exhausted as to be unable to walk for many days.

I had a distinct recollection of the gust of wind, and the boat's so capsizing, bottom up, as to cover me completely over, as well as of my having sunk to the bottom and risen again more than once; and as my eyes were open during this submersion, and the water was beautifully transparent, as it usually is in this western harbour, I saw distinctly a number of floating fishes, creeping crabs, large heaps of bones, and other refuse cast from time to time from the ships; and having read and recited several times to mj mother and sisters, who were fond of exhibiting my powers of memory and elocution in this way, the well-known description of Clarence's dream, in the elegant extracts from Shakspeare, I seemed to realise all its horrors, if not its splendours; and even now, at this great distance of time, I can remember distinctly the gurgling of the waters in the throat, and the fearful ringing in the ears, which are the usual accompaniments of drowning.

"Lord, Lord, methougbt what pain it was to drown! What dreadful noise of waters in mine ears! What sights of uglj death within mine eyes! I thought I saw a thousand fearful wrecks: A thousand men that fishes gnawed upon; Wedges of gold, great anchors, heaps of pearl, Inestimable stones, unvalued jewels; Some lay in dead men's skulls, and in those holes As ' twere in scorn of eyes, reflected gems That wooed the slimy bottom of the deep. And mocked the dead bones that lay scattered by."

It was fondly hoped that such a warning as this would give me a distaste for the sea, or at least abate somewhat of my former ardour to embrace that profession; but its effect was just the reverse; and the more frequent and earnest were the attempts made to dissuade me from entering on such a course, the more enthusiastically and perseveringly did I cling to it.

It was my mother's desire that I should be brought up to the Church; and having a relative of the same name then in orders, as rector of one of the adjoining parishes, his influence was brought to bear upon me to give me a taste for the clerical profession. But it was all in vain. The sea seemed to me to be my destiny, and it was the only career I could contemplate with any satisfaction. The passion for it too was fostered by a combination of circumstances, the influence of which it was impossible to resist. From the friendly intimacy that existed between Sir Edward Pellew and my father, previous to his death, I was a frequent visitor, as a child, to the house of the commodore, and mingled in play with his children Fleetwood, Pownall, and the rest one late an admiral on the East India station, and another, I believe. Dean of Norwich; and Sir Edward himself, having observed my love of boats and boating, ofl'ered to place me on his ship's books as a midshipman, it being then the custom to do this at even an earlier age than mine; some, indeed, I have heard, while quite infants, that their seven years of noviciate might pass over while they were at school a practice long since become obsolete; but my dear mother, always entertaining a hope that I might still be weaned from my sea-love, was unwilling to consent to this, lest, being once on the books of the navy, it might be difficult to obtain my discharge.

Sir Edward, however, often took me on board with him in his barge, vliich was sent ashore from the Indefatigable every morning at ten; and having the run of the gun-room, the cock-)it, and the 'tween decks, while on board, I soon became a favourite with officers and men. The first lieutenant now Admiral Pellow was the brother of my elder brother's wife. The master, Mr. William Pitt, bearing a striking resemblance to the great minister, and who was afterwards master attendant at IMalta, was an admirer and suitor of my elder sister; and the surgeon was an intimate friend and constant visitor of our family; while one of our female servants had been married to the coxswain of the commodore's barge, and another to one of Sir John Warren's crew, so that all these were additional links in the fascinating chain that bound me so irresistibly in its fetters. The Naval Ch'onide, then in high popularity, and tales of shipwreck and battle, had more interest for me than any other kind of reading, and I was never more happy than when dwelling on their romantic details.

Though I had not yet been at any but a dame's day-school in the village, and that more to keep me out of harm's way, than for any education I could receive there, and from which I may now freely confess that I was more frequently absent than present, suffering only the mildest rebuke when a truant, and the miserable year that I passed at Hubbarton, yet I had a strong love of reading, literally devouring whatever books fell in my way, and a sufficient knowledge of writing to bring both into useful exercise. In those days of simple village life, there was not so great a gulf between the members of the household and their servants as more recent times have created; and ours had lived so many years with us, and been present at the birth of all the children, that they formed part and parcel of the family. It was therefore thought no breach of the strictest decorum, that I should pass an hour or two in the evenings with them, reading such narratives and tales as delighted us equally; and this was one of my chief pleasures. But my services were soon put into requisition for other purposes. Neither of the maids could write: and as each had a lover in the squadron, whose visits were necessarily "few and far between," correspondence with them was an object of mutual desire. The schoolmasters of the two frigates (for the lovers were not shipmates) wrote the letters for the amorous tars; and I was called upon, not merely to read their contents to their innamoratas, but also to write the answers. I was not averse to this confidential secretaryship, as it helped to feed my passion for the sea, by the details which the sailor-lovers gave of their encountering heavy gales on such a day, and weathering them successfully; of their letting out all reefs to give chace to an enemy on the lee-bow on such another; of a desperate fight, but triumphant victory, over a French frigate of more guns and men than their own; and of their capture of several rich prizes, French West-Indiamen, in the chops of the Channel; winding up with a verse or two from Dibdin's sea-songs, which all seamen then knew by heart, to prove that the only lovers whose fidelity could be relied on were "the jolly tai's of Old England," who drank to their wives and sweethearts every " Saturday-night at sea," and relieved the tedium of the mid-watch and the raging tempest by singing

"The 11710(1 and rain, the inconstant main, My ardent passion prove. Lash'd to the helm, should seas o'erwhelm, I'll think on thee, my love!"

I may add that by this time I knew almost all this "matchless collection" of Dibdin's, for so I considered it, by heart; and the first of these songs I ever learned to sing, which I did with all my heart, was " The Post-Captain," or by some called " The Cabin-Boy," beginning thus:

"When Steerwell heard me first impart Our brave commander's story, With ardent zeal his youthful heart Beat high for naval glory."

The whole song was a complete epitome of what I constantly flattered myself would be my happy destiny, namely, to commence as a cabin-boy, as the hero of the song had done, and, rising like him through all the necessary grades of rank, to reach at last the distinguished elevation of a post-captain. With such a youthful training my longing to embark on the fickle element increased in intensity the longer it was delayed: and

Dibdin's songs and Falconer's Shipwreck had more charms for me than all the poetry in the world besides.

My going to sea at length determined on. Sent accordingly to a Naval Academy at Falmouth. Contemporaries at thia school, and characteristic portraits. Early victim of love. Romantic display of passion. First conception of religious feelino-s and views. Attractions of a sea-life absorbincr all others. Appointed to the Lady Harriett, Government packet. First outfit for sea: pride and delight in the costume. Ambition to excel in all boat evolutions. Preparations for departure on my first voyage to Lisbon. Mercantile adventure for trading with the Portuguese.

Necessity rather than choice at length led my dear mother to consent to my being indulged with my wish, but always with the secret hojoe that I might yet be cured of what she deemed my folly. One of my elder sisters was married to Mr. Samuel Steele, then master of one of the Government packets, the Lady Harriett, commanded by Captain Dillon, and it w as arranged that I should make my first voyage with him; it being expressly designed, as was afterwards admitted to me, but then, of course, concealed, that he should exercise towards me the highest degree of rigour that the discipline of the service would admit, by making me keep watch with some subordinate officer who should hold a tight hand over me, with as many "mast-headings" as reasonable excuses could be found for, and thus break my stubborn spirit into submission.

I was accordingly sent to the only academy then existing at Falmouth, kept by Mr. Duckham, a native of Taunton in Somersetshire, to learn navigation at least so much of its preliminary theory as should make the practical part more easy of acquisition afloat. I was overjoyed at this announcement, and never entered on any task before or since with greater zest and alacrity. I looked upon my volume of "Hamilton Moore's Navigator" as the greatest treasure I had ever possessed, and encased its leather covers with an envelope of cartridge paper, that no blot or stain should defile it. My case of mathematical instruments was so jorecious in my eyes, that I constantly took it to bed with me, and placed it under my pillow; and my Book of Problems and geometrical diagrams and figures, containing also my sums worked ou. t by logarithms, was admired as the neatest and most perfect in the class.

As this school occupied an elevated and airy situation on the slope of the hill overlooking the town of Falmouth, which lay below it, and commanded a complete view of the harbour, Carrick-roads, the castles of St. Mawes and Penclennis, guarding the entrance, with the Black-rock and its pole in the centre, and the signal station at St. Anne's Head to the eastward, every time that my laew was turned in that direction (and my bedroom looked right out upon it), I was gratified by the sight of ships and smaller craft in every variety of position. Sometimes as many as ten frigates and several smaller vessels of war would be in the outer roads at once, with a crowded fleet of merchant ships wind-bound, and waiting for a change, to sail under convoy to the East or West Indies, North or South America, or the Mediterranean: while the inner habour w ould be crowded with the handsome packets in their gayest trim, each distinguished by a special signal, and constantly exercising their crews in bending and unbending sails, reefing, sending up or down top-gallant yards, striking lower yards and topmasts, hoisting in boats, water, or provisions, and on a calm day the shrill whistle of the boatswain was distinctly heard from the school, as well as the cheering cry of " All's well," at the relieving of the watch, and the morning and evening gun at sunrise and sunset. All this was delicious food for my sight and music for my ears, and made me relish my studies with intense delight, so that in a very short period of about three months, I was pronounced competent to pass my examination, and somewhat surprised the old officers by whom that ordeal was conducted. In the enthusiasm of success I had a ship's anchor imprinted on my left hand, by the puncture of needles, drawing blood at each stroke, and the infusion of gunpowder under the skin, producing a permanent blue colour, according to the practice of sailors at that time; and this blue anchor I have borne on my hand through life, and shall retain it, no doubt, till the end of my days.

At this school, I may mention, were then two youths, contemporaries of mine in age, but of very different habits, who have since attained deservedly distinguished positions: namely, the Reverend Henry Melvill, the eloquent and popular preacher of Cam-berwell; and his brother, Philip Melvill, chief-secretary of the East India Company in London. Their father. Governor Melvill, as he was always called, was Governor of Pendennis Castle, and Commander of the corps of Invalids by whom it was garrisoned. He was of very diminutive stature, but always wore his military uniform, with the square cocked hat of the period. He had seen much hard service, and had lost an arm and an eye, the stump of the former being suspended by a black silk handkerchief as a sling, and the socket of the other being covered with a black silk patch fastened by a ribbon round the head, his hair powdered and tied in a short military queue or tail hanging over a well powdered scarlet uniform coat. His appearance was striking, and at the same time interesting and venerable. The most publicly known and prominent trait of his character was his practical piety. The clergyman of the church at Falmouth was then a Mr. Hitchins, a man of unusually evangelical religion for a churchman of that day, and who was universally admired and beloved, except by some of the orthodox high-church rectors and vicars, by whom he was denounced as ' a methodist," a term of the bitterest reproach in their vocabulary. But the best answer to their denunciation was a constantly full church, a most devout congregation, and a degree of beneficial influence exercised by this amiable and holy pastor over the society of his flock, such as few of his fellow clergymen could then command. Governor Melvill was one of his most constant attendants and communicants, and his sons appeared to partake of their father's spirit, as they were amongst the most devout and orderly of all the pupils and students occupying the large square pew devoted to us, as Mr. Duckham's scholars, near the altar.

VOL. I. B

An accident occurred at this period which is too characteristic of my temperament to be omitted. Even at this early period of my life about eight years of age I had formed an ardent and sincere attachment to a young girl of Flushing, about my own age, and was never so happy as when in her society, or corresponding with her during our separation, which never exceeded a few days, as I was always permitted to go home after the morning service at church, on Sundays, and thus to spend the remainder of the day with the members of my own family, and this cherished object of my early affections, who was always permitted to be with us.

There are many who will no doubt smile at the idea of love at such an age as this; but the passion existing between us was as strong as it was pure, and Avas manifested by all the usual feelings that mark its existence in maturer age. It happened that the young lady was taken ill, and, when the intelligence was communicated to me, I was anxious to be permitted to visit her; but this being forbidden by the medical attendant, as likely to produce an excitement which mio-ht aggravate the fever under which she suffered, I became distracted, locked myself up in nj bedroom, overcome with the most profound grief, refused all sustenance, was deprived of all sleep, and in a few days was reduced to the brink of danger myself.

At length her death was announced to me; and, in the strong conviction that her pure spirit would pass at once into the regions of bliss, as an angel of light, I became from that moment calm and resigned, and recovered my strength sufficiently to attend her funeral which I was permitted both by her parents and my own to do in mourning, though no relationship existed between our respective families. The interment of the body took place in the churchyard of the parish of IMylor, about two miles distant from Flushing, and close by the sea-shore. In the simplicity of those bygone times, all the relatives and mourners followed the corpse on foot, and the coffin was carried by six young girls dressed in white, relieved by an equal number of others at intervals on the way. The service was conducted in the usual manner, first within the church, and afterwards at the grave; and I appeared to bear this trial less moved than was expected, the truth being that my grief was really too deep for tears.

After the close of the ceremony, the attendants separated into groups, for their return home on foot, as they had come; but after proceeding about halfway back, all engaged in conversation, my sisters who had accompanied me, and who were each several years older than myself, found me missing from their party, and supposed I had gone home by another route, for the purpose of being alone. Finding, however, on reaching home, that I had not arrived, they became alarmed for my safety, as the churchyard was washed by the sea; but on returning to it in search of me, I was found in a state of torpor amounting almost to insensibility, stretched along upon the grave of the departed, and clinging to the earth of her new-made grave, as if to realise the scriptural expression," they were lovely and pleasant in their lives; and in their deaths they were not divided."

Happily, the natural elasticity of youth at length recovered even from this severe shock; but not without many a painful struggle.

The earliest developed of all my tendencies were the enterprising, the devotional, the sympathising, and the amatory. The first evinced itself in an irrepressible desire to visit foreign and distant lands, to encounter dangers at sea, and to undertake whatever was said to be difficult, without fear or hesitation. The second was shown in feelings of profound adoration for the Almighty, an intense pleasure in reading the sublimer passages of the Prophets and the Psalms, and, above all, the Book of Job; witli such a love for the person and attributes of the Saviour, as to make silent meditation on his divine countenance and figure in the Scriptural engravings illustrating the New Testament an exquisite enjoyment. The third was manifested in the deep interest I took in all pathetic stories, shedding copious tears over the tales of " The Babes in the Wood," and " The Beggar's Petition," both of which I could very early recite by heart, and the saving up pence for poor people, and feeling intense pleasure in bestowing them, a trait of my father's disposition, which in him was regarded as a weakness. The last found vent in the admiration of every beautiful female face, and such susceptibility to the influence of female fascination, especially when combined with song or music, as to bind me continually in fetters, till these were loosed by some new charm, and then reimposed and riveted afresh.

I make this early and frank confession of my propensities and failings, not only because truth requires such a statement, but because a recollection of these characteristics will form a clue to the explanation of many subsequent events in my chequered career: for though reason and experience, and still more, perhaps, increasing age, have greatly modified them, at least in intensity or degree, giving additional strength to some, and lessening tlie force of others; yet, on the whole, the influence of these propensities have, more or less, been felt by me at every period of life, and entered largely into the motives by which I have been impelled towards certain courses of action, and restrained from entering on others.

One of the earliest recollections of my youth, is that of the intense admiration with which I used to dv. ell on a series of engravings of the ruins of Baalbeck and Palmyra, which adorned the folding screen of a neighbouring lady, Mrs. Lang, at whose house we were frequent visitors; and the equal enthusiasm with which I would pore for hours at a time over the plates of Calmet's Dictionary of the Bible, giving views of Jerusalem and the Holy Places of Palestine, longing to visit such scenes, and see them with my own eyes, but not venturing so far as to hope that this could ever be my happy lot; and this, coupled with my desire to follow the ships that left the harbour through all the length of their voyages, only strengthened this early passion for travel into distant and foreign lands.

Of the devotional spirit, I had also very early manifestations, chiefly inspired and fed by attendance, Avhile quite a child, on the methodist ministers who at this period from 1792 to 1794 frequently preached at a small chapel in our village. Prior to this, bj a few vears only, John Wesley had himself visited Cornwall, and produced, both here and in every other place in which he preached, effects only comparable to those resulting from the preaching of the apostles of old; so that all ranks and classes of society were deeply imbued with a religious spirit. The celebrated Dr. Cook, and other eminent ministers, who from time to time embarked from Falmouth for the United Stales of America in the packets sailing from hence, usually held prayer meetings, and preached a few sermons at Flushing during their stay. The enthusiasm excited by their labours was such, that meetings commenced at six o'clock in the evening would be sometimes protracted till daybreak on the following morning; and, as at the revivals in America, there were frequent faintings and hysterics, among the female portion of the congregation especially, with outpourings of the confession of sins from the men; and, sometimes, spontaneous prayers and extemporaneous hymns, even from children. Such manifestations as these were of frequent occurrence, and not unfrequently led to aberration of intellect in some highly sensitive minds, whose powers of reason were absorbed by intensity of feeling, some of whom as I myself had witnessed would leave the chapel, with their arms extended, exclaiming that they felt themselves upborne by winged angels who floated them through the air, and singing with countenances beaming with joy, "Ho-sannah to the Lord." That tliese feelings were perfectly genuine and sincere no one doubted, and that they were highly contagious and communicable, even I was not too young to feel; nor do I remember any state of being, that it has ever been my lot to experience, more exquisitely delicious than this ecstatic elevation above all earthlv things.

The state of my mind and disposition at this period led my widowed mother to hope that I might be induced to meet her wishes by being educated for the Church, especially as there was a relative of the family, and of the same name, who held a living in one of the adjoining parishes, and who would have directed and superintended the course of education required. I was accordingly encouraged by every means of persuasion to look to this as my future vocation in life; and having been ever a diligent reader of the Old and New Testament, but especially the latter, I was furnished with controversial sermons and writings of the early English divines to strengthen my attachment to the Establishment. But the more I read on this subject the more it seemed to me difficult to reconcile the power, and rank, and riches of the Church, and even its forms and ceremonies, with the humilitjj equality, poverty, and self-denial of the disciples and apostles of Christianity, as well as with the character, conduct, and precepts of its Divine Founder himself. I could not, therefore, be prevailed upon to look to the Established Church as one of its ministers at least, though from habit and weekly attendance, liking the beauty, simplicity, and devotional spirit of many of its prayers, in the recital of which I always fervently joined.

My passion for the sea continued to increase by every opportunity I had of enjoying or sharing in any of its occupations; and these were now frequent, as my studies in navigation being completed, I no longer attended the academy; and scarcely a day passed that I was not on board one or other of the ships of war, or the packets then in the harbour, and never so happy as when permitted to join in any of the labours going on, whether on deck or aloft, thus familiarising myself with at least all harbour evolutions. I may add that, with that resistance to coercion, which seemed a part of the nature of my youth as it has ever been of my manliood, every attempt to force my tastes into another channel only made it run the stronger in this.

It was at length decided tliat to sea I should go; and no reprieve to a condemned convict, or opening the prison doors to a long-immured captive, was ever more Avelcome than this decision was to me. I was not, however, aware at the time, that a sort of friendly conspiracy was formed among the different members of my own family to make my first voyage as disagreeable as possible, so as to disgust me, as they vainly hoped, with the profession, and make me abandon it of my own accord. For this purpose, I was shipped in the King's packet The Lady Harriett, commanded by Captain Dillon, and of which my eldest sister's husband, Mr. Steele, was the sailing master, under whose special care I was placed; and he was charged with the office of making my life as uncomfortable as possible, by the severest exactions of duty at all times and seasons, by extra watchings, frequent mast-headings, and all the most disagreeable labours that could be decently assigned to me.

Mr. Steele had himself been brought up in the packet-service from a boy, and was accounted one of the ablest of its officers as a seaman, as he was undoubtedly one of the most popular as a man. His father, when acting commander of one of the packets many years before, had fought a most gallant action with two French privateers, each of greatly superior force to his own ship; but though beating them both off, and thus escaping victorious, he was himself severely wounded and given up for dead. Indeed his body was about to be thrown over board, with the rest of the killed in the action, when his son, then a youth of twelve years old, and a universal favourite on board, interceded so warmly for the preservation of his father's body that it might be buried on shore, that his wishes were complied with. The body was therefore placed in his cot, covered up all but the face, and lay in this condition for three or four days, under the impression that life was entirely extinct. The son, however, watched it incessantly, and on the arrival of the ship in port, thought he saw indications of the vital spark not being yet entirely extinct. The surgeon of the packet was accordingly summoned to examine it, and found that life still remained, but at the lowest point of possible existence; and immediate measures were taken for its recovery, which by due care and time was happily effected. The wound was in the head; a piece of an iron crowbar several inches in length, and more than an inch in circumference, had entered one of the eyes and remained imbedded in the skull. It was successfully extracted after being there several days, though the loss of both ejes was the consequence. The piece of iron was so much larger than had ever been known to remain in the head of any individual without causing death, that it excited great curiosity; and a lady of distinction desiring to possess it, her wish was gratified, in return for which she settled on the wounded and blind officer a small pension for life, which, in addition to a pension granted from the Post-office, rendered him independent of further aid. He then retired to Plymouth, where he lived with his brother, then one of the officers of that garrison, for a great number of years, one of the serenest and happiest of men. He cultivated music, which he enjoyed intensely; and 1 remember passing a day with him in his brother's quarters in the garrison, and thinking him one of the most contented and happy individuals, then far advanced in age, that it had ever been my lot to be in company with for so great a length of time.

The son of this gentleman, who married my eldest sister, was as worthy and as popular as his father; and, I have reason to believe, that the task he had to perform with myself was in every way repugnant to his natural disposition; but his profound respect for the wishes of my parent, and that of his wife, as w ell as the rest of my family, who were all equally opposed to my going to sea, made him undertake it against his inclination, and I must admit that he performed it with great fidelitj, though far from attaining the end desired, as the sequel will show.

I was now to receive my outfit as a sailor-boy, and never did field-marshal, king, or emperor don his robes of state with more pride or gratification than I, for the first time, wore my suit of blue jacket, striped Guernsey frock, loose black silk tie, and turned down collar, white duck trowsers, long-quartered shoes, and ribbed coloured stockings, with low-crowned hat, and flowing bands or ribbons. Having had early practice in rowing, and being considered rather skilful and accomplished in handling the oars, I was first appointed to the jolly boat, and took the bow-oar, which it was then the custom, on leaving the landing place or arriving at it, to toss perpendicularly with a sudden twirling in the air, before laying it in-board; and in the adroitness with which this was done, and the boat-hook managed by the bow-oarsman, as he stood on the forecastle to fend off or hook on as required, consisted the pre-eminence of one youth over another. In this art, I may say, without arrogance, that I took my place as " senior wrangler " from the first, and in the course of a few weeks only, was promoted to the rank of rowing the after or stroke-oar of the cutter; and, subsequently, to be the coxswain or steersman of the captain's barge, for gigs were not then in use.

I was, at this time, little more than nine years of age in the early part of 1796 but was as tall, stout, and full grown as youths of the present day of 14 or 15; and stronger, from the athletic sports in which I delighted, than many young men of 16 or 18. I could swim nearly two miles on a stretch, without exhaustion, could ascend, " hand over hand," as it is termed, from the ship's deck to the main-top, by a single rope, lifting my own weight at every successive handling; and could reach the main-truck, the flying-jib-boom end, or the royal yard-arm, in a shorter time than any of the youths on board; all which I owed, partly to the agility and flexibility acquired by constant exercise, and partly to the ambition which I felt to excel all competitors in every thing that could qualify me for an able seaman.

At length the day of sailing arrived, and the signal gun in the morning, blue Peter the flag at the fore, and the fore-topsail loose, were the visible indications of our preparation for departure. My chest and hammock were on board some days before, my nautical instruments well packed and in beautiful order, and a small supply of books furnished me for the voyage, as well as a little trading stock of velveteens, muslins, and other articles sure to find a ready sale in Lisbon the port to which the ship was bound.

In explanation of the latter provision it should be mentioned, that though it was the object of the packets to convey the mails with the utmost expedition, and of the officers to confine their attention exclusively to this duty, a system had been permitted to grow up which made the ship in fact a merchant vessel, and all the officers and men traders. Mercantile houses were established at Falmouth in correspondence wuth others in London, by whom were furnished every description of goods suited to the markets of the several ports to which the packets sailed. As the officers and crews of these packets were permanently employed, and most of them married and settled or belonging to families residing at Falmouth, they were all safe to be entrusted with any reasonable amount of goods on credit: and custom having established the space or tonnage which each individual in the ship might occupy with his private freight, there being no cargo of merchandise on board, except the articles thus shipped by the crew, it would often happen that the captain would take 5000. worth of general goods, with watches and jewellery, the offi- cers their 3000. and 2000. each, and the men frequently 1000. and rarely less than 500. each on sale or return. As there would have been a drawback payable by the Custom-house on most of these articles if shipped in the regular way in merchant vessels, and this payment was avoided by such irregular shipments, the Government winked at the practice, and all parties thus profited by its continuance. My own adventure on this first voyage was a very humble one, not exceeding In value 50. sterling; for in this, as in everything else, it was desired that the experiment on my sea-going propensity should be made as disagreeable and as little profitable as possible.

Sailing from Falmouth, after adieus and struggles. First impressions of the grandeur of the Ocean. Coasting along the shores of Spain and Portugal. Entrance to Lisbon, bar of the Tagus. Magnificent aspect of the Portuguese capital. Escort of Guarda-Costas, or revenue vessels. Singular scene of official smuggling. Peculiarities of the Portuguese Population. Public edifices and other objects of interest. Opportunities for reading afforded at sea.

After many fond adieus and tender maternal tears, which for a time abnost svibdued my resolution, and well nigh awakened a feeling of repentance at resolving on any course of life that could give pain to so fond a mother; and, accompanied by my sisters to the ship's boat in waiting at the quay, I at length embarked in the packet, and set sail, with bright weather, and a fresh and fair wind from the north-east, for Lisbon. Before sunset we were out of sight of land; and the solitude and grandeur of the ocean was witnessed by me for the first time, with feelings of awe and solemnity difficult to be described. I was stationed in the middle watch, so that I had to leave my hammock at midnight and remain on deck till four o'clock in the morning. The night was lovely, VOL. I. r beyond all that I had ever before witnessed. The water, from its increased depth, w as intensely blue, the firmament seemed more thickly paved with stars, of greater size and brightness than I had ever seen them on shore, and there was an exhilaration in the breeze, the bounding motion, the followhig of the white-crested waves, and the lustrous track left by the ship in her course through the phosphorescent sea, which filled me with admiration and delight.

As the wind was fresh and favourable, we made rapid progress, and the more I was sent aloft in setting and taking in studding sails, loosing and furling royals, and the other light work for which boys are sometimes better adapted than men, the more I felt proud of my achievements, and the very steps taken to disgust me with the service only increased my attachment to it.

On the third day after leaving port we made Cape Finisterre, and sailed along the coasts of Spain and Portugal, within two or three leagues of the shore. This first sight of a foreign land, with its brown aspect, rocky eminences, and the absence of all green fields and hedge-rows, which form so mateial a part of the beauty of an English landscape, was full of pleasing novelty; while the shoals of bonitas and grampuses gamboling around our vessel's prow, and leaping occasionally several feet out of the water, the strange-rigged boats and craft standing out from the various creeks and ports of the coast to sea, all produced an exquisite sensation of pleasureable excitement, such as I had never felt before.

We passed in succession the bay of Vigo, the entrance to Oporto by the river Douro, and on the fourth day got among the cluster of islands called the Burlingas, not far from Lisbon, to which the Portuguese send their convicts for hard labour and scanty fare, and their bare rocky aspect seemed to fit them for such an appropriation.

Passing by Torres Vedras, Bucellas, and Cintra, all since memorable in the Peninsular campaigns, we at length beheld the Rock of Lisbon, as a lofty overhanging peak of the mountain chain within the line of coast is termed. Here we were soon surrounded by at least a dozen large fishing-boats, with their picturesque but ungainly hulls, immense lateen sails, with crews in every variety of dress and colour, in which brown and bright scarlet predominated, and such a Babel of tongues as had never before saluted my ear. Every individual in every boat, to the number of twenty or thirty at least in each, seemed to be screaming at the top of the voice, and the object of all this clamorous vociferation was to prevail on the captain of the packet to take his pilot from the boat whose crew could clamour loudest. The war of words was followed up by the running alongside of half-a-dozen boats at once, and at least twenty well qualified pilots each claimed precedence. After a hard struo-o-le three were selected from the whole number to remain on board; and this being now settled, quiet was at length restored, when all the boats but the three to which these pilots belonged left us to pursue their fishing, till some other vessel should heave in sight, when the same scene would be repeated.

The passage over the bar of Lisbon was terrific. The accumulated and ever shifting sands at the rnouth of the Tagus, present far greater difficulties to the navigator than the Goodwin and other sands at the mouth of the Thames. The breakers seemed at one time ready to engulph iis on every side in channels of the narrowest dimensions; and it required all the skill of the three pilots one at the prow, one at the gangway, and one on the taffrail with the silence and attention of every man and boy at his post, to execute the orders given, and bring us through the peril, which at last was happily accomplished.

We then passed close under Fort St. Julian, sufficiently near to hear and answer, with speaking trum- pets, the challenge of the officer on guard; and from this point we were accompanied, in our entrance to the Tagus and passage by the old castle of Belem to our anchorage abreast the city, by two revenue vessels, or Guarda-costas one on each side, and within pistol-shot of our ship.

In my inexperience of the world never having before seen anything beyond my native country I was quite overwhelmed with the majestic grandeur of Lisbon; and, looking back upon it now, after an interval of sixty years, it seems to my mind's eye one of the noblest marine cities in the world. The ample breadth of the Tagus at least three miles immediately in front of the city, the massive build- ings, and numerous churches, which rise up in successive elevations from the water's edge to the heights that crown its crest, the undulated hills of the opposite shore, with long lines of factories and warehouses fringing the water's edge, the numerous fleet of Portuguese sliips of war, large Indiamen as they were called from the Brazils, and vessels and flags of every nation crowding the stream, made up a picture of surprising beauty and magnificence; while the continual clangour of the bells on shore, which never seemed to cease night or day, from one church or monastery or the other, kept up a kind of excite- ment whicli put all my faculties on the stretch, and hardly permitted me to sleep in tranquillity.

We were scarcely anchored and our sails furled, before the commanding officers of the two revenue crafts that were stationed, one on each side, to prevent our smuggling, paid a formal visit to our commander and his officers. Each came in full uniform, with cocked hats, gold epaulets, and swords, and both were received with what appeared to me wonderful cordiality for spies upon our conduct, for such they Avere. In the dining saloon below, the table was laid out for their refreshment with all the choicest articles on board; and the hospitality offered and courtesies exchancred were such as would become the sio-nlna; a treaty of amity between the ambassadors of two great nations.

All this excited my wonder, which was increased rather than diminished when I was told by one of the crew that this was a friendly meeting between the Portuguese revenue officers and the English smugglers or contrabandistas, to settle the amount of the bribe which should be paid by the latter to secure the connivance of the former in their smuggling transactions!

At the usual hour of eight o'clock the harbour watch for the night was set; and all remained tran- quil till midnight, the general silence being only broken by the sound of the ships' bells at every half hour, and the cheering cry of-"All's well!" from the English vessels in port. About midnight, however, there dropped down with the current of the Tagus, which at the ebb-tide runs from five to six miles an hour, two low launches or galleys, each as long as the packet, and each rowed by sixteen oars. Immediately the crew were all out of their hammocks, each bringing the boxes and bales containing his mercantile adventure on deck, and those of the officers being hoisted out of the hold, when the whole was bundled over the ship's side into the smuggling galleys; and in less than half an hour both were filled. No account seemed to be taken by any one of the goods thus put on board them, or receipt given by those to whose care they were consigned. The kind of " honour " which is said to " exist among thieves," was the sole bond of reliance for the fidelity of the smugglers, who were said to be most punctual and exact in all their dealings.

At length the boats pushed off from the packet, and the stout-armed boatmen plying their oars vigorously, began to make great progress against the stream, making obliquely for the shore to land their contraband cargo. They had not proceeded far, however, before a signal gun from one of the guarda-costas indicated that thej were discovered; and forthwith there was opened a cannonade from each of them, supposed to be directed against the smugglers, but the cannon were not shotted, and therefore no harm was done. Two boats were then sent from the revenue craft in chase; and these contrived not to overtake the pretended objects of their pursuit, but a tremendous shouting and execration was kept up against the vile and heretical smueglers, muskets and pistols were discharged without bullets, and swords were clashed against each other, striking fire at every stroke, and giving those in the ships near the idea of a fierce combat hand to hand between the patriotic guardians of the revenue and the flying-contrabandists!

This farce was kept up for at least an hour, to the great mirth and entertainment of our own officers and crew, who understood it perfectly; and on the following day the Official Gazette the only newspaper then published in Lisbon gave a glowing account of the devotedness of the officers and crew of the guarda-costas in pursuing and capturing tlie audacious smuggler, after a hard contest, in wliich some were killed and others wounded, these casualties being wholly in the ranks of the enemy. The price paid for these mendacious bulletins, which nohoclj had an interest in correcting, was a fixed share in the profits made on each successful smuggling transaction.

It was asserted and believed that the highest officers of the state, as well as the clergy, were participators in these frauds on the revenue, and that it was thought all fair game; and, as the duties on imported o'oods of the kind thus introduced were then one third of their estimated value, there was a sufficiently large margin for legitimate profit, and a bonus to set aside for the conspirators in these frauds besides. The taste for smuoffrlino; seemed to be universal; and, even in the returns for these goods, though they were generally paid for in hard, dollars, or doubloons, the contraband trade still prevailed, as the money was mostly laid out in Havannah segars, port wine, and other articles paying a high duty in England, which were again smuggled on shore, on the ship's arriving in the British Channel, either by the fishing and pilot boats from the Scilly Islands, Mount's Bay, and the west coast of Cornwall, or after the ship had anchored, in night visits to the shore.

Among the peculiarities which made the most forcible impression on me in Lisbon, and which I therefore most vividly remember now, the following may be named: The holiday dress of the sailors belonging to the ships of war and large-class merchant vessels, when on liberty ashore, was composed of a jacket and trowsers of olive-green velvet, with gay waistcoats embroidered with gold, white stockings, glossy black shoes with massive silver buckles, a long queue or tail of hair bound tight with ribbon, and hanging as low as the bottom of the jacket, like the English sailors of that day, and with immensely large cocked hats. Even the caulkers employed in repairing the ships along shore wore these huge and inconvenient head-coverings, and presented, on the whole, a most grotesque appearance. On shore the gentry and professional classes all wore dress swords, tight small clothes and silk stockings, with long, sharp-pointed tailed coats, reaching almost to the ground, and cocked hats of rather smaller dimensions. The ladies wore hooped petticoats, damask gay-coloured silk gowns, open in front, Avith embroidered stomachers, long waists, high peaked head-dresses with abundance of powder, and enormous fans. Even the respectable shopkeepers dressed in a similar style; and it was not unusual to meet mere boys of eight or ten years old dressed exactly like the men, and little girls of six or eight years old arrayed like matured matrons among the women. It seemed to me a new world, with an entirely different sort of inhabitants from those of England.

The public edifices of Lisbon being lofty and grand, and rather in the florid style of Roman architecture, the palatial residences of the nobles, the numerous and handsome churches, were very striking objects; but in contrast to these were many dark and narrow lanes of streets, and these, as well as the more public thoroughfares, were in a state of such extreme filth, and gave forth such offensive odours as to mark their great inferiority in this respect to England. The delicious climate; the abundance of fruit; the gay coffee-houses; the cooling drinks, sold even in the streets by itinerant ice-venders; and the sparkling and brilliant colours seen in the costume of all classes, leave on my recollection an impression of the gayest and most agreeable kind, so unlike the excessive toil, dirty apparel, and careworn countenances of the labouring classes, especially, of our own overworked population, as to convince me that the masses of Portugal enjoyed more of the pleasures, and fewer of the cares, of life than similar classes in our own country, while their universal sobriety presented an agreeable contrast to the frequent drunkenness of the labouring classes in England.

Our stay at Lisbon was short, and our return voyage a favourable one; and, though every means had been taken to disgust me with a sea life, my attachment to it was much stronger then when I first embarked, to the great sorrow and disappointment of my dear mother, and the other members of onr family.

I returned all the books which I had taken with me on the voyage, having read them all, by diligently devoting the hours of the watch below during the daytime to study, instead of idling or sleeping the more frequent course so that on being examined as to their contents, I was able to give so satisfactory an analysis of them, that I had a new supply of entirely different books for th second vojage; the stipulation being, that so long as I could give good proof, on each return, of having mastered the subjects of the books sent with me, I should always have a new supply for the next outfit; and I attribute to this judicious arrangement, the intense love of reading on grave and instructive subjects, which afforded me so much gi-atification then, and has continued unabated from that early period of youth to this. Indeed, I rarely ever returned from a voyage without having read, considered, and fairly understood the contents of ten or twelve volumes at least, and, in the longer passages, perhaps twenty, Avhich, considering that every one in a well-manned ship has four, six, or even eight hours of the watch below (that is, an entire relief from deck-dutv, unless "all hands" should be called) in each day, and that this time is free from the interruptions that break in upon studies on shore, such as letters by the post to answer, morning calls, the news of the day, public exhibitions and amusements, c. (none of which distract the attention at sea) may be easily accomplished, so as to enable a diligent reader, loving the occupation, to get through from fifty to sixty volumes in a year,

Second voyage to Lisbon in the same ship. Anecdote of a celebrated Portuguese wrestler. Encounter with this hero, and his triumph. Singular mode of enforcing payment of debt. Efficiency of this maritime machinery of justice. Splendid barge of the Queen of Portugal. Bathing parties of ladies and gentlemen of the Court. Reminiscence of Cleopatra's voyage on the Cydnus. Free manners of the Court and general society. Sacred names of wine-shops and ships of war. Anecdote of a smuggler and revenue searcher. Enthusiastic enjoyments of seamen on shore.

Mr second voyage to the same port, in the same ship, and with the same officers and crew, was quite as agreeable as the first; and as I became more familiar with the ship's duties, and acquired greater skill and activity in the performance of them, I rose in my own estimation as well as in that of my shipmates; for sailors are never backward to award their meed of praise to smart boys or able seamen, and to evince their admiration of courage, skill, and defiance of danger, the highest of all virtues in their estimation.

Two anecdotes of life and manners amonsc seamen, which occurred at Lisbon during this second voyage, may not be deemed unworthy of mention. As a na- tive of Cornwall, I had acquired an early taste for the athletic exercise of wrestling: and was known among my youthful contemporaries as a kind of champion ready and able to throw or master any boy of my own age and weight. My skill in this respect was often put to the test among the lads aboard, and with the invariable satisfaction of being declared the victor. The boatswain of the packet, named Waters, a thorough seaman, but a rough wag, delighting in the perpetration of personal or practical jokes, said to me, however, on one occasion of these triumphs, that he knew a Portuguese lad, one Antonio Calcavella, who would be more than a match for me, and would lay me prostrate without much trouble. As I had never yet been conquered in this exercise of wrestlino-, I felt a mixture of indignation and contempt at the idea of being vanquished by a Portuguese, as in that spirit of national prejudice with which all classes were then accustomed to regard foreigners of every description, I looked especially upon the Portuguese as decidedly our inferiors in physical strength. I therefore accepted the boatswain's challenge to encounter this redoubtable youth on the banks of the Taous, and longed for the day to come, on which I anticipated another victory to be added to the many I had already won.

On the first clay after our anchoring at Lisbon, I was among tlie party to whom leave was granted to go on shore, and the boatswain was also among the same group. It was resolved that we should make a holiday excursion along the banks of the river opposite to Lisbon, where this celebrated Portuguese wrestler lived; and, if we met with him, the trial of strength and agility was to be put to the test, and our comparative athletic powers at once decided on. We went, therefore, to an extensive range of buildings, forming a depot for wines, where he was said to be employed, and on our passage through the long lines of wine casks which occupied the ground floor, the boatswain, who had provided himself with a gimblet and reed for the purpose, bored a hole in one of the casks, inserted the reed, and drew from it draughts of the excellent wine it contained. He soon persuaded me to follow his example, and never having before tried the experiment, so as to be aw are of its effects, I fovmd the sweet wine so agreeable after a long and hot walk which excited unusual thirst, that before I was aware of it I became quite giddy, the fumes of the wine mounting to my head, and the next step of the process was to fall helpless on the ground. Li this state I was taken up by the sailors, carried into an adjoining shed, had draughts of lukewarm water freely administered, so as to act as an emetic, and in tlie course of an hour or two I was sufficiently recovered to be able to walk with them to the boat and returning on board, but terribly exhausted, and thoroughly ashamed, at having, for the first time in my life, been literally " overtaken in liquor," as the phrase is On reaching the ship, I was asked " who won in the struggle, Antonio Calca-vella or myself?" to which I replied, "We had never met with the youth at all, so that there had been no trial of our strength." The boatswain, however, with the loud hoarse voice which his vocation so often requires when giving orders to the men aloft amid the howling storm, said, "Avast, there, my lad! You did meet with him, and were fairly thrown." I repelled the calumny, as I then deemed it, with the loudest protestations against its truth; when the seamen of the party, to my surprise and astonishment, chimed in with the boatswain, and, amid hearty shouts of laughter, declared that they had seen me laid perfectly prostrate by my antagonist, and carried off the field in a state of complete insensibility, from which it took me two or three hours to recover. I felt as if it were all a dream; till the solution of the mystery came, in the explanation that the famous wrestler, Antonio Calcavella, was the cask of Calcavella wine,

VOL. I. G of which I had drank through the reed, and that by it I was completely thrown as described! It was a standing joke against me for the rest of the voyage; but, though I felt ashamed of having been thus betrayed, I had some consolation in the feeling that I had not been completely thrown, and that my championship as a wrestler was yet unshaken and unstained.

The other incident was this. Though the contra-bandists of the Tagus were generally most punctual in their payments for the goods taken by them out of the packets to be smuggled on shore, yet there were now and then persons in arrear, and some who were suspected of being wilful or fraudulent defaulters, perfectly able but unwilling to pay. One of these, who owed sums of different amounts to several of the crew, came on board one morning to open a new account on credit before he had settled the old; and there being a general feeling that he was a dishonest trader, the sailors, after finding all remonstrance vain to get any payment out of him on the spot, had recourse to this violent remedy, by exercising a species of Lynch law on the culprit. They stretched him along at full length over that part of the cable which lies between the windlass and the hawseholes, on the ship's forecastle, entirely unknown to the officers as they threatened instant punishment if the victim made the least noise. To this cable (then vibrating like a tremulous harp string, by the rapid motion of the current, which in the Tao; us runs at the rate of five or six miles in the hour it being the cable of the best bower anchor, by which the ship rode in the stream) the men lashed him fast, hand and foot, declaring they would keep him there until a messenger, authorised by him, should go on shore, call on any friend of his that he might name, and bring oflp the whole of the amount he owed the sailors, about two hundred and fifty dollars, in hard cash. With this only should he be released; but if the messenger returned without the money, the men threatened him with instant death, by veering out the cable through the hawsehole, by which he would be either crushed together in going through it, or, if he escaped that danger, he would be drowned in the Tagus, by being completely immersed beneath the surface, without the possibility of escape. The poor wretch was in a tremor of fear, and perspired as if he were being roasted.

The messenger was then sent ashore, urged to use all despatch, to w ait on a certain friend living near the landing-place, and tell the tale. In less than an hour he returned, with a large bag of silver 84 THE queen's state barge.

dollars, to the full amount required, and something over, if the released debtor should be disposed to treat his creditors, for having spared his life for future operations. The result was a gay and happy evening on the forecastle; the debtor going on shore with a light purse, but a light heart to bear it, and the sailors enchanted with the success of their experiment.

Another incident, which made a deep impression on me during our stay in the Tagus, was the frequent passing and repassing of the Royal barge to and from the bathing-place at the mouth of the river, to which the Queen of Portugal and her Court resorted every three or four days for sea-bathing. The barge was of the most splendid description, of great length and size, and adorned with carvings and gold. It was covered with silken awnings, and rowed by twenty-four handsome and athletic rowers, evidently selected for their manly beauty, dressed in snow-white shirts and trowsers, with scarlet sashes round their waists, and raven-black curly hair all harmonising well with their rich bronze complexions, brawny arms, naked and hairy breasts, and dark fiery eyes. The Queen was constantly surrounded by a bevy of fair maids of honour, and some dozen courtiers and favourites of the other sex; and judging from the peals of laughter which every now and then broke forth from the party, as well as from the character of the songs sang by the rowers in keeping time with their oars, feminine delicacy formed no part of the equipage. It was said, indeed, that the ladies and gentlemen bathed freely and nudely in the presence of each other, and that no scruples prevented even the rowers from exhibiting their fine proportions to the admiration of their superiors. Soft strains of music and delicious perfumes wafted in the air as the barge passed through the crowded ships at their anchorage; and the whole strikingly brought to mind the gorgeous description by Shakspeare, of Cleopatra in her barge sailing up the Cydnu. s to meet Mark Antony at Tarsus:

"The bai'ge she sat in, like a burnished throne, Burnt on the water the poop was beaten gold, Purple the sails, and so perfumed, that The winds were love-sick with them the oars were silver. Which to the tune of flutes kept stroke, and made The water which they beat to follow faster, As amorous of their strokes."

The free manners of the Court were thought to have great influence in relaxing the rigour of social relations on shore; and tales were in every one's mouth of such connections between persons of tlie higher rank as would not be tolerated in England: while among the humbler classes the dissoluteness was almost universal. Exclamations and expressions such as could not be named, and which in England would be confined to the most abandoned, saluted the ear at the landing-places and in the public markets, from women as well as men; and our sailors appeared to be familiar with all the haunts of vice, which were generally designated by the most sacred names; as the street of the Holy Trinity, the lane of the Blessed Virgin, the alley of the Sacred Heart, the court of St. Peter and St. Paul, the piazza of the Holy Sacrament. Most of the lowest wine shops, too, where aqua ardiente or aniseed brandy was as abundantly supplied as wine, had for their signboards the portrait of some favourite saint, particularly Saint Antonio, Joseph and Mary, the Bleeding Lamb, the Eternal Father, the Holy Ghost, and similar associations of the most awful and venerable names with the vilest of practices. In the same manner, their largest ships of war, both among the Portuguese and Spaniards, are called the Santissima Trinidada and the Salvador del Mundo, the most inappropriate that could well be conceived: and certainly less in harmony with the death-dealing and destroying powers they are intended to exercise than the English names of the Terrible, the Revenge, the Spitfire, the Arrogant, the Implacable, the Lion, the Tiger, the Wolf, and the Bull-dog, the Etna, the Vesuvius, and the Stromboli, all of which sufficiently proclaim the nature of their mission.

In our perambulations on shore it was impossible not to be struck with the contrasts presented by different parts of the city of Lisbon, in salubrity,-beauty, cleanliness, and the character of their occupants. In the upper parts, at Buenos Ayres and its environs, space, air, and purity might be enjoyed in perfection, while the views over the distant hills and the broad bosom of the Tagus were magnificent. In the steep acclivities of the intermediate region between the river and the upper ridge, the shops, stores, and private dwellings were often substantial and appropriate to the purposes they were intended to answer. But in the lower portions of the town, along the w ater's edge, dark, narrow, tortuous, and filthy lanes and alleys, leading off from the great thoroughfare, sent forth such bad odours, and exhibited such a squalid and miserable population, as to lessen one's wonder at the ravages which fever makes among them every year, notwithstanding the general healthfulness of this beautiful climate.

We left Lisbon for England, after a stay of about three weeks in port, and had a long voyage from much contrary winds; but, on the whole, not a disagreeable one. As usual, all the officers and crew had laid in a stock of wine and segars, from the proceeds of their outward adventure, to be smuggled on shore at Falmouth as opportunities might offer; and on our first making the Lizard lights it was amusing to observe the bustle and ingenuity of every one on board to conceal, in the places least likely to be suspected, the various commodities belonging to them; for though the ship's pennant protected her against the visits and inspection of the revenue officers in Portugal, this privilege was not enjoyed at home, and boats from the Customs and Excise were alongside as soon as we were at anchor. An instance occurred in which one of the seamen, who had had some of his tobacco seized on a previous voyage, was determined to be avenged on the unhappy searcher by whom it had been detected, and the stratagem to which he had recourse was the following: While the same searcher was on deck, the seaman went up the main rigging, carrying with him four empty bottles, which the searcher however believed to be full ones, and going out on the main topgallant yard, he pretended to hide two of them in the folds of the topgallant sail, which was furled, on the starboard side, and two others in the same sail on the larboard side, eacli nearly out to the yard-arm. He then descended on deck, and joined the rest of the crew. The searcher then asked the sailing master of the ship to send a man aloft to take out from the main topgallant sail four bottles of wine, which he declared that he had seen with his own eyes one of the seamen secrete there, for the purpose of smuggling. The officer refused to comply with such a request, adding that if they were worth seizing they were worth going after by himself. Not to be defeated in his purpose, the searcher mounted the rio; i; ino- reached the mast-head, and lay out on the starboard yard-arm, to take the bottles there concealed; when the seaman who had hid them there, watching the searcher's movements, let go the starboard lift from on deck, by which the yard was topped up in a perpendicular, instead of a horizontal, position; in consequence of which the searcher fell from the vard; and but that his fall was broken by his body lighting on several of the ropes that intercepted his descent, and landed him at last on the stretched-out netting spread like an awning across the quarter deck, he would have, in all probability, broken his neck, and dislocated every bone in his body. Nobody appeared to pity the victim of this practical joke; the only observation that escaped from officers and crew being, "Served him right," for all felt gratified at his failure, and applauded the seaman for the ingenuity of the device.

I remained on shore for three or four weeks after this, the harbour duty being so light as not to require the presence of all the crew, and I enjoyed the rural walks and rides by day, and the evening parties and the dance by night, with infinitely greater zest than is possible to be felt by those who are always on land. This, indeed, constitutes one of the charms of a sailor's life, that every time he returns from a voyage it is like the beginning of a new existence; he comes charged brimful of enthusiasm to enjoy the society of females especially, from which he has been so long cut off, and to enter with animation into every kind of entertainment; it is this also which makes the society of seamen so agreeable to all parties, and to young girls and women especially, with whom sailors are in general such favourites, from their frankness, ardour, and actual devotion to the sex.

Disastrous issue of my third voyage to Lisbon. Capture bj a French corvette. English mutineers. Seamen from the Enclish frisrate Hermione among the crew. Confinement of prisoners in the ship's hold. Suffocation. Short supply of water, and increased difficulties of drinking. Arrival at the Spanish port of Corunna. Imprisonment there, and scanty supplies of food. Love adventure with the daughter of the Superintendant. Orders for our release, to march to Oporto and Lisbon. General joy at the prospect of regaining our liberty.

My third voyage was disastrous, and caused me to become acquainted, rather earlier than I wished, with an entirely new phase of life, namely, captivity. We sailed from Falmouth under the usual circumstances, and for the first few days had favourable weather, but on the third or fourth day we had a contrary wind and dense fog. On the clearing up of this, when we were not very distant from Cape Finisterre, we beheld a large French corvette, of the leno-th and size of our first-class frioates, and filled with men, within gun-shot range on our weather beam. She fired a gun across our bow, the signal for heaving to, and hoisted the tricolor flag.

The corvette running close under our lee, the com- mander hailed us by the question " D'ou venez vous? " and our commander. Captain Dillon, not knowing a word of French which was indeed rarely understood in those days of national isolation except by highly educated or travelled individuals called out to our own ship's company, ' Is there any man aboard that knows French?" to which the gunner, Peter Wakeham, who was stationed at the gangway, answered, "I do. Sir, having been in a French prison for three years." " Then tell me," said the commander, " what does the Frenchman say." " Say, Sir," replied the gunner," why he says," Haul down your colours, or I'll sink ye, by God!"" " Damn the fellow," rejoined the Captain (who was nevertheless a professedly pious man, and brother of the rector of the parish of Mylor, but swearing was universal with gentlemen in those days), " does he say all that in three words? " " Ay! that he does," said Peter, " and a great deal more if I had time to translate it, but he is in a hurry for an answer." Several of the officers knew this could not be true, when my brother-in-law, Mr. Steele, the sailing-master of the packet, called out to me, "Here, youngster, you know French better than this, don't you, what does the officer say?" I replied, " ' From whence came you?" only:" to which an immediate answer was given, 'From Falmouth,"

and I was immediately placed by the Captain's side to interpret the remainder of the questions asked, till the order was given to lower the colours, " a has le pavilion," and consider ourselves as prize. This little incident raised me considerably in the estimation of our own ship's company, and exalted me not a little in my owai. The truth is, my elder brother, who was educated and brought up in France, had very early instructed me in the elements of that lanffuacre, so that I could read any book in it as easily as in English, and this greatly facilitated my subsequent acquisition of Spanish and Portugvtese.

All hands had been piped to quarters, and it was the captain's first intention to offer resistance or give battle, so that the crew were stationed at their guns. But a short deliberation among the oflicers soon led to the decision that it would be madness to make the attempt against such superior odds. Our own force was only 6 guns, short 6 pounders, and a crew of about 30 men. The enemy mounted 30 guns, long 18-

pounders, with a crew of more than 300 men. The first broadside, from her favourable position, just under our lee, would probably have dismasted us, and killed half the crew, and with a second we should have been annihilated: so that reluctant as all appeared to be to submit without a struggle, the order was given to back the main topsail, and lower the mizen peak, at which our flag was displayed. It was a moment of almost breathless sadness along our decks, as nothina; but a low and stifled murmur of minsjled sorrow and discontent was heard. On the other hand, as the corvette neared us, her crew manned the rigging, and waving their red caps of liberty in the air, shouted 'Vive la Republique," in sounds that at once mortified and thrilled us, bv their oftensivelj triumphant tone.

Boats with the requisite number of officers and men were immediately despatched from the corvette to take possession of the prize; and though the officers behaved with all the courtesy and politeness of gentlemen to their captives, the men, among whom we were shocked to find several English, were under no such restraint, but manifested considerable rudeness and severity. The officers and crew of the packet were then ordered into the boats that brought our captors to us, and we were all transferred, excepting only the passengers, among whom were several ladies and children, to the corvette, where we were not uncourteously received; the officers having berths allotted to them in the low er deck of the vessel, and the crew being transferred to the hold.

There the first painful fact we learnt was, that a very large portion of the crew of this French corvette, which was named the Mars, and which we understood sailed from Nantes, was composed of English mutineers, who had belonged to the English frigate Hermione, stationed in the Gulf of Mexico or the West Indies, in which ship they mutinied a few years before, and after murdering the greater number of their officers, by whom tliere is reason to believe they had been very cruelly tyrannised over and often undeservedly flogged, they took the ship into Vera Cruz, then a Spanish port, and gave her up as prize. From hence they had become gradually dispersed; some going into the American, some into the Spanish, and some into the French serv ice, and a few venturing back to England, hoping to escape detection, but several of whom were subsequently identified, and hung at the yard-arm the mutineer's usual fate.

I remember well, how much we were all revolted at findino; these English mutineers far less kind and civil to us than the French portion of the crew, who on the whole treated us with as much kindness as was compatible with their own safety, and often endeavoured to lighten our burdens, by saying it was only " the fortune of war," and that it might be their turn next to become prisoners to the English.

The second painful discovery was, that as the corvette had already made several captures of English vessels, chiefly merchant traders, before our own, there were already a considerable number of English prisoners on board: and there being no room for them among the crew they were of necessity sent into the hold, where they were battened down under grating hatchways; Sentries were placed with drawn swords to prevent an escape, and only a few could be permitted to come on deck for half an hour at a time to breathe the free air, and then return to give place to a similar number of their fellow-captives, that all might enjoy this privilege in their turn. In consequence of this confinement, several had died in the hold for want of air; and this would in all probability have been my own fate, had I remained long in this position; but being the youngest person on board not yet quite ten years old, it being in the summer of 1796, in the August of which my tenth year was completed and being related to the sailing-master of the packet, who was my eldest sister's husband, I was exempted from this confinement, messed with the younger grade of officers, and had free range on deck.

There was yet another hardship, liowever, to which even the most favoured were subject, and this was a deficiencj of Avatcr. Owing to the great number of prisoners on board, and a very large crew, the consumption of water was enormous; and it liad been progressively reduced, from a gallon per day, which is the usual full allowance for every purpose cooking, drinking, washing and all to half a pint per head only for officers and men; for there is this kind of equality on board all ships, that the highest admiral can draw no more biscuit, beef, or water than the humblest seaman, when the ship's company " goes on allowance," as it is termed; the similarity in the actual wants of all, for mere nutriment and sustenance, reducing all to a state of nature in this respect, and making any privilege of extra-quantity to any parties, on the score of more elevated rank, too odious to be permitted. It would have been easy, no doubt, for the ship to run into port, land her prisoners, fill up her water, and return to her cruisino-ground again; but as this would have involved, perhaps, the loss of a week, and prevented their adding three or four more prizes to the list of their captures during these days, the passion of avarice, which almost invariably increases with the extension of possession, overcame all other considerations, and VOL. I. H it was left till the last moment to quit the mine of wealth which these almost daily captures afforded. The ship was so fast a sailer, that when once she gave chase to any vessel within sight from the mast-head, nothing could escape her; and while everything within the range of her vision was sure to fall a prey, if an English frigate hove in sight, her amazing speed enabled her as easily to bid her enemy defiance, and to " run her out of sight," as sailors say, between sunrise and sunset.

During the last week of our stay on board, therefore, this contrivance was had recourse to, to diminish the consumption of water: The officers and crew of the ship had their allowance of half a pint each served regularly in the morning at eight o'clock, at the relief of the watch; but for the prisoners, a water-butt was placed before the mainmast, on its bilge, or lying athwart the deck. Into the bung-hole of this cask was inserted a long musket-barrel, with its muzzle at the bottom resting in the muddy deposit, which is sure to accumulate in all ships' water-casks that are sta-tionarv or at rest. The touch-hole of the musket-barrel was about three inches above or outside the bung-hole; and over this was a metal cap, secured by a padlock. The key of the padlock was placed in a small but secure iron box at the maintop mast-head.

attaclied to the cross-trees. Every prisoner, therefore, who wanted to drink, had first to go to the mast-head to get the key; then, after unlocking the cap over the gun-barrel, to suck as much moisture as he could, the first half-dozen mouthfuls being as much mud as water; and when he had slaked his thirst by the thin thread of water he could suck up through the touch-hole, he liad to relock the cap, and take the key to the mast-head, there to be deposited for the next comer; and severe punishment was threatened to any one who passed the key on to another without taking it to the mast-head as ordered. The result of this ingenious arrangement was, that no one ever went aloft for the key till he was so parched with thirst as to find it unendurable, while the mud-diness of the deposit, and the extreme fatigue to the lungs and mouth in drawing up water through such a tube as a gun-barrel, soon tired the drinker and oblifted him to desist.

At length the welcome order was given to make all sail and shape our course for the port of Corunna in Spain, that being the nearest harbour to our actual position, and Spain being then in friendly alliance with the new Republic of France. The boatswain's shrill whistle, repeated at each hatchway by the boatswain's mates, soon brought all hands on deck, and the rigging literally swarmed with men; all reefs were shaken out, studding sails set below and aloft, and with the wind two points abaft the beam, and every stitch of canvass spread, the ship shot through the water like an arrow, giving fourteen knots by the log, then deemed, as it really was, an almost unattainable speed; so that on the second day we made the land, passed by the entrance to the great naval arsenal of Spain, Ferrol, and soon entered the harbour of Corunna, the French band on board playing " The Marseillaise," then the national republican air, and the batteries of Corunna saluting a ship that had sent in so many prizes for condemnation and sale at its port. I remember well the mixed feeling of curiosity, sorrow, and shame, with which I was alternately possessed, while being transported with the rest of the crew to the shore in the ship's boats, for the purpose of being transferred to the building set apart for our confinement. To be a prisoner of war, and, perhaps, for many years before liberty would be regained, was a painful and mortifying event; but such is the elasticity of youthful spirits, that the novelty of all I saw about me soon absorbed my whole attention, and the sorrow and shame of my captivity was drowned in the exciting interest of all the scenes and people by whom I was surrounded.

We landed at a fine quay in tlie harbour, and were marched through the lower town there beuig an upper one on an elevated site, stronglj fortified; and we observed Fort Anthony protecting the harbour, and the Iron Tower of Hercules, nearly 100 feet high, independently of the elevated site on which it stands, formino; a liodithouse which is said to be visible at the great distance of twenty leagues at sea our English lighthouses being rarely visible more than a third of that distance, or twenty miles. We saw also the royal manufactory of cigars (tobacco being a royal monopoly in Spain), where more than five hundred women and children are said to be employed in preparing these articles in a manner so filthy and disgusting that it is said those who witness tlie process are often deterred from using them.

The population of Corunna, exceeding 20,000, afforded an infinite variety of figures, complexions, and costumes all characterised by greater variety and brighter colours tlian in England, and inter-spersed with such a number of priests, monks, and. nuns, in the varied dresses of their respective orders, as to mark, by this change more than any other, the diflperence between an English and a Spanish crowd. The noises in the streets, from the screaming cries of all tlie vendors of different articles, especially fresh

LIBRARY
UNIVERSITY OF CALIFORNIA

SANTA BARBARA water, ices, and fruits, and the continued clang of bells, as at Lisbon, at all hours of the day and night, was another marked feature of contrast with the more sober quiet of English towns.

We arrived at length at the large building appropriated for our reception, apparently an old palace or mansion then vacant; and as far as room or space was concerned, we had no reason to complain. Each man slung his hammock from wall to wall when night came. In the morning they were taken down and lashed up as on board ship; while cleanliness was strictly enforced, by frequent washing of the floors, as the ship's decks are washed, and ventilation was amply secured by open windows day and night continuously.

The provender supplied to us by the government authorities was, however, miserably stinted in quantity, and, to our well-fed stomachs and English taste, abominable in quality. Pulse, small beans, called calavances, coarse vegetables, oil and garlic, formed the chief ingredients, bread so rough and sandy as to grit against the teeth, and a thin wine, more like vinegar, constituted our daily food. The men soon began to catch young dogs, cats, and even rats, and convert them into soups, stews, and ragouts, which were far from unpalatable, and which extreme hun- ger made most acceptable; and when these failed, they parted, day by day, with some article of apparel in barter for something to eke ont their scanty meal. For myself I was fortunate enough to be amply provided, not merely with abundance, but with even delicacies, from another source. The governor or superintendent of the prison had a handsome and dark-eyed young daughter about my own age a little past ten years old but in Spain girls at ten are as mature as English girls at sixteen. She oc-casionally attended the prisoners with their food, and conceived, as she afterwards confessed, a violent passion for me, which she found it impossible to control. I may observe that even in England I was considered to be a very handsome boy, and the charm of a clear complexion, rosy cheeks, light blue eyes, and light brown curly hair, so unusual in Spain, made me appear, it would seem, a perfect x donis in her love-seeing eyes. She therefore revealed to me her inmost thoughts in her own impassioned language, which I had learnt during my voyages to Lisbon in conjunction with the Portuguese, and which I now sufficiently understood to comprehend every one of her burning phrases, impressed as they often were by kisses of the most thrilling intensity. By her kind hand I was furnished at every meal with all the delicacies of her father's table, of which she contrived to abstract some portion dailj; and with an ingenuity which left all my inventive powers far in the rear, she contrived twenty times a day to find some pretext for calling me out of the room for some pretended message or errand, to get a squeeze of the hand only if others were near, or if in any passage where we were not likelv to be seen, a warm and fond embrace, by which she pressed me to her bosom as if never intending to relax her grasp, and kisses and tears rained in equal abundance.

At length the fascinated vsenorita actually devised a mode of escape for me, and offered to accompany me in my flight. But though I was scarcely less enamoured than herself, I had yet sufficient prudence left to think where we should go to escape detection and capture liow we should subsist, even if we were fortunate enough to elude discovery and how I could answer to her parents and the authorities for yielding to an elopement under such hopeless circumstances, I was obliged therefore to temporise with my tender-hearted Donna Isabella Dolores (for such was her name), and, under pretence of waiting for some safer opportunity, to procrastinate and defer what I had not the courage or the cruelty to oppose.

Several months passed away in this agreeable manner for surely never did a captive's fetters sit more lightly on a prisoner of war than mine did on me when the avithorities of Corunna, finding our maintenance, scanty as it was, too burthensome to bo continued, proposed to give us our liberty, on condition of our leaving their city and going by land to Oporto or Lisbon, where we might find the means of returning to our native country, they paying the expenses of our journey and giving us an escort to the Portuguese frontier, and leaving to the government of Portugal, or to the British consuls in that countryj, to provide for us when we had passed the Spanish borders; for at this period (1797), though Spain was allied to France, Portugal still maintained her friendly relations with England.

The proposition was received with the greatest joy by all the prisoners and not with entire indifference by myself; for, attached as I now began to feel to the young' heroine who had done so much to lighten the evils of my captivity, still the love of home and the desire to return to it was not wholly extinguished within me. To her, however, the tidings came like a death-warrant, and its first announcement, which was made by myself, was met with a shriek and a swoon, wdiicli called the members of the family to her relief. An explanation was demanded, and it could not be rofused. There was a little manifestation of anger on the part of the father, but much more of sympathy and pity on the part of the mother; and in the end all was forgiven, as our separation was so near, and as no evil consequences were now likely to ensue.

Setting out ou our march tlirougli Galicia. Description of our party. Scanty travelling allowance. Scenery of the way. Benevolence of Spanish women. Lodging in stables, Costume and manners of muleteers.-Fires lighted to defend us from wolves on the snowy mo ntains. Kindness of the seamen towards ladies and children. Arrival at the city of Santiago di Compostella. Midnight serenade of a Spanish lover. Journey to Vigo. Fraternization of Spanish and English sailors. March to Oporto. Frontiers of Spain and Portugal. Description of Oporto, Coimbra, and Ab-rantes. Descent of the Tagus from Santarem to Lisbon.

When the day of our departure arrived, as all were to march on foot, everjone reduced his baggage to the smallest possible dimensions, so as to be carried in a knapsack on his back, as no cart or waggon was to be provided to accompany us. A sort of public sale, therefore, took place at the door of the prison, of the surplus shirts, jackets, trowsers, hammocks, bedding, and other articles impossible to be taken in the journey; but as the sale was known to be one of necessity, in which there could be no reservation, the prices produced were ridiculously small; and the whole united mass of things sold produced only a few pistareens.

In my own case, I was here again favoured by my enthusiastic young admirer. My stock of wearing apparel, books, nautical instruments, c., with which I had been liberally supplied by my dear mother and sisters, could not have cost less than 100?. sterling. For the whole, except the change of linen and a few small articles retained for my knapsack, a dealer ofiered five Spanish dollars! The mother of Donna Isabella vented on him such a volley of invectives for his cruelty, in thus seeking to take advantage of a poor little stranger, whom everybody ought to help instead of to wrong, that he slunk away in shame, amid the hisses and reproaches of the bystanders; and the Spanish is richer in opprobrious epithets than most other languages of Europe. Not content with this, she consented to take the whole of my stock herself, and risk the chance of sellino; it after we w ere gone, putting into my hands about a dozen gold coins, in pistoles and half-pistoles, with strict injunctions to take care not to lose them on the journey but reserve them to, buy food whenever the rations allowed to the prisoners should be insufficient. The daughter, who witnessed this, fell on her mother's neck and wept bitterly, gratitude for her bounty and pain at our parting mingling together in her sobs. I too was permitted, even in the presence of her motlicr (an unusual pinvilege in Spain), to kiss the sorrowing Seilorita's hand though we had secretly embraced and sio'hed out our adieus before and when we started on our march, I believe my heart was as heavy as her own, as there was no longer for either that " hope of return " which is said to " take tlie sting from adieu."

Our party consisted of about fifty seamen, with half-a-dozen passengers, only two boys, myself and a young relative of one of the officers, Mr. James Tilly, a year or two older than I, and a guard of some twenty soldiers armed with muskets and sabi es. It was understood that the stipulated allowance for our maintenance on the road was to be a crusada nova per head about two shillings English, for every hundred miles which, considering that distance to occupy eight ordinary days' march, made about threepence halfpenny per day for each person.

Our route was directed southward to Santiago di Compostella, in the province of Galicia, of which I remember the followins; most strikino; features. The scenery of the country appeared to me most romantically varied with mountain, valley, and plain, but destitute of the softer beauties of English landscape. The cattle and peasants, mules and muleteers, that we met on the way were all more picturesque than at home; and the contrabanclistas or smugglers, who were numerous, were all well mounted, well armed, and seemed a splendid race of men.

In our march we started always at or before daybreak, halted at the first village for an hour for the first meal of the day, which was often noon or past, when many of us were faint and weary; and started again after refreshment, always halting an hour or two before sunset, making from twelve to fifteen miles per day in these two short marches. Our evening meal was more substantial, because here we had generally an opportunity of exciting some interest among the population, who sent us small contributions, in fowls and eggs especially, to eke out our scanty government allowance. In this work of charity, the young women and children were conspicuous; the men were often indifferent or churlish, and the priests invariably hostile and insulting towards the " hereticos," so that the women were obliged to be very careful to bestow their kindnesses in secret. In all cases, as being the youngest of the party, I used to come in for a large share of female sympathy: the mothers would pat me on the head and cheek, and ask me if I had a mother, and why she permitted me to leave her for the war

SO young; whether I had brothers and sisters, whether I was the youngest of the family, both of which questions were answered in the affirmative, and seemed to stimulate their kindness. These repeated acts of bounty, added to the occasional use which I could make of the pistoles which the mother of the Senorita Donna Isabella had furnished me on leaving Corunna, made my fate very enviable compared with that of my companions; though I had, in addition to a good stock of natural generosity so much of the sailors' proverbial unselfishness, that I never enjoyed a meal apart, but always had some one or more to share my good fortune with me.

Our lodging at night was almost invariably in the stables with the mules; and a bed of clean straw and a roof over our heads for shelter were accounted luxuries. We rarely undressed, but, placing our knapsacks as pillows and heaping the straw above us as well as beneath us, we slept more sweetly than many crowned heads in Europe.

The muleteers wore a singular kind of cloak, formed of woven straw in a mat-like form for the groundwork or interior, but with a succession of projecting capes formed of loose straw for the exterior, each cape being about a foot deep, and proceeding in regular gradation from the neck to the lower edge near the ankle, presented a series of projecting ledges like the over-lapping planks of a clinker-built boat, or of a wooden dwellinii;, so that the rain falling from one ledije to another never touched the Pi'oundwork of the cloak, and thus kept the wearer dry In the heaviest torrents of rain. The cloak had a hood like tliat worn by monks, which equally protected the head from cold or wet; and the sight of a man so apparelled pacing up and down the stable with a lantern, when the mules were to be caparisoned for the march at daybreak, looked like a moving pyramid of straw for the cloaks expanded widely at the bottom and, seen for the first time, had something supernatural in its aspect.

On some nisi; hts in the mountains we were unable to reach a village within the day's march, and in such cases we bivouacked in the open air. As wolves, however, were here abundant, and their howlino; s at nio; ht left no doubt of their numbers, the precaution was taken to collect together as much dry fuel as possible during the march or before sunset, and form a circle of fire around us. AVithin this circle we slept, guards and all, having a sentry changed every hour, in comparative tranquillity, though the cold was bitter in the more elevated portions of the mountains; and melted snow water was our only drink.

At one portion of the journey, where a forced march of twenty-five miles in the day, in order to cross a mountain range, fatigued us all excessively, my young companion Tilly and myself, being quite overcome with sleep, found, on our awakening in the morning, that all our companions were gone, and having started probably before it was quite daylight, had not observed that we were left behind. Great was our consternation and sorrow; but there was not a moment to be lost. We knew the general direction of our route to be southerlv; and we could tell by the position of the rising sun in what quarter the south lay. We therefore braced on our knapsacks and ran with all speed for nearly an hour, till we were both ready to sink from exhaustion of breath, when, lo! to our intense delight, we perceived the whole party just rounding a rocky projection in a valley beneath us; and by shouting at the top of our voices, we attracted their attention, and they halted till we rejoined them.

For myself, I was quite done up, and would willingly have lai i down and died rather than proceed further. But this was not permitted. My old and kind friend the boatswain. Waters, though himself past

VOL. T. I fiftj, and with a very heavy body of his own to drag along, made a belt round his waist with a rope, and formed another round mine with a fragment of the same, and then linking the two together by an intervening rope, literally took me in tow, amid the cheering of our shipmates at this act of generosity; so that all the fatigue of my walking consisted merely in lifting my feet from the ground, as the impetus of forward motion was communicated to me by the tow rope by which I was drawn along. The kind-hearted sailors, however, would not allow the boatswain to have the monopoly of this generous assistance, but each took it in turn for half an hour at a time, by which I was wonderfully relieved; and being a great favourite with the men, to whom " smart boys " are always useful auxiliaries in setting light sails at sea, when heavier men could hardly effect the same objects so well, it was with them really a " labour of love."

Another striking proof of their generosity and gallantry of feeling was manifested during this journey in their treatment of one of the passengers, a lady of distinction and her children, who, being taken captive with us in the packet, in which she was going to Lisbon to join her husband, was subject to the same conditions of the march as ourselves.

For tills lady and her children, the seamen voluntarily made a capacious sedan-chair out of the branches of trees by the way-side, assisted by the carpenter and his mates. To this was attached two long poles, one on each side, by which the chair containing the party could be lifted from the ground; and eight men, two at each pole before and two behind, carried this litter on their shoulders the whole of the way, to the intense delight of the children and to the great relief of their mother, who could never have performed the journey without such aid.

At length, after many days' marching and many nights' bivouacking, we reached the city of Santiago di Compostella, the capital of Galicia, and were deeply impressed with the beauty of its public squares, its numerous churches, and conventual edifices, this being a city of great renown as a place of religious pilgrimage, from its being supposed to contain the body of St. James the apostle; and its ecclesiastical revenues are said to be the largest in all Spain.

Here we were permitted to halt for a few days to recruit our strength, and we were as well lodged as at Corunna in a barrack of the town then happening to be empty. We had full liberty, also, in company with one of the guards to each party, to roam about the city between our meals, and to visit all the churches, which, in comparison to the bare and naked edifices of Protestant worship in our own country, seemed to us of overwhelming splendour; while the services of the matins, vespers, and masses, one or other continually performing, the constant coming and going of devotees to and from the churches, the perfumes of the silver censers, the glowing pictures, the rich painted glass of the windows,-and the enchanting music of the organs and tlie choirs, were fascinations which it was impossible not to enjoy, and the influence of which it would have been difficult, if long continued, to resist. As for ourselves, in comparison with such a people, we seemed to have no religion at all.

One of the most interesting incidents which I remember during our stay at Santiago di Compostella, was that of a Spanish serenade, one of the last relics of the old romantic days of Spanish gallantry and intrigue. Not far from our place of lodging was a spacious mansion, evidently the abode of some person of note, the front of which was perfectly visible to us from our windows. About midnight, when most of our party were buried in profound sleep, the sound of a fine voice accompanied by a guitar awoke me from my slumbers. I hastened to tlie window, where I was soon joined by others, and we were richly rewarded for this interruption of our vigils, by the sight we beheld.

Before the front of this mansion was a party of minstrels and choristers, about a dozen in number, all in the ancient Spanish costume, the principal one of the group being dressed in white satin (for it was bright moonlight which enabled us to see the picture in detail) with slashed hose and jacket in scarlet relief, a broad-brimmed slouch hat, turned up in front by a diamond loop, and a graceful plume of white feathers, having round his neck, suspended by a light blue ribbon, a guitar, and over his shoulder and waist a blue scarf, with a steel-hilted dress sword. It was this hero of the party whom we heard singing in a fine voice and with rich accompaniments, and ever and anon the choristers joined in to repeat the refrain.

Presently there appeared at one of the upper windows an elderly looking dame, such as we should picture as a duenna; and after certain apparent scoldings and threatenings, to some one within as well as to the serenaders without, she vanished. In a few moments afterwards a young lady witli a black veil thrown over her head, but without cap or bonnet, opened the casement, and kissincr her hand to the innamorato below, let fall a rope-ladder, three or four feet of which rested on the ground, so that the musicians speedily pulled it out a little distance from the front wall of tlie house, fastened its ends into the ground, by some means with which they were already provided; and in a minute or two of time, the lover, unslinging his guitar, and handing it to one of his companions, mounted by the ladder with wonderful agility, gave the young lady in the window several hearty kisses, and descended still more rapidly than he had gone up; when the whole party suddenly dispersed, as if apprehensive that some pursuit would be made, or some vengeance inflicted. With the exception, however, of considerable scolding and vituperation within the house, and a number of persons moving about with lights in their hands, all went off quietly, there being scarcely any persons walking in the streets at this late hour of the night, so that soon after the silence was profound. The whole scene Avas perfectly dramatic, and such as I have subsequently witnessed on the stage; but since then now "sixty years since" the costume and manners of the Spaniards have greatly changed, and in Spain, as in most other countries of Europe, the most striking characteristics have generally disappeared.

After a few days' halt at Santiago di Compostella, ill Yllich we enjoyed the pleasure of gratified curiosity, from the novelties with which we were every hour surrounded, as well as most welcome repose, we resumed our march, and went by El Padron and Pon-tevedra to Vi o. The first two of these were small towns on the banks of rivers, and the last, a sea port, on a good bay, but with very few vessels in it at the time of our visit. In this place, however, an occurrence took place, which is too characteristic of the fraternity of seamen to be omitted. About this period, several richly laden Spanish galleons conveying treasure from Acapulco in Mexico to Old Spain, had been captured by British ships of war, and the Spanish crews were accordingly made prisoners. After a short stay in England they had been exchanged for a corresponding number of British prisoners in Spain, and had been landed at Vigo, from whence to reach their own homes as they best could. They might therefore be fairly supposed to be in no very favourable mood of mind to fraternise with the seamen of England, by whom they had been captured, as many of them had lost all the earnings of their long and perilous voyage, in the gold and silver they were bringing from Mexico, all of which became prize to their captors. Nevertheless, as soon as they heard of our arrival at Vigo, and (consignment to a large empty bviilding there, as prisoners of war, on our march to Lisbon, a large party of them called upon us, and, after a conversation in broken English and broken Spanish by such among them as could thus imperfectly understand each other, they actually proposed to give us a banquet! alleging that "seamen were brothers all the world over;" though it seemed to me then, as it has done ever since, to be an odd way of exhibiting their ties of brotherhood, by burning, sinking, and destroying the property of each other, and either putting each other to death, if resistance be offered, or rew arding the most quiet surrender by captivity and miserable fare.

As the guests of these warm-hearted Spaniards, we, of course, readily accepted their proffered hospitality; but there was one obstacle which at first appeared insuperable. Neither the entertainers nor the guests could muster more than a few dollars between them. Perseverance, however, conquers most difficulties; and the Spanish seamen, forming themselves into groups of three or four, actually went round from house to house among the inhabitants of Vigo, to solicit aid for the purpose of fulfilling their design, and they succeeded. Accordingly on the evening following our arrival, a goodly store of provisions was brought to our quarters, consisting of fishj flesh, and fowl, with vegetables, fruit, and wine in abundance. The cookery was Spanish; and therefore oil and garlic predominated in almost every dish; but we were not in a condition to be fastidious, and all appeared to eat heartily the givers of the feast as well as the receivers. But in the matter of drinking, there was a marked and disadvantageous contrast. The Spaniards drank the wine mixed with water, though it was the thin, and what would be called the weak, wine of the country, and when they had satisfied their thirst they drank no more. The English sailors, on the contrary, added brandy, or aqua ardiente, to their wine to make it stronger, and then drank to such excess that there were not half a dozen of the whole number who were not helplessly drunk by midnight, and in that state of unreason or temporary madness would actually have fought with each other but for the intervention of the soldiers, by whom we were still guarded. I remember distinctly the keen disgust I felt at this exhibition of my shipmates' indiscretion, and my countrymen's weakness, if not vice; and I have reason to believe that this scene had a large share in giving me the early dislike 1 have ever since felt to the companionship of men of intemperate habits.

From Vigo, our march was towards Oporto; and at the end of our second day's journey in tliis direction, we readied the banl s of the Minho river, which rises in the north of Spain, runs through all Galicia, the province we had been traversing, and as it approaches the sea, forms the southern boundary line separating Spain from Portugal. On each side the river, at the place where we crossed it in a ferry-boat, there were forts within less than half a mile of each other; and it was curious to us, who had never passed a land frontier between two countries before, to see the Spanish flag waving from one and the Portuguese from the other, with the sentries of each in different uniforms; a little thread of water, so to speak, thus dividing the tnVO nations who have frequently been engaged in war. The Spanish and Portuguese languages the latter appearing to be a corruption of the former were equally spoken in both these frontier forts; but we learnt from each, that instead of close proximity making their occupants friends, a most deadly hatred and even contempt was felt by each towards its opposite neighbour. The near approach of France to England seems, to one who sees the cliffs of Calais from the heights of Dover, to be a strange reason to be assigned for the two countries being natural enemies, by position to each other; a doctrine so prevalent at the period of which I am writing, that it would liave been deemed most unpatriotic, if not actually treasonable, to have doubted its correctness; but here, the few feet of distance from Spain to Portugal, measuring from the centre of the river Minho to each, seemed to make this doctrine of juxtaposition begetting natural enmity still more absurd.

The frontier town and fortress on the Spanish side is named Tuy: it appeared about as large as Falmouth, but more regularly built, with many open squares and large public buildings and churches. It occupied a commanding height, and was deemed a place of considerable strength in a military point of view. The Portuguese town, whose name I have forgotten, seemed greatly inferior, and its population of a less favourable aspect.

From hence our journey lay through the rich province of Entre Minho e Douro, accounted one of the most fertile in Portugal; and nothing could exceed the luxuriance of vegetable production in every variety of form, or the beauty of the landscapes. The peasantry, however, appeared to us more indolent and more dirty than the Spaniards; and, though, since quitting the Spanish frontier we were no longer in an enemy's country, or guarded by sentinels, but in a neutral and even friendly territory our ftire and accommodation were mucli worse, and our admiration of the country liardly sufficient to reconcile us to the change. Here, as in Spain, smuggling seemed to be all but universal; and wherever we arrived, either in the smallest villages or larger towns, inquiries were constantly made as to whether we did not do a little business on a small scale as contrabandistas; and great disappointment generally ensued at the negative given to the question. With a view to interrupt the carrying trade of the smugglers as much as possible, the government had made an absurd regulation that the axles of the wheels of carts and waggons should neither be greased nor oiled to lessen their friction, and thus prevent their being heard when on the road; so that the creaking noise made by these vehicles on their journeys from one town to another could be heard more than a mile off, and when near was quite intolerable. The bells on the mules and oxen used for drawing them seemed to have had a similar origin, though this was far from being offensive. The peasants, however, seemed reconciled to both, and frequently declared that the harsh discord, as we deemed it, was so agreeable to the cattle that thev would not work half so well without it: so readily do bad habits become rooted, amonc; brute creatures as among mankind.

The only town of note that we passed through in our way was Barcelos, on the Cavado river, which was walled, round, with towers at the angles, and had broad and regular streets, and several fine buildiniis, with a brido; e across the stream. Here the Enfrlish seemed to be better known and in higher esteem, and we had several marks of kindness shown to us, by presents of fruit and provisions, especially from females, chiefly of the lower classes, but also from two or three of higher position.

Two days' march from hence about thirty miles brought us at length to Oporto, where it was arranged that we should halt for a week. As there were here a British consul, and many English merchants engaged in the wine trade with England, and as it was a place of considerable opulence as well as population, our condition was much sympathised with, and materially relieved by better quarters and provisions than we had yet enjoyed since our captivity; and as we had free liberty to roam about during the day wherever we pleased, on condition only of our being at home by sunset, we had ample opportunity for enjoyment; and some pocket-money given to me by an English lady, who had a son about my own age, and who felt for me therefore the more keenly, put me quite at my ease, and made the week passed at Oporto one of extreme pleasure. It is difficult to describe, at this distance of time, the impression which Oporto made upon my young and untravelled mind. Next to Lisbon it was the largest and most beautiful city I had ever seen. Standino; on the north bank of the Douro on several undulating hills, and having numerous churches with lofty spires, many la 'ge public buildings, noble and spacious squares surrounded with trees, and gardens, and foliage mingled with the dwellings, on the heights it has a most imposing appearance; while the rapid stream flowing before it, and reaching the sea at a distance of about twenty miles below the town, con-tainino; a great number of vessels of different nations, waiting for their cargoes of wine and other products; the opposite suburbs of Villanova and Gaya, united by a bridge of boats; and the gaiety of cloudless skies, floating flags, and peals of bells from the numerous churches and convents, all then in full possession of their wealth and influence, produced a fascination which contrasted most agreeably with the dulness and privations of our journey thus far. The number of priests and monks seemed to us al- most as great as at Lisbon; and the nuns were said to be even more numerous still. The shaven crowns, long beards, loose coarse brown and black robes, fastened round the body with white cords, the enormous hats, some with the broad brims expanded like umbrellas, others with the sides rolled up like tubes or scrolls, making the hats three or four feet long and not a foot broad; the numerous water carriers in the streets, crying and vending their cooling drinks, and the sparkling jets of the fountains in the public places of the city, were all objects of novelty and interest. With considerable difficulty, we (that is, my young shipmate Tilly of my own age and myself only, for the men could not be permitted) obtained the privilege of visiting two of the nunneries; but instead of seeing the lovely young creatures that our inexperienced and fertile imaginations had pictured as the inmates of these establishments, we saw chiefly aged women, very old and shrivelled, and not one that could be called handsome or good-looking, so that we felt no disposition to visit more.

As there were many English vessels at Oporto, about to sail soon for England, we had hoped to have obtained a passage in some of them. But it appeared difficult, for reasons which I never knew, to accomplish this; so that we w ere obliged to continue our march towards Lisbon, and, leaving all the comforts by which we were surrounded in the citj of our week's sojourn, we had to resume our weary and foot-sore journey. We were a full week in passing from Oporto to Coimbra, feeding scantily and coarsely all the way, and rarely getting even a temporary lift in cart or on mule on the road; sleeping sometimes in stables or other out-hovises, sometimes in the open air, accounting ourselves most lucky if we could get a little clean straw for our litter.

We remained at Coimbra for two or three days, and enjoyed the rest it afforded us exceedingly. It presented us with fresh novelties, which made our stay agreeable. Being the seat of the chief, if not the only University in Portugal, it was crowded with students, between the ages of sixteen and twenty-one; and, as these included, like our Oxford and Cambridge, the sons of the chief nobility and gentry of the country, they furnished the best specimens of Portuguese stature, physiognomy, and manners; and had an evidently superior air to the inhabitants generally. The city abounded also with churches, monasteries, and ecclesiastics; the females appeared to us handsomer than elsewhere in Portugal; and both the town and surrounding country were full of objects of interest and beauty.

We vere now, however, anxious to push on to tlie place of our desthiation, being thoroughly weary of this tiresome journey. All our English shoes had long since been worn out, and the cheap Portuguese ones, with which we could alone afford to replace them, were so flimsy in material and workmanship, that three or four days' travel on rough and stony roads was enough to tear them to pieces, so that we were all now barefooted, and our only wardrobe was the garments we had on our backs, and these mostly in rags and tatters. We hastened on, therefore, by daily marches of ten or twelve miles each, towards Abrantes, on the Tagus, where we found boats descending that stream to Lisbon, giving us the luxury of water conveyance, for which we now longed. In this journey we had to cross a lofty range of mountains, running through Estramadura, and the toilsome ascent, rocky passes, and sudden declivities of this great barrier made its traverse infinitely tedious and painful. We felt, therefore, as if we had reached a paradise, when we came to Abrantes, as there our rugged and fatiguing land journey was to end.

The town of Abrantes is much smaller than either Corunna, St. lago. Oporto, or Coiambra; but it was strongly fortified, and, being the highest point of navigation on the Tagus for boats of large size, is the,

VOL. T. K seat of a most active commerce for conveying by water the produce of the interior to the capital. Here we embarked our whole party in two laden barges, keeping company all the way, and floated down the stream in a dreamy and languid repose, which was like a new existence to us. The whole distance was abovit a hundred miles from Abrantes to Lisbon; but the slow and indolent habits of the Portuguese, the frequent stoppages at the smallest villages, and a stay of a day and night at Santarem an ancient and decayed city, which, we were told, was once the residence of the Court, before the royal family removed to Lisbon, made our voyage as tardy as our foot journey. We were in no impatience, however, to hurry it over, as it was really delicious to sit or lie along on the cargo, to gaze around upon the many beautiful scenes which the Tagus presents on either side, and feel that the hours of breakfast, dinner, and supper, and afterwards those of sleep, would come, without requiring a single effort on our parts to provide or prepare for either. I never felt the luxury of perfect idleness so much before; and I have hardly had an opportunity since, to know whether a similar absence of all occupation would now be as agreeable to me or not, but I am inclined to think it would be painful.

The English fleet of Sir John Jervis entering the Tagus. Followed by the prizes taken by him off Cape St. Vincent. Impressment of our own party by the ships of war. Embark in the Prince of Wales packet for England. Happy stay at home after my captivity. Reluctance of my mother to permit me to go to sea again. Placed with a Bookseller at Plymouth Dock. Life led there. Association with naval officers. Extravagant expenditure. Story of a Negro cook. Visits to the Theatre. Composition of a five act Di-ama. Reasons for its not being presented for representation.

Our arrival at Lisbon was at a moment of great interest and excitement. On the very day when we were descendino; the last reacli of the Tagus to effect our landing at the wharf of the busy city, the victorious English admiral, Sir John Jervis, was sailing up from the mouth of this majestic river, with the French and Spanish prizes he had captured, after a hard-fought struggle oflp Cape St. Vincent, the promontory between Lisbon and Cadiz. Several line-of-battle ships, all more or less bearing in their shattered hulls, broken masts, and fluttering rao-s of sails, external evidences of the ravages of war, with, no doubt, many in agonies from wounds still lin- gering among their crews, and envying perhaps their comrades who had been consigned to the deep, came foaming up against the downward stream, with the English ensign over the French and Spanish flags; while the bells of the churches and convents appeared to be all in motion, and heard at intervals between the salutes from the batteries and ships afloat, gave a tone of exultation and rejoicing, as at once a welcome to the living and a requiem to the dead.

As Englishmen, ourselves just escaped from a painful captivity, we could not but share the general joy; but alas! how soon was it damped by the intelligence the first we had on landing, that already from the ships that had anchored first, there were pressgangs prowling along the river and the shore, seizing all Englishmen that could be found, to fill the places of the dead and wounded, and help to navigate the fleet and the prizes to England. As no protection or excuse for exemption was admitted, some of our party were seized, handcuffed, and dragged into the boats by the pressgangs, or forced at the point of the cutlass, as if they had been enemies and not fellow-countrymen. A few only escaped by concealment, among whom I fortunately happened to be one. In the midst of the struggle between the press- gang and our men I ran into the first open doorway I saw, mounted up stairs, was met by two women of the labouring class, and, speaking Portuguese pretty fluently, I explained that I was endeavouring to escape from the pressgang, the terrors of which they seemed to understand and feel, so that with many exclamations of sympathy and expressions of shame that such youths should be kidnapped and torn away by ruffians, they kept me concealed in bed in an upper attic for three days and nights, till the press-gang had scoured the locality and was not expected to return. To this incident, perhaps, I owe my early abhorrence of the system of impressment, which has continued with me through life. How compassionate are the women of all countries and towards children and youths especially! and how grateful did I feel for their protection!

About a week after our reaching Lisbon, the victorious fleet and their prizes were all out of the river on their way to England; and the danger of impressment being thus past, I sought and obtained a berth on board the British packet Prince of Wales, Captain Todd, to whom I was well known, as well as to most of his officers and crew; so that my return by her to Falmouth, after a pleasant voyage, brought me once more into the bosom of my family and friends, with whom I spent some happy months in all the enjoyments of home, before thinking of any preparations for resuming my nautical career.

When the period arrived for doing this, the reluctance of my dear mother always very strong was now increased by ill-health and depressed spirits to such a degree, that no effort of mine could prevail upon her to let me go to sea again. Indeed, after many long-repeated conferences with her and my sisters at her bed-side, my father being dead and my brothers both abroad, the female tenderness and persuasiveness so prevailed in these domestic councils, as to draw from me a solemn promise that, during my mother's life at least, I would never again venture to trust the fickle element of the sea, at least as a profession.

To live in idleness would iave been for me impossible; and the next thing then was to determine what my future pursuit should be. For the Church I had not, in my own mind, the requisite amount of zeal to enter it heartily, nor sufficient apathy or indifference to recrard it as a mere mode of obtahiino; a livelihood, without any regard to higher considerations. Of the Law I had seen a little, for a short period, and was sufficiently disgusted with it to deter me from choosing it as a profession. I had a great love of books, and had already acquired some knowledge of charts and nautical instruments, and thought I should like very well to be placed with a person connected by inter-marriage with our family, who then had a larce booksellino- and nautical instrument establish-ment at Devonport (then called Plymouth Dock). This being mutually arranged, I repaired to my new abode, and for three or four years enjoyed the occupation exceedingly. It by no means, however, extinguished my passion for the sea; on the contrary, I felt it daily fed by all the bustle and excitement of a great naval port, by personal intercourse with officers of all ranks, frequent visits to them on board line-of-battle ships in Cawsand Bay, frigates in the Sound, and vessels of every class refitting in the dockyard and Hamoaze: while every Sunday afternoon and evening's walk on Mountwise, in the garrison or on the Hoe at Plymouth, in the grounds of Mount-Edge-combe, or in visits to Maker Tower, Torpoint, and Saltash, bringing me in sight of ships in every variety of action and repose, made me long intensely to go to sea again. On one occasion during this period, between 1798 and 1800, I dined with a naval party at the Fountain Hotel, in Fore Street, in which were three of the most remarkable naval heroes of the day Lord Nelson, Sir Edward Pellew (afterwards

Lordexmouth), and Captain Jeremiah Coglan, a sort of fire-eater, as he was called, who had done more daring things than any man of his rank and length of service. Sir Sydney Smith alone perhaps excepted. The theatres, too, of Plymouth, and Plymouth Dock, which were continually filled with naval officers in the boxes, and sailors in the galleries, and at which naval pieces and sea songs were in constant request, all aided to increase the spell under which I seemed to labour.

During this period I was thrown constantly into the company of naval officers and seamen of every class; and their very recklessness had for me something irresistibly attractive. The transport of delight into which men are thrown when they first come on shore aft er months and years of solitary confinement at sea, speedily communicates itself to those by whom they are surrounded; and the recitals of their perilous adventures, whether of battles or shipwrecks, makes them heroes in the estimation especially of females and young persons. At this period the streets of Plymouth Dock were daily crowded with officers and seamen on shore on liberty, after receiving pay and prize-money to an extent beyond their power to spend in a short time without some unusual modes of extravagance, as the idea of hoarding or laying by for a future day was never entertained apparently, by either officers or men. By both, carriages of all descriptions were in request at enormous prices; and cases were described in which young midshipmen, having perhaps 200. to spend in a week, would have one carriage for themselves, another for their gold-laced cocked-hats, and another for their hangers, or dirks. The seamen would sometimes hire three or four coaches to remain on the stand, and in groups of three or four on the roofs of each, dance hornpipes and reels to a violin player seated on the box; and when the dance was over, drive a furious race against each other for ten or twenty guineas a side, till the horses became exhausted.

As the ordinary clothing of themselves was not sufficiently expensive, the finest broad cloths were used for their jackets and trousers; scarlet velvet and gold lace for their waistcoats; golden guineas fitted with eyes were used for the larger buttons of their trousers, which had gold fringe at the bottom; rows of half guineas, similarly fitted, and so close as to overlap each other, like scale armour, were used for the jackets, and seven-shilling gold pieces, just then introduced, were used in double rows on each side the velvet waistcoat. In addition to all this, every sailor had one, and many two or three, female favourites to share his favours, so that a few days was sufficient to exhaust their funds, all parties being in a state of excitement during the whole period, from the frequent use of grog, milk-punch, and other " necessary refreshments," as they were called. The admirals and captains were not at all desirous of checking this extravagance in any way, as their maxim and belief was, that so long as a sailor had any money left, there was no hope of his return to duty; but that, when everything was gone, he was sure to come aboard, and after four-and-twenty hours of sleep and idleness, would become a fresh man, and resume his ordinary labours with pleasure and contentment.

One of the most remarkable cases of this extravagance that I remember, was that of a cook of a lineof-battle ship, who had returned to England after an absence of seven years on the West India and South America stations. It was then the custom to withhold all pay and prize-money from officers and men while the ships were abroad; so that the long arrears of both due in this case, with the gains arising from the cook's privilege of " slush-money" as it is called, that is, the sale or supply to the ship's purser of all the " grease" made in cooking operations, which is used for many purposes at sea.

and for the value of which credit was given in the ship's accounts exceeded 3,000., and all this was dissipated in less than three weeks! The cook was a negro, but a fine man of his race, and proud of his person. As a warrant officer, he was entitled to wear the naval uniform, and having taken an extensive suite of rooms in one of the principal hotels, he was fitted out by the most fashionable tailor with two or three rich suits of broadcloth, kerseymere, satin linings, and gold. His hair was dressed every morning, and well powdered, and he had a carriage and four for his daily exercise. He took the stage-box at the theatre every night, invifed his tradesmen to dinner before going to the play, and after the performance brought home with him sometimes as many as half-a-dozen ladies of compliant character to sup and spend the night with him. At the end of the first week he engaged one of the Portsmouth sloop packets, which sailed daily from Plymouth, and gave a general invitation to as many ladies as chose to avail themselves of it, offering a free passage there and back, as a cruise, with ample entertainment on board. Of course the sloop was crowded, and the cost of this experiment exhausted all his funds. At the end of the third week, having sold or pawned what remained of his wardrobe and ornaments to keep up the game, he was at last so destitute as to be unable to pay for a bed, and was literally found, by a shopman who went to open his place of business in the morning, stowed away in the hollow space into which the shutters were placed during the night. From thence he was taken to the hospital, and in another week he was dead!

Having, on my frequent visits to the theatre, become acquainted with the manager and admitted to the green room and behind the scenes, and finding this a very agreeable relaxation after the drudgery of the day, I became so fascinated with the drama and all its accessories that I conceived the idea of becoming a dramatic author; and reading with great diligence all the plays of Shakspeare, with those of Ford, Beaumont and Fletcher, Massinger, Deckar, Ben Jonson, and other ancient writers, as well as those of Lee and Otway, and of Mrs. Inchbald, and all the moderns, I wrought myself up to the belief that I was fully competent to produce something original in a dramatic form. The subject I selected was an imaginary Invasion of Circassia by the Russians; and the title of the piece was, "The Conquest of Circassia." It was furnished with an ample number of characters, witli a principal hero and heroine of the conquered tribes, something after the model of Rolla and Cora in Pizarro, a play which, at that time, enjoyed immense popularity. It was written in blank verse, extended to five acts, with most elaborate provisions of scenery and costume, and engaged all the leisure I could command at intervals during about three months, the greater portion being written between midnight and three or four o'clock in the morning, in my solitary bedroom, and by the flickering light of a single tallow candle, requiring perpetual snuffing, as moulds, spermaceti, or wax were too extravagant luxuries for such a household as that of which I was then an inmate.

When the piece was finished, and had been gone over and corrected many times, I took it to the manager of the theatre, who promised to read it, and give it his best consideration. It was with him about a month, and was then returned to me, with the highest commendations on its excellence, whether sincerely or not, I had no means of testing, but with the observation that to put such a drama properly on the stage would require an outlay of from 300. to 500Z. to do justice to its scenery, costume, and decorations, and that only a first-rate London company could furnish the requisite amount and variety of talent to perform it well.

The piece was ultimately destroyed, in a subsequent period of my career, when all such compositions were regarded by me as a profane waste of precious time, and a perversion of powers that should be devoted to higher objects: but I record the fact as an instance of erj early though misdirected ambition, and as the first literary production of my pen.

Complete cliange In the current of my life. Sincere repentance. Strong religious impressions. Intense study of controversial divinity. Public baptism in the meeting-house of Devon-port. Conviction of the truth of Calvinistic doctrines. Public preaching of these doctrines in the pulpit at fifteen. Intimacy with the Rev. Dr. Hawker, of Plymouth. Gradual relaxation and relapse into worldliness. Revival of my passion for a sea-life again. Entry as a volunteer on board a ship of war. Severe discipline. Frequent and capricious punishments. Horrid spectacle of a deserter flogged round the fleet. Risked a similar fate, by running from the ship. Successful concealment and disguise, and final escape. Safe arrival once more in the bosom of my family. Attempt to induce me to follow the profession of the Law.

At length the smooth flow of the current of my life was partially broken by the intervention of a new feeling and a new phase in my existence. I was at this period about fifteen years of age; and having for ' some time led a life of as much gaiety as was possible in the position in which I was placed, I found now and then, especially in the gloom of the evening and the early hours of the morning between waking and leaving my bed, something very like shame for misspent time, and a desire to repair it, gradually stealing over me. This feeling reached its culminating point, by what might be called an accident, or at least an unexpected and unpremeditated event. On the evening of a day in Lent, I was walking alone through St. Aubyn Street, and seeing that service was performing in the church there, I went in, and took my place in one of the pews near the pulpit. After the evening prayer, the clergyman, whose name I think was Williams, preached a most touching sermon on the story of the Prodigal Son. It took deep root in my heart. I thought of my dear indulgent mother, and felt that I had disregarded her wishes and injunctions in feeding rather than repressing my inclination for a sea-life; and that in the hours spent with young officers at the Fountain, and Prince William Henry (the latter the favourite hotel of the young Duke of Clarence, afterwards King William the Fourth), as well as in the boxes and the greefei room of the theatre, I had misapplied many precious hours which could now never be redeemed. My repentance was most sincere. I determined to begin a new life, and applied myself with all practicable diligence to the abandonment of my old connections and the formation of new.

Not being of a disposition then, any more than since, to take up opinions on trust, or to have sufficient reverence for authority as to be able to place entire reliance thereon, I read earnestly, not merely tlie Old and New Testaments, but all the conniien-taries on them within my reach; and books of controversial theology soon became to me the most delicious food. I rose constantly in the morning at four o'clock, though not required to attend to business till nine, after breakfasting at eight. I rarely ever went to bed till midnight, reading therefore at least eight hours every day, attending vforship three times on Sundays, and twice and thrice on the evenings of the week; so that in a year or so I had devoured perhaps a hundred volumes, large and small, on theology, no other subject having then the least attraction for me. The book of all others that fascinated me most was the celebrated treatise on Free Will, by the Reverend Jonathan Edwards, the American Puritan divine. The writings of Bunyan, Baxter, Cotton Mather, Jeremy Taylor, Fuller, and most of the old Nonconformist divines, were all agreeable to me, but Jonathan Edwards bore away the palm. I became, therefore, a confirmed Calvinist of the most rigid school, as firmly believing myself to be one of the Elect as any of the teachers of unconditional predestination; and I am free to confess, that though the ground on which I could dare to think myself thus favoured appears te me

VOL. I. L now most hollow and insufficient, it was a belief which made me inexpressibly happy, and reconciled me entirely (at which I cannot now but be astonished) to the perfect justice of the eternal damnation of all the millions upon millions not included within that sacred circle.

The only doubt I had yet to solve was that which related to the rite of baptism. To settle this in my own mind, I read, as diligently as before, all accessible works on that subject. I referred, first, of course to every mention of baptism in the New Testament; and I there found that the rite was administered only to adults, and to those only, as an outward sign of the new birth or regeneration which had taken place within those partaking of it. I referred to the Catechism of the Established Church, and found there also, that baptism is declared to be an " outward and visible sign of an inward and spiritual grace, whereby we have a death unto sin and a new birth unto righteousness" all which seemed to me perfectly inapplicable to infants, unconscious both of the feeling of sin or repentance, and incapable, therefore, of any mental participation in such a rite. I felt it my duty, therefore, to undergo the form of adult baptism; which was performed on me with other converts, by a very Avorthy minister, the Rev Mr. Birt, in the

Baptist Chapel of Plymouth Dock, on one of the coldest days of winter; and never could the powerful influence of mental emotions to ward off physical danger be more manifested than in this case, where neither of the baptized individuals some very old, and others of the most delicate constitutions suffered the least inconvenience from being immersed in the icy water, and standing in it during the ceremony for a considerable period. For myself, I can truly say I felt a holy glow inexpressibly agreeable, and thought that if religious duty demanded it, I could have borne a baptism of fire with the same equanimity. I could understand and appreciate by this, the exultation and the joy of the martyrs.

An event which occurred about this time and was much talked of in society, contributed largely to my convictions of the irrationality of infant baptism. It appears, that a party composed of an infant, its parents, and the usual number of sponsors, went to one of the Plymouth churches to have their child baptized. The godfather, who stood next the infant while in its nurse's arms, was, in the course of the service, addressed by the clergyman, who read over to him the usual articles of the Christian creed from the Prayer Book, and then said to him, "Dost tliou believe all this?" To which the sponsor answered, "I do." The next question was: ' Wilt thou be baptized in this faith? " To which the godfather replied, "Sir, I have been baptized already." The clergyman rejoined, "But this question is addressed to the child through you."

The sponsor asked, "And was the question relating to the belief in the Christian doctrine also addressed to the child? " The clergyman replied, "Yes, through you."' " Then," said the sponsor, " the mistake was mine, since I answered as for myself, seeing that I really do understand and believe all that you recited; but as for the child, it is impossible for me to communicate to it the requisite degree of intelligence to comprehend your questions, or to answer them: and in this state of its ignorance, it is perfectly passive. I think, Sir, therefore, with your permission, that we had better take the child home; and when it is sufficiently advanced in years and knowledge to comprehend what you say, and to understand the nature and object of the baptismal rite, it can come again and answer for itself, and be thus a voluntary agent in this solemn profession of the Christian faith." The clergyman made no reply; and the party retired, to the great surprise and disappointment of the mother and nurse, who tliouglit these scruples most ill-timed and unreasonable.

This incident led me to search the Scriptures thoroughly on the subject; and as I could find no instance of any other baptism recorded in them than those of adults who, following the example of the Saviour, used this rite as a public profession of their renouncing an erroneous life and doctrine and embracing the Christian faith while the little children brought to Christ, on which so much stress is laid, were not baptized by him or by any of his disciples my convictions were confirmed as to the irrationality and inefficiency of inf xnt baptism, and the superiority of the adult initiation into the Christian fold.

Soon after this an occasion arose in which a Cal-vinistic minister, Mr. Reece, a Welch gentleman of great theological learning and eloquence, whose miit-istry I preferred to all others because of its absolute and unconditional or uncompromising predestinarian-ism, was taken suddenly ill, and he sent for me to take his place in the pulpit. I was not then sixteen, and had never anticipated such an event. Instead of being, however, in the least degree embarrassed, I considered this to be a distinct call from Heaven or an occurrence decreed, like every other, from all eternity, or before the foundations of the world were laid, and that I had no power to resist it. I went, without fear or hesitation, and (what now seems to me most marvellous) without the most remote idea of there being any presumption or impropriety in such a step, ascended the pulpit with the firmness of an apostle, preached what was deemed and declared to be a powerful and convincing extemporaneous sermon on the principal texts of the 10th chapter of Paul's Epistle to the Romans, and continued the subject on the evening of the same day.

The effect of this effort or exhibition gave me such a degree of religious popularity among the Calvinists of the town and neio; libourhood, that I was fre-quently called upon by other ministers to supply their places in cases of absence or illness; and always did so with the greatest readiness; thinking it sinful to make any preparation for any discourse to be delivered, depending entirely on what I believed to be the " inspiration" that would be sure to be given me at the moment required; and the fulness of this confidence was never disappointed.

Among other distinguished persons to whom soon became known, were the Rev-erend Dr. Hawker, of Plymouth, then in the very zenith of his popularity as Vicar of the New Church, Plymouth, and his son, the Reverend John Hawker, Rector of Stoke

Damerell, between Plymouth and P4ymouth Dock. These pious and excellent men were regarded by the majority of the Church party, laity as well as clergy, as little better than Dissenters, and by many, indeed, were abused as Methodists, the term being meant as one of reproach. They were, however, strict Cal-vinists, but at the same time so genuinely pious and holy in their lives and conduct, and so zealous and earnest in their evangelical labours, that no two men perhaps were ever more beloved and honoured by all who knew them than this worthy father and son. I spent many evenings with each in their libraries and family circles; was a frequent communicant at the churches of both; attended their private prayer meetings and recital of religious experiences, and was never more happy than when so engaged.

But, alas for poor human nature! It would seem to be a law in mental, as it is in natural philosophy, that when the pendulum of the heart or mind is forced with 2; reat violence to the one side of the scale, the responding oscillation will carry it speedily to the opposite extreme: at least, I found it so in my own case. The perfect reliance which I felt in my eternal safety, as one of the Elect, soon begat a relax ation of effort, as none seem needed to attain to what had been already accomplished; and another twelve months was sufficient to bring me back to nearly the same condition as that in which I was before hearing? the sermon on the stoiy of the Prodigal Son.

During all this period of gradual descent from the glddj height to which I had reached, my old passion for the sea returned; and having now been for some time separated from the personal influence and sympathy of my dear parent, her injunctions had less firm hold of me tlian before; so that an occasion of difference arising between myself and the bookseller with whom I was placed, I quitted him against his will, and going alongside a corvette then fitting out in Hamoaze (which turned out to be the identical French ship of war, the Mars, by which I had been captured in 1795, but being since made prize by some Eno; lish frio-ate, was taken for her fast-sailino; qualities into the British service), I entered as a volunteer, and my previous short experience at sea obtained me an appointment to the mizen-top, the active duties of which were sufficiently familiar to me to make them perfectly agreeable.

I did not remain long, however, on board this ship of war. Though rather a favourite with the officers and boatswain's mates, from my being a volunleer, as well as strong, active, able, and willing to discharge all that was required of me, the tyranny and cruelty exercised on the greater part of the crew was really revolting. Floggings on the naked back at the gangway were of almost daily occurrence; and " starting," or " rope's ending " as it is called, by the petty officers, especially on the youngsters, happened almost every hour. As the greater number of the crew not more than half complete had been brought on board against their will by the pressgang some dragged out of their beds at night, others torn from merchant ships where they were earning five pounds a month, to serve for two pounds and be deprived of their personal liberty to go on shore and see their friends there was everywhere among them the sullen murmur of discontent, and the silent broodino; of revenge: so that the officers seemed to be in daily dread of a mutiny, and thought the only way to repress this was by severity of discipline, which only added fuel to the flame. From the first dawn of day, therefore, when the daylight-gun summoned all to the washing of decks, up to the evening-gun, which gave the signal for all but the watch to repair to their hammocks, and put out all lights, it was one continued scene of hoarse blasphemy among the officers an order hardly ever being given unaccompanied by an oath and dogged obstinacy and complaint among the men. In short.

I had never before so completely realised the meaning of the expression, " a perfect hell upon earth," as in what I saw before me, and I longed for some oppor- ' tunity to make my escape.

My resolution, however, was sadly shaken by two scenes which it was my lot to witness during this short period of service, which to me seemed an age. The first was the hanoiino; a mutineer at the yard-arm of the Pique frigate, then anchored in Barn Pool, near Mount Edgecombe, which a boat's crew from every ship in the port of Plymouth was summoned to witness, and in one of which I was an unhappy and disgusted spectator, it being the first instance of hanging I had ever witnessed, and this under peculiarly horrifying circumstances. The second was the floo-o-infr a deserter round the fleet, an exhibition of barbaric cruelty which no nation would now tolerate, and which it is astonishing that Englishmen could ever have permitted after its first exhibition. The deserter was said to be a young waterman who had been forcibly dragged by a press-gang from his home, his wife, and children, in the dead of the night; and who did the most natural and laudable thing in the world, as soon after as was practicable, namely, escaped back to them again; but having, in addition to the desertion, struck the officer who seized him at his re-capture, might lawfully, as the naval code then stood, have been shot dead on the spot, or condemned by court-martial to be hung! In this instance, however, it was " commuted," such was the phrase for the milder punishment of being flogged round the fleet. On the day appointed for this legalised torture, a signal gun was fired from the guard-ship in Hamoaze, and the yellow-flag appropriately the signal for punishment as it is for the plague hoisted at the main. Another signal then ordered a boat's crew with an officer from every ship in the port to repair to the scene of punishment, not only to witness its execution, but to form part of the melancholy procession. The wind was blowing a fresh breeze from the westward, and the first infliction of the lash was to take place alongside the easternmost ship, or to leeward, from whence the victim was to be towed in succession to all the ships lying to windward, and receive a certain number of lashes at each, thus eking out and prolonging the anguish of the sufferer by this protracted process. The prisoner was in the launcli, one of the largest boats of his own ship, in the centre of which was erected a triangulai' framework, made of handspikes or poles. To this he was " seized" or fastened, by the arms being extended upwards and outwards, and his wrists bound tightly to the framework by cords, his body being perfectly naked down to the waist. In this boat were about a dozen of his own shipmates, the officer superintending the punishment, a lieutenant of his own ship, and the surgeon of the same, whose duty it was to see that the punishment was kept short of inflicting; death.

On reaching the leeward ship, the launch was hauled alongside, and at least twenty boats, in one of which I was stationed at the bow, clustered round the vessel on tlie starboard side, a few yards only from the launch, so that we could see every lash as it fell, and hear every shriek and groan of the sufferer.

From the ship there descended an officer, with two boatswain's mates, and an assistant surgeon. The naked body of the victim was exposedj and we heard the order given: " The prisoner is to receive a dozen lashes from each ship. Boatswain's mates, do your duty I" meaning by this dignified but here most vilely prostituted phrase, "Lay it on with the lash, with all the force of arm you can command! and at your peril neither shrink nor falter!" It should be understood that the naval lash, or " cat-o'-nine tails"

as it is called, is far heavier in the cords used in its nine filaments than the military; besides which, every one of the nine cords is full of knots (such was the case at least in these by-gone days), so that a dozen lashes on a seaman's back was deemed equal to a liundred on a soldier's, from the mere difference of the instrument of torture alone. The strokes of the lash fell heavily, and at what to me seemed long intervals (a minute between each at least); the very first brought blood; the sufferer restrained his utterance till about the fifth or sixth, but then the pent-up agony had vent in a shriek, enough to rend a heart of stone. As the youngest in the boat, though having had a week's experience of seeing flogging almost daily on board our own ship, I became faint and deadly sick at the murderous scene before me; but a " rope's ending," inflicted on me by order of the officer, soon roused me, and I felt strong with indignation, but dared not even look it, if it were possible to repress it. The rest of the boat's crew pressed their lips closely, and ground their teeth, and not a man among them all but seemed ripe for mutiny. At the end of the first instalment of a dozen lashes, the victim's back was one mass of lacerated flesh and blood; and over this was spread a blanket, which we were assured was steeped in vinegar and brine, as some said to augment the suffering, as others contended to prevent mortification.

The boats now all fell into line, each towino; the one next behind her at an interval of about a boat's length apart, and the last having the launch with the prisoner in tow, all pulling against a stiff head wind o the ship next in order to windward, occupying from fifteen to twenty minutes. Here the same horrible scene was repeated, and so onward till about ten or twelve ships had been visited, there being still six or eight more to go to: when the victim having several times fainted, and his voice having ceased to give forth either shrieks or groans, he was reported by the surgeon to be incapable of bearing any further infliction, and was ordered to be rowed ashore to the hospital, before reaching which he was discovered to be dead; and some declared that he had received the last heavy lashes on his body, after the spirit had quitted its earthly tenement J It is impossible to describe the impression which this, the most horrible scene it has ever been my lot to witness, made on my mind: and though it at first terrified me into the temporary abandonment of my resolution to escape from such a demoniacal service, in the end it only strengthened my determination, even at the risk of a similar punishment, to abandon it for ever; for I consoled myself with the belief that if caught I should be able to find means of self-destruction, and thus escape this fearful torture.

On the day before that appointed for our sailing, therefore, being sent, as steersman of the jolly-boat with a midshipman, to the landing-place called Mutton Cove, and there left in charge of the boat, while the crew were lounging about the quays waiting the officer's return, I took the favourable opportunity which this presented of deserting. Threading my way through all the back streets and lanes, dreading at every step to meet any one by whom I might be recognised, and without a sixpence in my pocket,

I at length got across the ferry to Torpoint, by promising to pay on my return, walked a few miles from thence in the direction of the western road, but through fields and over hedges; until, completely tired out, as much with anxiety as fatigue, I lay down under a hay-rick, with no covering but the sky, and slept profoundly till morning.

I was awakened, even before my rest was complete, by a farmer's son, about my own age, who at first considered me to be a tramp or trespasser, and therefore accosted me in no friendly manner. I told him, however, my whole story; by which he was so moved that he said if he could help me to secure my escape he would willingly do so, and he was sure his father and mother would do the same. He at first proposed to take me to the farmhouse; but knowing that heavy penalties awaited those who harboured deserters, I was unwilling to make so unsuitable a return for so much hospitality. On conferring together, however, it was agreed that he should bring me where I then was, under the shelter and concealment of the hav-rick, some meat and drink, for I was famishing with hunger, a set of his own working clothes, a smock frock, thick hob-nailed shoes, a coarse felt hat, c., which were soon produced. In these I dressed myself, giving him my sea garments in return, which, however, he would not receive as an equivalent, but insisted on paying for them, and taking me in my new garb to his father's house, I there made a hearty supper, slept sweetly, and after a breakfast sufficient for the day, and about twenty shillings in my pocket, given me by the good housewife at her son's request for my clothes, as being liberally estimated to be worth that amount above the value of his own, I set forth on my way.

My object was of course to get to my own home at Flushing as speedily as possible; and as I knew the chief towns that lay in the route, Liskeard, Lostwithiel, St. Austell, Grampound, Truro, Penryn, and Falmouth, I had only to inquire the way from one of these to the other, and shouhl be sure to find carts, horses, and foot-passengers on the road to direct me. I proceeded, therefore, with a hght heart and a firm step, and before night I reached Liskeard, a distance of about fifteen miles, on foot. To avoid as much as possible all chances of detection, I sought the most obscure inn in the place for a lodging, and having made a hearty supper, for which my funds were ample, I repaired to the only bed vacant, one of three in a large barn-like room, the other two being occupied by other lodgers.

About midnight we were all roused and alarmed by the visit of a constable, with his staff, a marine with his naked bayonet, and two seamen, who had come to search for deserters. My heart sank within me, and I was literally struck dumb with fear. I soon heard, however, by their conversation, that they were not in quest of any individual deserters from any particular vessels, but as there was great difficulty in manning ships at Plymouth, and many were known to have run away after having been impressed, this detachment, at the head of which was a sergeant of marines, who, however, left the duty to his corporal, was stationed at Liskeard, to examine the low inns and tramp lodging-houses, and pick up such stray deserters as they might find: so I gathered

VOL. I. M courage at this discovery, and by the time they came to my bed, accosted them in the broadest Cornish dialect I could command, and how unintelligible this is, even to the natives of the county itself, who have not had much intercourse with the peasantry, most of its residents know: so that if they had entertained any suspicions respecting me, of which they gave no evidence, this was sufficient to allay it; and after a short parley, they left the room to my great relief and satisfaction.

Bv the end of a week, walkino- eio-ht or ten miles a day (for since my long marches as a prisoner in Spain I had never been a good walker), getting an occasional lift on a waijo'on or cart, and subsist-ing comfortably by the way at the rate of lialf-a-crown a day, which was a liberal allowance, I reached Flushing about ten o'clock at night. Our family were all in bed, for early hours of rising and rest were general in those primitive times, and I had some difficulty in rousing any one. When the servant opened the door, however, and saw a rough country lad, as she supposed me, pretending to be the son of her mistress, she thought me an impostor, and shut the door in my face. I desired one of my sisters to be called, by whom I was immediately recognised, and embraced with many tears of joy and congratulation. I was soon in bed, where I had to remain three whole dajs and nights till new clothes could be made for me, for I had not a garment save those of the farmer's boy that I had worn as a disguise, and village tailors could not equal London ones in making a complete suit in a night.

On being duly equipped with these essentials, I was permitted to see my dear mother, then ill in bed, and wholly ignorant of all that had transpired, as all my correspondence was confined to my sisters, and nothing of this was communicated lest it should give pain or anxiety. I was received with all the tenderness of a younger son and favourite, and soon forgot all the hardships and sufferings through which this ease and comfort was obtained.

Another attempt was now made to wean me, if possible, from all thoughts of the sea as a profession, and every member of mj family used their utmost endeavours to attach me to some other pursuit. The attractions of the Church had been tried and failed; the more recent experiment of trade had been attended with no greater success. It was now determined, therefore, to try the Law; and I was accordingly placed in the office of Mr. Tippctt, the principal attorney in Falmouth, with a view to being articled with him. lie was, in reality, one of the magnates of the town, being employed by nearly all the nobility and gentry of the county, and, as it used to be said, " carrying the corporation in his pocket;" and being reputed to be wealthy, being universally popular, living in a fine mansion, having the handsomest wife, and a large family of the finest daughters in the county he was more sought after for his influence than any nobleman or baronet west of the Tamar.

I remained with him about a year, was petted, indulged, and coaxed by the greatest personal kindness to make me in love with the Law, but I felt a repugnance to it that I could not overcome. I was much too young, no doubt, to form any accurate judgment on what was passing before and around me; but still I saw so much of what appeared to my straightforward and unsophisticated mind, of unintelligible verbiage, of positive mis-statements and deception practised on clients and witnesses, and extolled as "wondei'fully clever" by the clerks, and so much feasting and carousing at the principal hotels, on divers occasions, at the expense of suitors, that I passed- a weary and miserable noviciate, and went back to my own home, declaring that I would never return to the office again.

CHAP. X.

Life of ease and pleasure passed on shore. Cultivation of music, and passion for the art. Remarkable history of a Negro musician. Liberality of London composers and artists towards him. Voyage of recreation and amusement to the Scilly Islands. Singularly primitive state of society there. Voyage from Scilly to Milford Ilaven. Agreeable associations, and gay life and manners. Death of my dear mother while absent here. Speedy return home. Property left in trust. Love at first sight. Marriage at nineteen. Establishment of a Bookselling and Nautical Depot at Falmouth. Sudden destruction of all our promising prospects.

The next two years of my life were passed in perfect freedom from any fixed occupation whatever, during whicli I was so amply supplied by my fond and indulgent parent with all the necessary means of purchasing whatever I desired, that my days and nights were devoted wholly to personal enjoyment, or the pursuit of pleasure in every accessible form. During this period I began the study of music, finding it a most agreeable recommendation in female society, of which I was always fond; and as I desired to be placed as speedily as possible in the way of turning this acquisition to practical account, I se- lected the flute as the instrument on which tolerable perfection is soonest attained, and as having the further advantage of portability and convenience. The only teacher procurable at Falmouth was an African negro, named Emidee, vho was a general proficient in the art, an exquisite violinist, a good composer, who led at all the concerts of the county, and who taught equally well the piano, violin, violoncello, clarionet, and flute. I placed myself under his tuition for an hour s daily lesson under his own eye, and four hours' daily practice besides; which I followed up with unbroken perseverance, and in two months I was perfectly competent to play any accompaniment to the piano, in three months to take a first flute's part in a concert, and in six to play Hoflpmeister's Grand Concerto in D, with full orchestral accompaniments, which I did with great ddat in one of the monthly concerts of the Harmonic Society of Falmouth, held at the Town Hall, where Emidee was the leader, Major Wall, of the Wiltshire militia, then in garrison at Pendennis Castle, playing the first violin; Mr. Jordan, Deputy Collector of Customs, the tenor; Mr. Lott, of the Post Office, second flute; and the rest of the orchestra made up of the militia band and amateurs.

The history of this negro musician, Emidee, is too remarkable to be passed over in silence. He was born in Guinea, on the west coast of Africa, sold into slavery to some Portuguese traders, taken by them to the Brazils when quite a boy, and ultimately came to Lisbon with his owner or master. Here he manifested such a love for music, that he was supplied with a violin and a teacher; and in the course of three or four years he became sufficiently proficient to be admitted as one of the second violins in the orchestra of the opera at Lisbon. While thus employed, it happened that Sir Edward Pellew, in his frigate the Indefatigable, visited the Tagus, and, with some of his officers, attended the Opera. They had long wanted for the frigate a good violin player, to furnish music for the sailors' dancing in their evening leisure, a recreation highly favourable to the preservation of their good spirits and contentment. Sir Edward, observing the energy with which the young negro plied his violin in the orchestra, conceived the idea of impressing him for the service. He accord-in o-ly instructed one of his lieutenants to take two or three of the boat's crew, then waiting to convey the officers on board, and, watching the boy's exit from the theatre, to kidnap him, violin and all, and take him off to the ship. This was done, and the next day the frigate sailed; so that all hope of his escape was vain. In what degree of turpitude this differed from the original stealing the youth from his native land, and keeping him in slavery, these gallant officers, perhaps, never condescended to consider: but surely man or boy-stealing, and carrying off to forced imprisonment, is equally criminal whether it be called " impressment" or " slave trading." Yet all England was roused by Clarkson, Wilberforce, and Sharpe, to protest against the African slave trade; while peers and commoners, legislators and judges, not only winked at, but gravely defended, in the legislature and from the bench, the crime of man-stealing for the British navy, at the same time teaching the men thus reduced to forced servitude and imprisonment, to sing of the country that had thus enslaved them

The nations not so blest as thee

Shall in their turns to tyrants fall; Whilst thou shalt flourish great and free, The dread enemy of them all.

Rule, Britannia, Britannia rule the waves. For Britons never shall be slaves!

Poor Emidee was thus forced, against his will, to descend from the higher regions of the music in which he delighted Gllick, Haydn, Cimarosa, and Mozart, to desecrate his violin to hornpipes, jigs, and reels, which he loathed and detested: and bemo;, moreover, the onlj negro on board, he had to mess bj himself, and was looked down upon as an inferior being except when playing to the sailors, when he was of course in high favour. As the captain and officers judged, from his conduct and expressions, that he was intensely disgusted with his present mode of life, and would escape at the first possible opportunity, he was never permitted to set his foot on shore for seven long years! and was only released by Sir Edward Pellew being appointed to the command of a line-of-battle ship, UImpetueux, when ho w as permitted to leave in the harbour of Falmouth, where he first landed, and remained, I believe, till the period of his death.

Here he first began by going out to parties to play the violin, which he did to a degree of perfection never before heard in Cornwall: this led to his being engaged as a teacher, and then a leader at concerts; so that, by degrees, he made rapid progress in reputation and means. Though he was one of the very ugliest negroes I ever remember to have seen, he had charms enough to fascinate a young white woman of a respectable tradesman's family, whom he married, and by whom he had a large family of children. Though anticipating by some years the proper period of this narrative, I may mention here, more appropriately than further on, tlie following anecdote connected with his life. Emidee had composed many instrumental pieces, as quartetts, quin-tetts, and symphonies for full orchestras, which had been played at the provincial concerts and were much admired. On my first leaving Falmouth to come to London about 1807, I brought with me several of these pieces in MS., to submit them to the judgment of London musical professors, in order to ascertain their opinion of their merits. At that period, Mr." Salomans, the well-known arranger of Haydn's symphonies as quintetts, was the principal leader of the fashionable concerts at the Hanover Square Rooms. I sought an interview with him, and was very courteously received. I told him the story of Emidee's life, and asked him to get some of his pieces tried. This he promised to do, and soon after I received an intimation from him that he had arranged a party of professional performers, to meet on a certain day and hour at the shop of Mr. Betts, a musical instrument maker, under the piazza of the Royal Exchange, where I repaired at the appointed time: and In an upper room a quartett, a quintett, and two symphonies with full accompaniments were tried, and all were highly approved. It was then suggested by Mr. Salomans, that Emidee should come to London and give a public performance. But Mr. Betts and all the others thought his colour would be so much against him, that there would be a great risk of failure; and that it would be a pity to take him from a sphere in which he was now making a handsome livelihood and enjoying a high reputation, on the risk of so uncertain a speculation. To show, however, the sincerity of their admiration for the man and for his works, they originated on the spot a private subscription, which, being extended for about a week among others of the profession not then present, realised a handsome sum, which I had great pleasure in transmitting to him, with several complimentary letters from those who had been present at the performance of his compositions, I record these facts with pleasure, as while they speak well for the liberality of the musical profession to their less fortunate brethren, they at the same time offer another splendid proof of the utter groundlessness of the fallacy which supposes the negro intellect to be incapable of cultivation, or arriving at an equal degree of excellence with that of the whites, if placed under equally favourable circumstances. With the same advantages as were enjoyed by most of the great composers of Europe, this man might have become a Mendelssohn or a Beethoven; but as it was, it was the achievement of extraordinary perfection, in spite of a thousand obstacles and difficulties.

To return to the narrative of my own life. I may now record a short episode in the career of imadul-terated and innocent enjoyment which these two years of complete leisure afforded me, in which I passed my time between reading, visiting, music, amatory poetry, riding, boating, and every other available pleasure, and in the possession of vigorous health. This episode was a visit to the Scilly Islands, to the south-west of the Land's End, and subsequently to Milford Haven. The Commander of the Active revenue cutter, belonging to the Falmouth station, Ir. John Millar, was a suitor for the hand of my eldest unmarried sister; and I received an invitation to accompany him on his next cruise, which I accepted with great delight. The cutter was a beautiful craft, a fast sailer, armed with ten guns, and a smart crew of fifty men, with an ample supply of boats for chasing smugglers in-shore, and all the appliances required for the fulfilment of their duty. We sailed from Falmouth with a fine breeze, gave chase to, and overhauled several suspicious vessels, having twice called " all hands to quarters," and had the guns run out for action, all of which was most agreeably exciting. After a week's cruise, and the capture of a few prizes bj the boats, w e anchored in the hay of Penzance, and passed a most delightful week in the hospitable society of that town, dining out every day, at different houses, and spending the evening with ladies, who everywhere seem to have a predilection for naval officers, and to be more frank and cordial in their attentions to them than to any other class, as if to compensate them for the dreary weeks and months they often pass at sea without hearing the sound of a female voice; while, on the other hand, it may be said, that this very privation of female society in their long voyages, makes sailors more enthusiastically happy in their enjoyment of it when it is placed within their reach, than is possible with any other class of men; so that mutual sympathy, admiration, and gratitude are all thus awakened, and more sudden and ardent attachments take place between sea officers and ladies than is ever effected in the same short space of time between the sexes in other circles; for few seamen quit the society of agreeable women without leaving their hearts behind them.

From Penzance we passed the Land's End and the romantic rocks of the Longships lighthouse, and steered for the Scilly Islands. We entered this vast cluster of visible and hidden rocks, thrown up as it were from the bottom of the ocean, and guarded on the south-west extremity by a group of black eminences, just above the water's edge, called " the bishop and his clerks," on which many a ship has been wrecked, and anchored safely in the harbour of St. Mary's, the principal island of this singular archipelago.

We remained here about a week, having, every morning, parties sent off in boats to scour the intricate channels in search of smugglers, and men on the heights with telescopes to watch their approach from a distance. When the duties of the day were all arranged, we dined at twelve o'clock, at the same hour with the crew, and then went on shore to spend the afternoon till sunset, when we always repaired on board to sleep. Nothing could be conceived more primitive than the state of society among which we were now thrown. The town of St. Mary's, though the largest of all within the islands, was very small; the population not exceeding fifteen hundred. It had however a governor, two clergymen, three doctors, two lawyers, several merchants, who were all smugglers, a collector of customs and his staff, and two military officers, with a single company of soldiers. These constitiitcd the aristocracy of the island; the rest were mere tradesmen, shopkeepers, and boatmen, who lived partly hy fishing, still more by smuggling, and, worst of all, it was said by visiting wrecked vessels and helping themselves freely to whatever could be saved from destruction. The mail-boat arrived only once a week from England when the weather was fine; but in winter, wath heavy south-west gales, they were sometimes three months without any advices from thence. A slieep was killed once a week, and a bullock once a month, for the gentry, the joints having to be bespoke to secure them; and pigs, poultry, and fish formed the chief food of all other classes. There was a splendid lighthouse, with revolving reflectors and thick plate glass, often encrusted with the spray of the sea, but so well kept and attended to, as to have its light visible for fifteen or twenty miles in clear weather.

Among the objects of interest in the eyes of the natives here, we were shown the spot where were interred the remains of the shipwrecked admiral Sir Cloudesley Shovel (to whom there is a monument in Westminster Abbey), his lifeless body being washed ashore with those of the seamen and recognised only by his uniform; to which they added the sage observation, that as a mark of the judgment of Divine Providence for his cruelties, no grass ever grew on his grave, the fact being that the spot Is just above high-water mark, and in spring tides or heavy gales it is frequently covered by the sea.

As an illustration of the primitive manners of the people, a current anecdote prevailed here to the following effect. That during a Sunday afternoon, a fearful wreck occurred in the island of St. Mary's, and not far from the church in which divine service was then celebrating. As all ranks and classes regarded such wrecks as fair subjects for plunder, since the underwriters must have to pay for all, the intelligence of the disaster had hardly reached the church, before the portion of the congregation nearest the door began to move off" pretty quickl3 The clergyman, being in the pulpit, demanded aloud the reason of this sudden movement, when several voices exclaimed, "A wreck! a wreck! " on which he instantly closed his sermon book, and said, ' Now, dearly beloved brethren, fair play is a jewel; wait till I have left the pulpit and put ofi my canonicals, and then let us all start fair together." This was professed to be believed as a truth by the narrators, and the period fixed for it occurring was less than fifty years ago.

The aristocracy of the island, as above described, met regularly at the principal inn, as early as two o'clock in the afternoon, every one dining at one; and here they usually spent their time till sunset or later, drinking, smoking, hearing and discussing general or local news, singing songs that would not now be tolerated in any decent society, varied now and then by a game at cards or backgammon. In all these daily diversions, the most perfect equality seemed to reign; the Governor was just as ready with his joke, and the clergymen with their songs, as the lawyer, the doctor, or the smuggler; all seemed loyal to the backbone; George the Third was the paragon of monarchs William Pitt the heaven-born minister the Americans were Yankee rebels, and the French a frotr-eatincr. wooden-shoe-wearing, dancing and capering set of Jacobins; yet, amidst all their loyalty, cheating the revenue by smuggling, and plundering wrecks when thrown within their reach, were not regarded as disreputable, since all classes there shared more or less in the profits of such occupations.

We grew thoroughly tired, however, of this monotony of mediocrity before the week was expired, each day being but little varied from the preceding, and were glad when the order was given to weigh anchor and sail for Milford Haven.

Our passage was delightful; the ample and noble harbour of Milford enchanting; and though the town

VOL. I. N was then in emhryo, there being ahnost as many houses in course of construction as finished, we found every thing in it delightful The liusband of my eldest sister, Mr. Samuel Steele, whose history as a youth, with that of his father, has been already alluded to, resided here, and commanded one of the packets sailing between Milford and Waterford, so that I was now quite at home as their guest, and introduced at once into the best society of the place. These consisted very largely of retired naval and military officers, families from Ireland, who sought a more tranquil place of residence, and many persons of good families and education who resided here from economy. Such materials could hardly fail to produce agreeable parties; and from the intimate relations maintained between the members of it, there were dinner parties, or evening parties, balls, concerts, and rude theatricals almost every evening. Boating, yachting, and swimming, in each of which, from constant practice, I was proficient formed an agreeable variety in the daytime, and not a moment hung heavy on my hands. Among the captains of the packets running between Milford and Waterford was one A hose acquaintance I was fortunate in making, Captain Pocock, a grandson of the famous marine painter of that name, and who inherited his ancestor's talent in this art. From him I received daily lessons, having some previous acquaintance with general drawing before: and ere I left Milford, I had obtained great freedom of pencil in sketching every description of sea-going craft, which my passion for the sea made more agreeable to me than any other subject, and which my technical knowledge of rigging and sails made accurate as well as easy.

This career of continual pleasure was, however, at length cut short by the sudden and sad intelligence of my dear mother's death. Her illness had been of many years' standing; indeed, she had never enjoyed either health or good spirits since the loss of her husband; and at length she sunk under her afflictions, falling gently to sleep and dying without pain. This was a sad blow to my happiness, for never was child more fondly attached to a parent than I was to one of the most indulgent of mothers; and the thought that I should never look again upon her beautiful and venerated countenance made me miserable in the extreme. I accordingly shut myself up from all society for nearly a month, waiting the return of the Active to her station at Falmouth, by which I came back to what seemed a most desolate home, having only my two sisters, each my seniors by a few years, as companions: and these as deeply inmerscd in sorrow for their loss as myself. One of my first duties was to visit her tomb, where she was deposited in the same grave that contained the dust of my father, in the parish churchyard of Myloi", about two miles from Flushing, on the very margin of the sea, opposite to the estuary of the river Fal, running from Truro to pour its waters into the Carrick Roads, the place of anchorage for all ships of war frequenting the port; and here in frequent visits, with my sisters, we passed many many hours, listening with a sort of melancholy pleasure to the ripple of the waves breaking against the shingly beach, and walking from thence home at the close of day along the margin of the sea, all the way round Trefusis point to Flushing, a distance of four or five miles, with the fine expanse of the harbour, and the opening into the British channel constantly in view.

As I was still in my minority, being then about eighteen (in 1804), the whole of the property left by my mother, consisting of lands, houses, shares in mines and fisheries, and several small vessels engaged in the coasting trade, was by her will placed in the hands of trustees, for the joint benefit of my two unmarried sisters and myself, to be held by these trustees until I should become of age, and then to be divided equally between the three. According to the best Information we could obtain as to its amount, it appeared likely to be quite sufficient, when tiius divided, to have afforded an income of several hundreds a year to each. In the meantime, we had a sufficient allowance from the trustees, who were the appointed receivers of all rents, dividends, and profits on our account, to enable us to live in great comfort, and without any anxiety as to the future.

After a year or so of mourning and general abstinence from gay society, time, the great healer of all sorrows, gradually assuaged our griefs, and we returned again to our usual free intercourse with the world. At this perii)d I became acquainted for the first time with the young lady who was destined to become the future partner of my life; and with both of us, it was really and truly " love at first sight." Miss Elizabeth Jennings was the daughter of a worthy and once wealthy farmer, who held the estate of Gwarder under the family of the Ennises of Ennis, near Penryn, but who, feeling a greater pride in the improvement of his farm, the excellent condition of its live and dead stock, and the comfort and happiness of its labourers, than in the profits it might yield, fell behind the woi'ld by his expenditure exceeding his receipts; and was so mortified at the result that he became broken in health and spirits, and soon after died, a victim to disappointed hopes. His sons had all early embraced the profession of the sea, and all rose rapidly in their profession, so that they were able to assist their widowed mother in her need, and her daughter kept her household and ministered to her comfort and happiness. It was in the bosom of their family circle that I first saw the object of my admiration and affection, and on my leaving the happy party, among whom I had passed the most delicious evening of my life, I felt all the enjoyment arising from the fullest confidence that my attentions were favourablv received.

As I was then without occupation, my visits were almost daily repeated; and though there were at first some scruples on the part of the mother as to my extreme youth, being then barely nineteen, yet this gradually wore away, and all parties in both our families became reconciled to our proposed marriage after a suitable time should have elapsed to give each the fullest opportunity of thoroughly knowing and appreciating the character and disposition of the other. I shall say nothing of the qualities of person or mind that thus powerfully won my aff ection, beyond this, that after fifty years of wedded life, which has now passed over our heads, while I write this, amidst every vicissitude of prosperity and adversity, absence and presence, health and disease, calumny and popularity, persecution and triumph, I have found such uniform and continued exhibition of all the virtues that first enchained me such aftection, such sweetness of temper, such prudence, intelligence, sound judgment, and fidelity, that our mutual attachment has never for a sinirle moment been even clouded with doubt or indifference, but we have loved on to the end, with the same fervour as we began; and at the approaching close of our lives find our constant presence more essential to each other's happiness than at any previous period of our existence.

It may be deemed anticipating a too remote period of my history from that here described, to carry it forward for a moment to the opening of the present year; but the episode will be a short one, and not inappropriate, as descriptive of my feelings after so great a lapse of time. They are here faithfully embodied, in the lines addressed to my wife on the G9th anniversary of her birth-day, January 1. 1855.

Hail, day of days! which nations in every clime revere As ushering in the dawn of a new auspicious year, But doubly dear to me, from its having given birth To her 1 value more than all treasures of the earth.

Yes, Dearest! tho' together we have trod the path of life, I, as thy loving husband thou, as ray faithful wife, No year has yet elapsed, that saw our fondness less, Or interposed indifference, to check Love's sweet caress.

When health has been our portion, we could mutually rejoice,
And lift to heaven our gratefal thanks, with one accordant voice;
And when sickness and suffering have been our frequent lot,
"We have borne each other's burthens, and watched each other's cot.

Whate'er has been our portion, in our declining years, Upon the sun-lit mountains, or thro' the vale of tears. We have linked our fate together, for sorrow and for joy. And thus our lives have passed, without Dissension's base alloy.

How many years of future life, to each may yet remain. Is shrouded in the future and to lift the veil were vain; But this at least we still may hope, let Death come when it may. We shall only pass from darkness here, to the more perfect day.

And oh! may those we leave behind, as pledges of our love, Rejoin us in the realms of bliss, reserved for them above, To dwell with us for ever in the assembly of the blest. Where "the wicked cease from troubling, and the weary are at rest."

TREraRATIONS FOR MATRIMONY. 185

To continue tlie narrative, after this anticipatory digression. It was tliouglit proper, however, as there might be some uncertainty in the ultimate value of such precarious property as mines and fisheries, by which as many fortunes are lost as won, and as a family of children might require to be provided for, that, previous to the marriage taking place, I should fix on some pursuit or profession, instead of living an entirely idle life. In thinking over this, strong as was still my passion for the sea, the idea of the almost constant absence from home which this would involve, was equally repugnant to both my betrothed and myself; and what we at last resolved upon was to ask the trustees to make a sufficient advance of capital to establish a business at Falmouth, Avhich should have for its principal feature a depot for nautical and astronomical instruments, with marine charts of all parts of the world, and the auxiliaries of a printing office and a good library. This would be an occupation to which I could bring some practical knowledge and experience acquired during my stay at a similar establishment at Plymouth Dock; it would also be quite congenial to my taste, and would be sure to bring around me, as visitors, the class of society in which I most deliglited that of naval officers, and nautical and literary men.

This proposition received the assent of my guardians; who, however, could not advance the required capital at once without effecting some sales of the property held in trust, which would require some time to do advantageously. They advised, therefore, that all the requisite supplies, up to a certain extent the amount of which was ample should be ordered on the usual terms of six or twelve months' credit, by which time funds would be provided to meet all claims.

In the course of a few months, therefore, the establishment was completed, our dwelling-house comfortably furnished, and being sufficiently encouraged at its outset to warrant expectations of ultimate success, all parties were content. Our marriage accordingly took place in the presence of all our relatives on both sides, in the parish church of Gluvias, at Pen-ryn, in the month of February, 1806 my own age being then just six months more than nineteen, and that of my wife a few months older than myself, both being born in the year 1786 our separate ages, and the slight difference between them, being as nearly as possible the same as those of her present Majesty and Prince Albert, at their nuptials.

If I had then been as well read in the literature of Greece as I was at a subsequent period of my life.

and had caught any of the spirit or feeling of the ancients, I should have lived in constant apprehension of some reverse, as our happiness seemed to he too great for mortals to endure for any length of time. But I had no such misoivino-s, and fondlv believed that our prosperity and enjoyment would be as lasting as our lives!

Oh! blindness to the future! kindly given That each may fill the circle marked by heaven.

This blindness made our happiness complete, as long as it endured. But at last came the heavy stroke that seemed to crush us with its fall.

Before the period of credit had expired, one of the trustees who, from the neglect and indifference of his colleague, got the whole management of our property into his hands, tempted by the hope of making a large and sudden fortune, entered into a gigantic speculation, no less than that of purchasing the entire cargo of a Swedish East Indiaman, which had put into the harbour of Falmouth, avowedly for repairs and provisions, but in reality to smuggle the whole of her valuable lading, if an opportunity occurred. The sum required for this was to be raised among four or five adventurers, and being placed in the hands of a third larty, in which all had confidence, the cargo was to be discharged at night in boats outside the harbour, and securely landed on different parts of the coast for safe custody. My trustee was one of the adventurers, and under pretence of selling the trust property held by him for our benefit, he disposed of the whole, vested the proceeds in this dangerous speculation (by which, if it had succeeded, he would have probably doubled his own fortune, and restored all that belonged to us also); but the scheme failing, by the vigilance of the revenue officers, who captured several detachments of the goods while landing, the parties engaged in the transaction were exchequered in double the auiount of the goods seized, and were obliged to seek safety in flight.

Here, then, were all our hopes blighted at a single stroke. The funds not being forthcoming to answer the various claims, everything had to be sold off at a great loss, and we were thrown penniless upon the world, just at the moment wlien our fii-st-born, a daughter, made us feel additionally the weight of our cares.

There is something in a first calamity which one experiences, as in a first love that one feels, which is never equalled in intensity by any subsequent recurrence of a similar event; and though I have lived since to experience many far heavier pecuniary losses than this in amount, yet to be thus thrown as it were from the very pinnacle of happiness to the very depth of despair, produced a feeling which no wrrds can describe, and which no subsequent calamity has equalled.

record this as the first inisfortune in life, of any pecuniary magnitude, that hefel me, icithont any fault of my own, hut entirely from the misconduct of others; and I place it thus emphatically by itself, as I shall have other, and even still greater, misfortunes of a similar hind to record, before this narrative is brought to a close.

We were so stunned and stupified by this reverse, that we were many weeks before we could bring ourselves to determine on the best course to be pursued. Help from friends was out of the question. My own father and mother had both descended to the tomb, and my two sisters were reduced to the same extremity as myself. My wife's father was dead, her widowed mother was supported by her sons, and there were no relatives on either side to whom we could now apply with any hope of more than temporary relief for the moment, till something better could be thought of.

Determination to resume ray original Sea-life. First visit to London to seek for a berth. Landing at Dover. Exorbitant charges. Ship Hotel. Journey on foot to London. First impressions. Cheap lodging in a humble garret, at 2. 6d. a week. Accidental visit to the British Forum in Piccadilly. Speech there. Introduction to John Gale Jones. Visit to an Amateur Theatre. Ridiculous scene there. An evening passed in the Fleet Prison. Mock Election. Profligate manners, and demoralizing effects.

After much deliberation I determined to return to my early profession of the sea, and to make the scene of my future operations a remote one from my former home and its associates, so as, in short, to begin the world entirely anew. My wife's second brother. Captain Thomas Jennings, commanded a West Indiaman sailing from the port of London, and we thought it best to repair at once to the great metropolis, where neither of us had ever been before await his arrival there, and then for me to join him as one of his officers. It was thought best, however, for me to proceed first to London alone, and, having made the necessary inquiries and due preparations, for my wife and her infant daiighter to join me afterwards. We parted with heavy hearts, and ahnost empty purses; and, for economy, I obtained a free passage in a coasting vessel, commanded by Captain Brokenshire, on condition of my working my way before the mast with the seamen, and sharing their fare, so that during the passage, which was a stormy one, I kept watch, hove at the windlass in weighing anchor, did duty aloft in reefing and making sail, and took my turn at the helm as steersman; which were all familiar to me, and valuable as practice.

We landed at Dover, as the vessel was likely to be a long time beating up to London; and, inquiring for a good inn to take tea and a bed before starting next morning for the capital, I was directed to the Ship Hotel, and in the morning after breakfast had a bill of nearly a guinea to pay for tea with cold meat, bed, breakfast, and servants a sum which I had calculated to last me a week at least; but it taught me a lesson to ask the scale of charges before putting up at any inn or hotel for the future, though the Ship, I believe, had the reputation (of which I was wholly ignorant) of being one of the dearest hotels in the kingdom.

To make up for this unexpected drain in my slender finances, I determined to make the journey to London on foot, which it took me three days to accomplish, my trunk having gone round by the coaster, so that we reached the Custom-house within a few hours of each other. Never shall I forget, however, the depressing and utter solitude in which I found myself in this huge metropolis. The continued stream of strange faces, not one of which I had ever seen before, or, perhaps, might ever see again, passing over London Bridge, up Fish Street Hill, and along Leadenhall Street, Cornhill, and Cheapside, with the tlirong of merchants, brokers, and ship captains on the Exchange between three and four o'clock in the afternoon, positively bewildered and oppressed me; and, in the humble garret I felt it my duty to choose for my lodging, at 2s. 6d. a week, I could get no sound sleep for many nights, from the never-ending din of the great thoroughfares. During this my first visit to London, while walking one evening along Piccadilly, 1 was attracted by a transparency over a doorway, on which were inscribed the words " British Forum." My curiosity was excited to inquire of the doorkeeper the nature of the institution thus described, and I learnt from him that it was a public debating society, and that the admission was a shilling. Though I had but few shillings to spare, I could not resist the inclination to devote one at least to a visit to this place of entertainment, as I had never been present at any debating society before.

I accordingly paid the admission fee, and, on entering, found a spacious and lofty room, well lighted, with from two to three hundred well-dressed ladies and gentlemen seated among the audience, and a sprinkling of working men in their undress costume. The chair was occupied by a grave elderly man; and, as the proceedings had not yet begun, he announced from the chair that the subject of debate for the evening was " Whether celibacy is more favourable to the cultivation and concentration of the intellectual faculties, and therefore advantageous to the progress of discovery and improvement in art, science, and literature, than married life with all its cares and anxieties? and whether a greater number of examples of high attainment could not be selected from history among; the former than amonc; the latter?"

There was some difficulty at first in getting an opener to the debate. At length, however, a middle-aged man rose from among the audience, and delivered a very fair speech, as regarded its matter, in favour of married life; and the marks of approbation from the female part of the audience were frequent and hearty. He was followed by a tall, thin, nervous person, apparently about fifty, with a jerking VOL. I. O movement of the limbs, and twitching of the head and face, not unlike what has been sometimes remarked in Lord Brougham when in an excited state of eloquence. He undertook to defend the superiority of celibacy, which he did in a style of fluent delivery, cogent argument, and abundant examples by way of illustration that seemed to carry all before it. I had never before heard such speaking; and though I could not divest myself of the idea that the pleader was not himself convinced of the truth of his position, but argued the matter as a paid counsel would do at the bar, it must be confessed that his oration made a deep impression on all who heard it, and it was impossible not to admire the extraordinary talent which it displayed. The orator resumed his seat amidst the loudest applause.

I deemed his views so erroneous, that, with the enthusiasm of a newly married husband and a most happy one I was strongly tempted to rise and reply, especially as there was a long pause without any speaker offering himself, and the chairman several times reminded the audience that any one was at liberty to take part in the discussion. But I shrunk from the idea of following such a man. I asked the person sitting next to me who the orator was, and he answered, "What! not know him? Why, that's the celebrated John Gale Jones, the editor of the Independent Wliig, the greatest thorn in the side of the Tories, who would hang, draw, and quarter him if they could." I was so unacquainted with j)olitics, that I had never heard his name before, though I was a constant reader of the Examiner, then recently established by John and Leigh Hunt, and rendered attractive to all lovers of wit, taste, and literature, independently of its bold assaults on its political opponents.

At length another rose, and then another, each speaking but for a few minutes, and each more feebly than the other, so that the meeting was becoming very dull, and the usual hour of adjournment had not yet arrived. Encouraged, therefore, by the mediocrity that had now tamed down the enthusiastic admiration of Mr. Gale Jones's speech, I took courage and rose to defend the state of married life as infinitely superior in all respects to that of celibacy, even including the successful cultivation of the intellectual faculties, and the production of great works in literature, science, and art. I was listened to with great attention, much applauded on all sides, but especially by the ladies, and after a speech of nearly an hour brouo; ht back the meetino; to its orio-inal state of enthusiasm; so that when the question was put from the chair, as it was too late for any one to follow me, it was carried in favour of Married Life by an overwhelming majority.

On retiring from the audience I was spoken to by one of the committee, who said Mr. Gale Jones had expressed a desire to see me; and I accordingly followed him into the committee-room for this purpose. Here I received a great many more compliments than I thought I deserved;' and after some conversation I was invited to join the committee, and become one of the regular visitors. I declared this to be impossible: when it was added, that they thought it so desirable to retain my services, that they were willing to admit me to a share of the profits of the undertaking. It was then explained, that the committee took upon themselves all the pecuniary arrangements; and the rule was, that when all the expenses of the evening were paid, the surplus was divided among the committee in equal portions, with a double one for the president, Mr. John Gale Jones, who was the chief speaker and most powerful attraction of the whole. I thanked them for this mark of their confidence, but felt it indispensable to decline it, and never repeated my visits, by which, perhaps, I escaped some trouble, as these societies were at that time illegal when they discussed politics, which was the chief topic of their debates; and, moreover, Mr. Gale Jones himself was subsequently imprisoned in Newgate, either for some speeches delivered here, or for some articles in the Independent Whig; and he fell subsequently, I believe, into great poverty, and died at an advanced age in want.

Another phase of London life became revealed to me about the same time. A number of young men and women, chiefly, I believe, of the class of assistants in shops, had formed themselves into an amateur theatrical company, and rented a theatre near Soho Square, to which I was invited, not as an actor, but a spectator, a box-ticket having been presented to mc. I understood from the person who gave me this, that all the parts to be performed were put up to competition within the body of performers, and whoever paid the highest price had the first choice of the character they would take, and so on of all the others. The fund thus raised was devoted to the payment of rent, scenery, dresses, lights, music, and attendants, as no money could be received for admission, since the theatre was not licensed. Attached to each character so purchased by the actor or actress there was a certain number of admission-tickets, proportioned to the price paid, for presents to their friends.

The play selected for this representation was Shakespeare's Romeo and Juliet, and the following ludicrous occurrence took place: In the scene where Romeo and Juliet meet on the stage for the first time, thouo-h there was but one Juliet, who was really very handsome, tliere were two Romeos, and each addressed her at the same time. This was at first thought to be a blunder, and was merely laughed at; but as soon as it was discovered to be designed, hissing succeeded, till a perfect storm of disapprobation drowned the voices of both. The manager was called for, and appeared, and the explanation he gave of it was tliis: The person who had bid the hio-hest price for the character of Romeo, and had paid his money down, happened to be a discarded lover of Juliet oif the stage, and he sought this mode of winning her, if possible, by his playing. But the lady had communicated this fact to her real lover, who happened to be one of the same company, and he, procuring a much handsomer dress, and being also the handsomer person of the two, determined to outshine the legitimate Romeo, which he really did in his acting, while Juliet exhibited towards him every mark of favour and affection, and turned upon her heel whenever the obnoxious rival approached her. The manager said it would therefore rest with the audience xohich should be the Romeo of the night; and he begged to put it to the vote for their decision. As every question has two sides to it, and something may always be said on either, there were many short speeches delivered on this. The advocates of mercantile integrity declared that it was dishonest to deny a man the enjoyment of what he had paid for. Those whose sympathetic feelings were stronger than their sense of justice, clamoured for the real lovers, as they only could best express the action and sentiment of the play, and this was desired by a large majority; after which the performance was resumed, and all passed off satisfactorily.

Though in the course of my wanderings in various parts of London, I had walked by the lofty blank walls of the Fleet Prison, and dropped my sixpences into the debtor's box at the grating, through which some of the unhappy inmates used to look into the street, and ask the sympathy of the passers by, I had never expected to enter it; but an occasion arose on which I did so, and the scenes it revealed were altogether so new to me as to make a very vivid impression on my feelings, and my memory has retained a perfect recollection of them ever since.

Having met unexpectedly in the street a young midshipman I had known at Plymouth, and who had since become a lieutenant, he asked me wlietlier I had any curiosity to see the interior of the Fleet Prison. I replied, " Yes, if I could readily get out again;" to which he replied he was going there on the following day as an invited guest, to be present at a contested election, and as he had permission to bring a friend with him, he would take me under his care. To this I readily assented, and in the morning we met as agreed, and went there together. I had expected to find the place full of gloom and sorrow, and every countenance sad and careworn, as it appeared to me that to be shut up within such impassable walls for debt, with so little hope of escape, must be a state of extreme misery. I was surprised to find, however, that the inmates were gayer, and appeared more happy than the crowds of free men which filled the streets outside. Here were groups of gentlemen playing at tennis and fives, others enjoying the games of back-gammon and cards, many drinking and smoking, some singing songs, and not a moody or melancholy person among them. The election was to take place at noon, and hustings were already erected for the candidates and their supporters in the open court-yard. It was to determine who should be the mayor or chief magistrate of the prison for the ensuing year, the elected person being chief justice of a court of appeal, or a sovereign on liis own bench, to settle all disputed cases referred to him of differences among the prisoners; but without any power to release either them or himself from their confinement.

There were several candidates, each with a proposer and seconder; and as all of them made speeches in succession, it occupied several hours of time. As there vas no politics involved, the speeches were chiefly satirical and witty, containing many allusions to prison anecdotes and personages, not intelligible to myself, but eliciting roars of laughter and applause from the crowd; indeed good humour seemed to reign universally, and though there were continual salvos of applause there was no hissing or other marks of disapprobation. At the close, a show of hands was taken for each candidate, and all had some supporters, but there was an overwhelming majority in favour of a little black-bearded, bronze-faced elderly man, about fifty, who wore a blue jacket and trousers, and a rough hairy cap, and whose speech was so interlarded with sea phrases and marine jokes as to make it certain that he was a sailor. He was then chaired as the mayor elect for the ensuing year, being carried in a chair on men's shoulders around the prison, and hailed in his progress by loud hurrahs, waving of handkerchiefs, and other demonstrations of satisfac- tion. In the evening we dined witli the hero of the day and a small party in his own apartment, when I learnt that he was a captain in the navy, with a large fortune, but believing his creditors to have imposed upon him, he preferred going to prison to paying their unjust demands, and his resources being ample he lived even extravagantly, and gave frequent drinking bouts in evening parties, which was the chief cause of his popularity. Among his remarks during our conversation, I remember his saying that he had enjoyed many pleasures in his life-time, winning victories by sea and races on land, being in at the death in hunting, with all the rest of the field behind, and he had enjoyed all the pleasures that women and wine could afford; but none of all these were half so excitingly agreeable as gaining a contested election by a single vote, which had happened to him but once in his lifetime, and was one of the pleasures he should most like to have an opportunity of enjoying again. We left the party at eight o'clock, when the prison doors were closed for the night, and they were even then so deep in their cups as to render it probable that all would be under the table before morning. No wonder that the popular belief should be that no man ever came out of a prison better than he went in, but many a oreat deal worse.

Delay in the arrival of an expected Ship. Procure employment in a London printing office. Disgust at London life and dissipated associates. Went into the country to escape from the contagion. Reach Oxford, and get lodgings at Is. Qd. per week. Obtain employment in the Clarendon Printing Office. Anecdote of students altering the marriage service. Return to London, and joined there by my family. Privations suffered. Acquaintance with Captain Hors-burgh. Correcting the press for his East India Navigators' Directory. Arrival of the long-expected ship from the West Indies. Appointed chief officer of the William Fenning for Port au Prince. Lines addressed to my wife on parting. Sudden change in our destination. Transferred to the Titus, bound for Trinidad.

On Inquiring at the owners of Captain Jennings' ship, I found that his arrival from the West Indies was not expected for three months, whicli was a sad disappointment, as I knew not how we should subsist in the interval. To return again to Falmouth would be foil '; to remain in London without funds for my own subsistence, and something to send ray dear wife and her infant, impossible. I applied to many places for employment as a clerk, and would have deemed myself fortunate to get oqL a year, but I found every house fully supplied. It then occurred to me that I might turn my practical knowledge of printing to some account, and I accordingly offered myself as a compositor at various offices, and at length, after many sickening refusals and delays, I obtained employment at the office of Messrs. Evans and Ruflfey, in Budge Row, near the Mansion House, great printers for the lottery, offices, then in full activity. Here the hours of attendance were from six in the mornincr till eight at night, the office dirty, the men dissipated, coarse, and boisterous, and regarding me as an unqualified interloper, greatly inferior, no doubt, in manual dexterity to the London-bred workmen in constant practice. I was scowled upon by some, and shunned by others, which last was the greatest favour they could confer on me. At this occupation, mainly from my own want of habit and skill, I could never earn more than twelve or fourteen shillings a week; yet I contrived to live on this, miserably enough indeed, and send at the end of each month a one pound Bank of England note to my wife in Cornwall.

I became, however, so sick of London life, London workmen, London fogs, and Loudon noise, that I determined to go into the country, and having heard that there was a great printing office at Oxford, wliere bibles and prayer books only were printed, with better wages, and cheaper living than in London, I set out one morning outside the stage-coach for Oxford, and was delighted with the whole journey, the fresh air, the green fields, the cattle, the birds, the bright streams, and gay flowers, all so familiar and so dear to me in childhood, but which in London never gratified my sight, as the slavery of toil from early morn till late at night would never admit of my visiting even the suburbs. An hour's walk after leaving the office in the open space of Moorfields, then a place without a blade of grass, and used chiefly for beating carpets, with secondhand furniture shops on the sides, and the lunatic asylum of Bedlam, with the occasional screams of its inmates, being the only sights and sounds of the locality was all I could command; but there was open space and air, and this was something. All this has since been built over with Finsbury Crescent, the London Institution, and other large buildiniis.

At Oxford I was fortunate in obtaining a single bed-room, a garret in a poor tailor's house for Is. 6d. a week; and as I had by this time learnt to breakfast on a penny loaf and a basin of milk, with potatoes and a little butter without flesh meat for dinner, milk and rice boiled for tea and supper

united, and animal food only on Sundays, a single mutton chop being deemed amply sufficient, 1 had brought my expenditure down to ten shillings a week, including lodging, food, and washing; and obtaining work immediately at the Clarendon printing office, at fixed wages of twenty shillings a week, I was comparatively rich; and could now send a one pound bank note every fortnight to my wife in Cornwall, instead of every month only.

I was charmed with Oxford in all other respects. Its fine old Gothic colleges and churches, its rich green lawns and noble avenues of trees, its bright atmosphere and gay streets, with the dignitaries and pupils in their college costume, and above all, the rich and beautiful country around it, made me often feel that if I had an independent income, there was no place in which I should like to settle for life so well as at Oxford.

While working at the Clarendon Printing Office, a story was current among the men, and generally believed to be authentic, to the following eff'ect. Some of the gay young students of the university who loved a practical joke, had made themselves sufficiently familiar with the manner in which the types are fixed in certain forms and laid on the press, and with the mode of opening such forms for correc- tions when required; and when the sheet containing the Marriage Service was about to be worked off, as finally corrected, they unlocked the form, took out a single letter, v, and substituted in its place the letter k, thus converting the word live into KJce. The result was, that when the sheets were printed, that part of the service which rendered the bond irrevocable, was so changed as to make it easily dissolved as the altered passage now read as follows: the minister asking the bridegroom, "Wilt thou have this woman to thy wedded wife, to live together after God's ordinance in the holy state of matrimony? Wilt thou love her, comfort her, honour her, and keep her in sickness and in health: and forsaking all others, keep thee only unto her, so long as ye both shall like? To which the man shall answer, ' I will."" The same change was made in the question put to the bride.

It was said that the change was not discovered till all the sheets were printed off, and was then detected by the compositor who distributed the types: the whole of the sheets had accordingly to be cancelled: but the real culprits were never discovered till they left the university, and then when they were beyond the authority of the proctors, they voluntarily confessed what they called their " lark." Many other college tricks were the frequent theme of conversation, but most of them were such as could not be described without offence.

It became necessary, however, to quit Oxford, as intelligence had arrived of Captain Jennings being daily expected, and it was thought desirable that I should be in London immediately. I accordingly repaired there; and as my dear wife was heart-sick at our separation, she intreated so earnestly to join me that I consented to it. I sold some of my apparel to raise the means for paying the expense of the journey; but as they fetched very little, I was obliged, with more reluctance than I ever felt at parting with anything before, to sell my flute, which had been a solace to me in many a weary hour. Means being thus provided, my wife and her infant daughter Virginia left Cornwall, and after their long journey, I met them at the Belle Sauvage Inn on Ludgate Hill, where we found it difficult to restrain the exuberant expressions of our joy in the presence of strangers. I may mention that the reason of our daughter being named Virginia was this. Dui'ing my stay at Plymouth, as recorded in a previous page, I had been appointed by my elder brother as joint prize-master with a young midshipman of the Impetueiix, of about my own age, named Alexander Young, wdiose father was a well- known physician at Rochester. We had formed a most romantic attachment to eacli other while shipmates and messmates, and among other pledges of friendship exchanged, we agreed that if either of us should many and have children, the first daughter should be called Virginia, the name of the French West Indiaman of which we were prize-masters: and the first sons should be called James or Alexander, after ourselves, which was faithfully adhered to.

In the expectation of my wife's joining me, I had procured two rooms in a small cottage at Hoxton for seven shillings a week furnished; but we could not afford to pay for the attendance of a servant, and accordingly all the heavy burthen of this duty, as well as the care of the child, now little more than a year old, fell upon her mother, and this was a greater grief to me than any sufferings or privations of my own.

Day after day, however, passing on, without Captain Jennings' arrival, and our scanty store being soon exhausted, I was obliged to remove again into London, where I obtained cheaper lodgings at a place called Shakespeare's Walk, in the very heart of

Wapping, in the house of a Mrs. Patterson, whose husband, the commander of a West Indiaman, had been captured by the French, and was then in prison

VOL. I. P at Verdun, so that she was oblio; ed to let lodmno-s and take in washing to support herself and infant daughter. In tlie meantime I obtained employment as a compositor in the office of Messrs. Plummer and Brewis, near Mincing Lane, where Horsburgh's East India Directory was being printed: and this for me was a most fortunate circumstance, for Captain Horsburgh calling one day to inquire as to the progress of the work, I got into conversation with him, and without revealing my whole story, I showed him that I was familiar with all the processes of navigation and nautical astronomy, was well versed in geometry and logarithms, and, therefore, more than usually competent to correct the proof sheets of his great work, (neither of us then dreaming that I should ever use this work, as I did afterwards, when commanding a ship in the Indian Seas, or that I should receive from him, while Hydrographer to the East India Company, many years afterwards, letters of thanks for the valuable hydrographical information I was enabled to give him from my own researches in the Persian Gulf and the Red Sea). This office was therefore assigned to me while I remained here, which w as but for a short period; for at length Captain Jennings arrived; and the intelli- gence of this event infused new life into our almost despairing bosoms.

I hastened on board his ship in the West India Docks: he was greatly moved at all that had happened to ns during his absence: he instantly repaired to his sister, and we were both put into more agreeable quarters; taking up our abode, indeed, with him at pleasant lodgings in a street leading out of the Minories, and feeling as if the dawn of a new life was opening upon us.

My outfit was speedily provided out of advances made on my future pay. I was appointed chief officer at once of the William Fenning, at 8 a month, with no expense for mess thus having board and lodging free, and with power to my wife to draw 4: a month as half-pay during my absence and till my return.

As Port-au-Prince had, however, at that time the reputation of being one of the most unhealthy ports in the West Indies, I was desirous of insuring my life for 500. as some provision for my family in case of death, but no office would take such a risk; and when a newly established one expressed a willingness to do so, the premium asked was 50 per cent.!-equivalent to saying, " the chances are just equal whether you will live to return or leave your bones

Oil the Island of San Domingo." This was a most disheartening discovery; and when the ship was reported ready for sea, and I had to take a farewell of my wife for the voyage, our parting was painfully embittered by the fear that we might never meet on earth again.

One of her favourite airs was that of Dr. Arne " The Soldier's Adieu:" and on the morning of leaving her, I placed in her hands the following lines adapted to that air, written amidst the conflicting feelings of the present and painful apprehensions of the future:

FORGET ME NOT.
Forget me not! the' Fate's decree
Has torn me from thy bosom, And duty calls me far from thee,

To cross a dangerous ocean: My soul shall smile at human fears,
And ill that may beset me. While the fond hope my bosom cheers That tho' between us billows roll, Thy fettered soul. Released by Love's resistless power, Will sometimes stray The pledge to pay Thou gavest me in the parting hour, That thou would'st ne'er forget me.

Forget me not! when festive joy-Dispels each trace of sorrow; When sparkling mirth thine hours employ,

One pensive moment borrow, To trace the happy hours we've passed, The scenes where oft thou'st met me, When as thy hand I warmly pressed, And on it breathed a burning kiss, Trembling with bliss, I felt thy glowing pulse beat high, And in thine eyes Saw pity rise. As thy last broken faltering sigh

Breathed that thou'dst ne'er forget me.
When evening shadows close the day,
And I, of home still dreaming. Shall watch the sun's last parting ray.
On thee still warmly beaming; I'll think that thus, when life shall cease,
With all the woes that fret me, Wlien my last sun descends in peace.
And sinks below the horizon's bound, Tho' all around Shall view me pale and cold in death, Thy fancied form My heart shall warm. Inspiring e'en my latest breath To liop thou'lt ne'er forget me.

As o'er old Ocean's foaming surge,
Our labouring bark is reeling, Where wild winds seem to howl my dirge,
And mock the pangs of feeling; When lightnings glare and thunders roll,
And beating torrents wet me. This hope shall cheer my drooping soul, That tho' by raging torrents torn On waves upborne. We mount on high and sink below. Still thou, my love! Wilt faithful prove. And oft fulfil the sacred vow

That thou would'st ne'er forget me.
But should our vessel prove a wreck,
Or fatal balls fly near me, When bleeding on the gore-stained deck,
With no soft hand to cheer me; While from me earthly prospects fly. And death's dark gloom awaits me, Thou'lt have my last expiring sigh: Yes! my spirit soars above To thee, my love! 'Twill fly to bid its last adieu; And then prepare To meet thee there, In the fond hope that vow was true That thou would'st ne'er forget me.

Wo parted In silence, our hearts being too full for utterance. But so strange arc the changes and turns in human affairs, that while we lay at Gravesend, preparing the ship for sea, getting all ready for weighing anchor, and waiting only the arrival of the captain from London with the ship's papers fi'om the custom-house, some disagreement had taken place between himself and his owners, which led him to resign his command. Tlie joyful intelligence came down by post, with the advice, that I had better resign also, as he would refund the two months' wages in advance, by which my outfit was provided; and, in a few weeks, no doubt, another ship might be obtained, and possibly for a less unhealthy destination. I accordingly followed his advice, and returning speedily to London, our meeting was intensely joyous, as it seemed like an vmexpected return from the grave.

Before a fortnight had elapsed, Captain Jennings obtained another command, being appointed to the Titus, a fine large West Lidiaman, destined for Trinidad. I joined him as his chief ofllicer, as before, and in the course of a month we had our cargo on board, and everything ready for sea.

First voyage to the West Indies in the Titus. Early capture by La Josephine, French privateer Release, after being plundered and stripped. Leisure at sea, and books read in the watches below. Recollections of Trinidad. Agreeable French society. Deplorable condition of most of the Negro Slaves. Advocate their Emancipation at some risk. Hurricane at Trinidad. Fearful conflict of the elements. Sir Walter Scott's poetical description of the Orinoco. Departure on the homeward voyage to England. Squally weather in beating up the windward passage. Mesmeric trance, and unconscious writing of poetry. " Starboard Watch! ahoy! " set to music. Tremendous hurricane on the banks of Newfoundland. Wreck and devastation in the fleet. Severe suifering. Circular theory of Storms. Safe arrival in the Thames.

We had a fine passage from Gravesend to the Downs, and all through the Channel, carrying a fair wind beyond Cape Finisterre, when, about a week after leaving London, we wei'e chased by a fast-sailing cruiser, that overhauled us with marvellous rapidity, and soon indicated her intentions by a shot from one of her bow chasers, which fell just under our quarter. She was soon alongside of us, and, with the French flag at her peak, declared herself to be La Josephine, of Nantes, showing, at the same time, a formidable battery of long brass twelve-pounders run out fur action, with matches lighted, and all prepared for a heavy broadside. A boat soon came on board, and, as we had but two guns, chiefly of use for signals rather than defence, and a crew of twenty men to oppose to her 200, resistance would have been folly; so we surrendered to her as prize. An examination of our papers showed the nature of our cargo, chiefly English manufactures of the coarser kind, with tools and implements for estates worked by negroes, things of so little value for sale in France as to make it hardly worth Avhile for the captors to take us into port, as it would necessarily require a diminution of their own crew to navigate the prize, and run great risk of re-capture. They contented themselves, therefore, with taking chiefly articles from the cabin, including the captain's and my own private adventure, consisting of articles adapted for the higher classes of the West India society, and comprising, therefore, more of value in less weight and space than the cargo generally. They also took our sextants, quadrants, and compasses, with most of our charts, threw the only two guns we had overboard, and then left us to our fate.

We were sadly mortified at being thus stripped of

SO much that was essential to our safety, though glad to escape imprisonment in France at any sacrifice; and, having a leading breeze to take us into the trade winds, which we caught a little to the south of Madeira, we rolled on before the steady east wind of the tropics; and, in four weeks after our capture, safely reached Trinidad, steering in through the intricate passage of the Dragon's Mouth, and anchoring in the Port of Spain opposite the chief town of the island.

During these four weeks of our outward voyage, having almost always six hours off duty, either the forenoon or afternoon watch of four hours, and one of the shorter dog-watches of the evening of two hours, and never having yielded to the frequent practice of sleeping or idling during the watch below, I read a large number of books, fourteen or fifteen volumes at least, including Bryan Edwards's History of the West

Indies, the voyages of Drake, Anson, and Cooke, as well as of Columbus and his companions, Don Ulloa's interesting voyage and journey to Quito to measure an arc of the meridian there, and several others relatino; to the western world. This was sub-sequcntly my constant practice, to furnish myself on every new voyage with all the books I could procure on the countries and seas about to be visited.

and in the leisure of release from duty, and often amidst the very scenes described, to read everything relating thereto, which made a much deeper impression on my mind than if read in the library or closet at home. To this habit I attribute largely my fondness for geographical, historical, and antiquarian studies; and it can readily be conceived that in the entire freedom from interruption which is enjoyed by officers in their watch below, when the weather is fine, with no letters to read or answer, no morning or evening visits to receive or pay, no long distances to walk, and no external cares to distract the attention, the closest studies may be most uninterruptedly pursued. Sometimes, when the sun was in the eastern quarter, as we rolled westward before the trade winds, I enjoyed the shade of the head sails, as I lay in the netting on the bowsprit for stowing the fore topmast staysail, and read at my ease there. In the after part of the day, when the sun was in the western quarter, I went into the main-top, and there, under the shade of the main-topsail, read equally at ease, though always ready for duty when the occasion demanded it. By most of the sailors I was regarded as a sort of astrologer, especially as I took frequent opportunities of observing the stars at night, and noting tlieir positions on the celestial map, and I was on this ac- count frequently consulted as to the probability of winds, weather, long or short passages, and so forth; nor was I always believed when I frankly declared my incapacity to look into the future, even for the space of a single day.

Though necessarily more occupied with the ship's duty in harbour than when at sea, as the discharge of the outward and the shipment of the homeward cargo engages the greater portion of the day for the chief officer's attention, besides the greater difficulty of maintaining discipline among the crew, and looking after the extra hands employed from the shore, yet I availed myself of such intervals of leisure as I could command to inquire and to learn.

The principal recollections that I have of the harbour of Trinidad and our stay there are these: I was charmed with the romantic scenery of the island, and the luxuriance of the vegetation everywhere, as well as with the bold views of the coast of Cumana, on the neighbouring continent of South America, which is full in sight from the ship's anchorage, and every part of the island. We were consigned to a French merchant's house, Messrs. Vance and Co., and nothing could be more agreeable or hospitable than the society of the head of the firm and his entertainments, of which I was a frequent participator.

There were two cliaracteristics of West India society, however, wliich were to me very revolting. One was the abundant use of rum and water, lime punch, sangaree, and other drinks, at all hours of the day, among the upper classes; and the fearful drunkenness, on new rum, of nearly all the sailors seen on shore, by which so many get their deaths rather than from any really deleterious qualities in the climate; but, above all, the constant sight of naked negroes working in gangs, many with chains on their legs, leaving sores by their friction, and others with iron collars round their necks, with great hooks projecting outwards fi'om them on all sides, to prevent the wearers from escaping through the forests or jungles. In my youthful enthusiasm for liberty, and with more zeal than prudence perhaps, I took frequent occasion to express my abhorrence of this state of degradation in which the negroes were kept, and once asked Mr. Vance what he thought would be the feeling of the population of Paris or London, if some of these gangs of negroes with their chains and iron collars could be paraded through the streets of these capitals, with slave drivers using their whips to accelerate their movements. He replied: " No doubt it would be thought very horrible; but it was impossible to cultivate sugar without negroes, and impos- sible to make negroes work without the whip." I said, "We had then better live without suo; ar, which, after all, is not an absolute necessary of life, than have it at such a price." To which he replied: " Young man, take my advice as a friend, and a sincere one: never utter such sentiments while yovi are in Trinidad, or some day you will find yourself in trouble." Notwithstanding this advice, which was well meant for my safety, I could not help now and then returning to the subject: and greatly softened his objections, by saying that I was no enemy to the planters; but was fully convinced that if the same motives of good wages and kind treatment were applied to the negroes as to other men, they would work far better when they were to be benefited in proportion to their labour, than if they saw all the profits of their labour taken from them by their masters. He doubted this, as apparently did every one else at that period in his position. But my convictions were as strong on this subject as at any subsequent period of my life; and I could not refrain from pressing this conviction on others.

During our stay at Trinidad, we had a hurricane, which was the most fearful thing I had yet seen. Ships half laden, and with yards and topmasts struck, were blown over on their beam ends at their anchors, as if they had been made of paper; an entire terrace of llg yly built liouses, not yet occupied, were levelled with the ground; ponderous casks of sugar, requiring four men to roll them along the wharf, were taken by the wind and sent forward with immense velocity; trees and plantations were rooted up by thousands; the sea had flowed over tlie flat part of the island near the coast, and two ships had been driven with the flood three miles inland, and there left high and dry when tlie floods subsided. The water of the harbour was tinged with the outpourings of the great American streams from the neighbouring continent, especially fx'om the Orinoco; and this discolouration of the water, with the conflict of counter-currents, the raging blast of the hurricane sweeping in all its fury, gave a perfect realisation of the splendid imagery of Sir Walter Scott, in his description of tlie fight on Marston Heath in his Poem of Rokeby.

"The battle's rage Was hke the strife which currents wage Where Orinoco, in his pride, Rolls to the main no tribute tide, But 'gainst broad Ocean urges far A rival sea of roaring war; While, in ten thousand eddies driven, The billows fling their foam to heaven, And the pale pilot seeks in vain, Where rolls the river, where the main."

We made an excursion after the hurricane was over, to a remarkable lake in the interior of Trinidad, called the Pitch Lake, from its being filled with liquid bitumen, or pitch, oozing up through the surface of the earth at the bottom of its bed, and presenting different degrees of liquidity and consistency at different seasons of the year, sometimes being like asphaltum, sufficiently solid to bear the weight of a man walking on it, at others so complete a fluid that a boat might float on it. The pitch is constantly used for covering the seams in caulkino- and for laying on the bottoms of coasting craft that are not coppered, and is therefore very useful.

On leaving Trinidad on our homeward voyage, we had to beat up to windward, in order to touch at Tobago and St. Thomas's, there to meet the convoy for the homeward-bound Windward Island fleet; and our passage was tedious and intricate, with squally weather, which required a constant good look-out, and frequent tacking, reefing, and shortening and making sail. We had taken on board two passengers the major of a West India regiment, and his wife; the former so confirmed a drunkard as to be wholly unfit for duty; and in a society where intemperance was never regarded as anything beyond a gentlemanly weakness, his conduct became so obnoxious that a subscription was raised by his brother officers to pay his expenses home; his wife was equally given to the bottle, so that we had no very agreeable companions. The captain, too, having, as was not then unusual in the West Indies, taken his parting glass of punch or sangaree at every house at which he had called during the day, to respond to the wishes of his friends for a successful voyage, was so overcome as to be fitter for his cot than any duty when he came on board, while the second officer next to me in rank was not of sufficient steadiness to rely on for such navigation and such weather as we had now to encounter.

In consequence of this I felt it my duty to remain on deck ail night, keeping three watches in succession instead of one, and that too after a most fatiguing day in getting the ship fairly out of port. My fatigue was such as to reduce me almost to a state of insensibility; though, when the morning broke upon us, and I heard the welcome sound of "Starboard watch, ahoy!" the summons for relief from the duty of the deck, I seemed to feel a thrill of delio; ht which gave me new life, though for a few moments only. And here I must record a singular pyscho-logical fact, unique in my own experience, though

VOL. I. Q since appearing to me, from what I have seen in others, to partake of the nature of a short mesmeric trance.

The log slate was brought to me by the boy entrusted with this duty, to enter the course and distance steered, and the usual remarks of the watch for subsequent entry into the regular log book of the ship. I was then seated in my own berth, intending to turn in and get some rest: and I sat with my pea-jacket still on, and wet to the skin from the constant squalls of wind and rain during the night. I made the proper entries with the pencil and fell asleep seated on the chest in my berth, with the slate in my hand: and four hours afterwards, when it was my turn to be on deck, I was found in that position, sleeping almost as heavily as death. Being roused by constant shaking, I changed my wet clothes and went on deck to resume my duty.

It is customary at sea for the log slate to be handed to the officer who has charge of the log book to transfer the entries from the one to the other; after which the slate has to be cleaned and hung up in its usual place under the companion hatchway, for the entries of the ensuing watch. When the second officer had made his entries therefore, he cleaned that side of the slate, but on turning to the other, he found some verses there, which he knew to be in my handwriting, and he brought the slate to me, to know whether this might be cleaned off also. I was perfectly amazed at what I saw; the writing was certainly mine: and the words forming the heading of the verses, "Starboard watch, ahoy!" I well remembered as having caused me a thrill of inexpressible delight; but of the lines that followed, I had not the most distant recollection. They had emanated, it was clear, from my brain, and expressed no doubt the genuine feelings of the moment; but I was as utterly unconscious of their being written by me, as a clairvoyant in a mesmeric trance is of what has been said and uttered during its existence, after he has been awakened from it. The lines, however, were copied by me from the slate, on paper, and when shown, after our return to England, to Mr. Dale, a music-seller in the Poultry, he thought they would become popular as a sea-song if set to music. He accordingly engaged Mr. Charles Horn, then a risnig young composer, to execute this task. It was published by Mr. Dale, had a good run, was sung at several places of public entertainment, and from a printed copy of the words and music now in my possession, I am able to present tlie following version of this unconsciously written effusion.

STARBOARD WATCH, AHOY!
At midnight's dark and dreary hour,
Deserted e'en by Cynthia's beam, When tempests beat, and torrents pour.
And twinkling stars no longer gleam, The weary seaman, spent with toil,
Hangs on upon the weather shrouds, And Time's slow progress to beguile.
Sings, as he views the gathering clouds, "Starboard watch-! ahoy!"
CHORUS.
But who can speak the joy he feels, While o'er the foam his vessel reels, As his tired eyelids slumbering fall. He rouses at the welcome call Of " Starboard Watch, ahoy!"

With anxious care he eyes each wave, That swelling threatens all to o'erwhelm,
And his storm-beaten bark to save Directs with skill the faithful helm.
With joy he di'inks the cheering grog 'Mid storms that bellow, loud and hoarse;
With joy lie heaves the reeling log,
And marks the distance and the course.
CHORUS.
But how much gi'eater joy he feels, While o'er the foam his vessel reels, As his tired eyelids slumbering fall, He rouses at the welcome call Of "Starboard Watch, ahoy!"

We completed our passage through the group of the Windward Islands in perfect safety, touching at Tobao; o, and rendezvoued at St. Thomas's, where we found a convoy with about twenty sail ready to start for England. To profit by the westerly winds and northern latitudes of short degrees of longitude, wo steered up the Gulf Stream for the banks of Newfoundland; and as we were passing over these, were

At this period no one apprehended the least evil from a moderate use of spirits, well diluted with water, In times of storm and rain; and the grog served out to seamen was always so diluted. The drinking of raw spirits unmixed with water, was that which generally caused intoxication. Subsequent experience, however, has shown that even diluted spirits are injurious to health; and that hot tea, cofIfee, good beef soup, and similar refreshments, are more permanently sustaining and beneficial when exhausted nature requires restoration.

assailed in the dead of the nio; ht with one of the most violent hurricanes that had been known to race for many years. In order to keep up with tlie commodore, whose ship was Lord Nelson's old two-decker, the Captain, 74, most of the fleet were under full sail, some even having their topmast-studding-sails, and royals set. But the blast came so violently as to carry everything before it. The Captain was running before the wind under bare poles, without a stitch of canvass set beyond a fore top-mast staysail to steady her steerage, yet her three top-masts went by the board, snapping off near the lower cap, as if they had been so many reeds. As our own vessel, the Titus, was not a heavy sailer, we had single reefed top-sails only set, the whole fleet going about seven knots, as the pace in convoys is necessarily regulated by the rate of the slowest, but we were thrown completely over on our beam-ends, so that the top-sails were in the water on the lee side, the horizontal deck was nearly perpendicular, the long-boat, caboose, hen-coops, and puncheons of fresh water stowed on deck to make room in the hold for cargo were all swept away, tearing the weather bulwarks and midship stanchions along with them, as if they had been made of paper or straw. Every one was paralysed by the helplessness of our situa- tioii, as no sails could be taken in, tlie helm was perfectly powerless, and there was no use in cutting away the masts, as their weight and lumber might have dragged the vessel over a few inches more, when we should unavoidably founder: a fate which befel three vessels close under our lee, one of them a man-of-w ar brig forming part of the convoy, another the Atlas of Bristol, and a third a fine ship from Lancaster, which then sent many large and handsome vessels to the West Indies, though Liverpool, I believe, has since absorbed all her colonial trade.

As to any help from boats, it was quite impossible, for none could live in such a raging sea; so that we passed the long hours from midnight to daybreak in the most painful suspense. Fortunately for us, a sudden shift of wind, blowing with equal violence, righted us on our keel again, but with the fury of the oscillation we were as nearly as possible capsized on the opposite board. All hands had new life inspired into them by this unexpected change; so that in a few minutes all were aloft, furling the topsails, striking top-gallant yards and masts, and pre-. paring the ship against a repetition of the calamity from which we had just escaped.

When daylight broke, the scene was most appalling. Not less than forty-five vessels were in sight, which arose, as we afterwards understood, from the Jamaica fleet under convoy having followed close in our wake, and become united with our own during the night. The wind had now abated, but the heavy swell was still such as to prevent communication by boats. Out of the forty-five vessels in sight, however, thirty-three had all their masts swept away by the board, the rest had lost one or more of their lower masts, and all were without a top-mast. We afterwards learnt that no less than eight had foundered in the hurricane and every soul on board perished.

On the second day a slight breeze springing up, the signal was made for each vessel to pass within hail under the stern of the Commodore, when it was ordered that every ship having more spare spars than she needed for her own use, should supply them to others in need; and the Commodore set the example by sending, towed by boats, all his spare spars, yards, topmasts, booms, and every other kind, to those most in want of them. By these means almost all were enabled to rig some kind of jury masts, and with their own spare sails put their ships again under canvass. Every vessel having the superiority in rate of sailing or in equipment, was next ordered to take some slower or less fortvmate ship in tow, and the Commodore had three in a line following in his track.

Water also was supplied in small quantities of a puncheon to each ship that most needed it, from the Commodore's own stock, and this was the greatest relief of all; but even with this, calculating the probability of a thirty days' passage from the Banks of Newfoundland to the Channel in our present crippled condition, in which we could make no progress except with a fair or leading wind, we deemed it prudent, if the stock was to last, to put ourselves and our own crew on a quarter of a pint of water per day for all purposes; and considering that our only food was salt beef and pork, with hard biscuits, it may easily be imagined how intensely we suffered from thirst.

There was one curious circumstance connected with this hurricane which no one could then explain; it was this: A large ship called the Pilgrim had all sail set when the storm came on, and was so entirely untouched by it, that she did not reduce an inch of canvass, as she felt nothing of its violence; and her captain and crew were amazed at day-break to find themselves surrounded with so many dismasted vessels while they remained perfectly unharmed. The sailors, who are usually very superstitious, attributed this exemption to the sacredness of her name, the Pilgrim, to which it was added, by conjecture, for no one had any communication with the ship, that the captain and all the crew were devoutly religious, and that she was exempted, as a special mark of divine favour to her occupants.

The circular theory of storms, as it is called, was not then at all known, though subsequently so well established by the observations of navigators, and the able work of Colonel Reid of the Royal Engineers, now Governor of Malta. But the law of storms was, of course, the same then as now, though our knowledge of this law is but of recent acquisition. By this theory the unharmed condition of the Pilgrim is perfectly intelligible. She happened to be in the centre or vortex of the whirlwind, which was a vacuum, while the spiral course of the hurricane swept everything in its course, and this accounted also for the sudden shift of wind, by which our own vessel was righted from her beam ends on one side, and nearly thrown over upon the opposite one.

After a long and tedious passage, the convoy keeping close together for mutual aid and protection, we reached England in about the time calculated, thirty days; and never were her shores more lovely in the sight of any of her children than they appeared to us on sailing up channel and on landing. Our friends, too, who had heard of the hurricane by some earlier arrivals, but who knew nothing of our fate, were happily relieved from all their anxieties; and our meeting with them was additionally delightful, from the cessation of the fears for our safety by which they had for many weeks been haunted.

Portuguese merchants from Lisbon and Oporto. Instance of tyranny and cruelty in Impressment. Impossibility of obtaining redress for such wrongs. Visit to the church of the celebrated Joanna Southcott. Pictures and Peculiarities seen and learnt there. Pregnancy on the expected Shiloh. Passports for heaven. Exhibition of Gully the prize-fighter as champion of England. Visit to the Plough public-house kept by him. Striking contrast in his condition in after life. Meeting with', him at the seat of Eai'l Fitzwilliam. Himself and his daughters " the observed of all observers." Entered as a member of the Royal Naval Lodge of Freemasons. Enthusiastic attention to the duties of the craft.

About tliis period of my stay in London, there arrived from Oporto and Lisbon two Portuguese merchants who boarded at the same house with us, and each spoke English perfectly well, having been engaged for many years in trade between their country and our own. We became extremely intimate, and 1 enjoyed their society very much. The history of one of these gentlemen is sufficiently remarkable to be adverted to. Being the owner of several vessels employed between Oporto and London, he had for some years past been in the habit of coming over to England in the winter, to enjoy the

Christmas festivities and public entertainments of that season; and being thus half a sailor, he usually wore, for convenience, the ordinary jacket and trousers of an officer, on the voyage. It happened that in the British Channel his vessel was brought-to by an

English frigate, when a boat with a lieutenant came on board to look for English seamen, and if found to impress them for his Majesty's navy. After a vigilant search none were found, at which the officer was excessively angry and disappointed, as his ship was greatly in want of men. As the lieutenant was pacing up and down the weather side of the quarter deck, while his boat's crew were searching the vessel below, he encountered in his walk the Portuguese owner of the ship himself, who was also walking on the weather side of the deck. He immediately ordered him to go to leeward, accompanying his command with a brutal and opprobrious oath. It should be understood that the weather side of the deck is the post of honour reserved for the commander or officer of the watch, as giving him the most perfect sight and command in all evolutions; and midshipmen and inferioi' officers walk the lee side of the deck, which is much less agreeable, especially when the mizen staysail is set and the weather is rainy, as then they get all the drippings from the foot of the sail as they walk the deck; and hence this sail, in a man-of-war, has acquired the unenviable name of " the midshipman's curse." Of this piece of naval etiquette, however, the Portuguese owner was wholly ignorant, and firing at the insulting language and conduct of the lieutenant, he asked whether any man could have a better right to walk on any side of the deck he chose, the weather or the lee, than he to whom the ship herself belonged? To this the only response of the lieutenant was, "Oh! oh! you mean to be saucy, do you? Here, coxswain, bundle this fellow into the boat."

No sooner said than done; the seamen with great alacrity handed the unfortunate owner, whose struggles were unavailing against a whole boat's crew, into the boat, in which he was speedily conveyed to the frigate. It appears, however, that during the transit from one ship to the other, the lieutenant began to be ashamed or afraid of the undoubtedly illegal, and as certainly tyrannical act that he had committed; for on arriving alongside, instead of reporting the incident to the captain, he had tlie Portuguese merchant bundled forward in charge of a boatswain's mate, with instructions to keep him before the mast, and send him into the fore-top for duty. The victim of this naval tyranny without a change of linen or a shilling in his pocket was thus hoisted into the fore-top, as he declared his inability to go there; and the frigate running afterwards into the North Sea, in the dead of winter, he was, after several hours' confinement there without extra clothing or food, taken down in a half-frozen state, and with difficulty warmed into life again. After a week's cruise the frigate anchored in the Downs, where the impressed merchant was landed in the jolly boat at Deal; when the frigate sailed for Portsmouth, and ultimately to the West Indies. At Deal he told his story to the innkeeper at whose house he put up, who consented to wait for a remittance from London. This arrived by return of post, so that he was enabled to get all he wanted in the way of apparel, and to come to London by the stage coach. Here he found his ship arrived some weeks before him, and, owing to his absence and the necessary detention of the cargo till his arrival, he was a loser of several hundred pounds, besides all the personal indignities and injuries to which he had been exposed.

If ever there was a case of naked and unjustifiable tyranny, this was one; but, strange to say, after every effort in his power, and the expenditure of a large sum of money to obtain redress, " the preroga- live of the crown," which assumed the right of naval officers to impress whom they pleased, and held them free from all responsibility for the manner in which this power was exercised, was too powerful for him, and he gave the matter up in despair.

This gentleman and his compatriot from Lisbon, expressed a strong desire to see some of the more remarkable things in England which had no parallel in their own country, and, having some leisure and a great inclination for new sights and subjects myself, I readily agreed to accompany them. The two to which they gave the preference, out of many submitted to their choice, were, a visit to the Church of Joanna Southcott, then in high popularity, and a visit to Gully, the most celebrated prize-fighter of the day, two things in striking contrast to each other, but both great novelties to myself as well as to the Portuguese.

We selected a Sundav-evenins; for the visit to the Church of Joanna Southcott. This was situated on the Southwark side of the Thames, near the well-known station of " The Elephant and Castle." It was an ordinary building without any pretensions to architecture, but it had on its front, in large raised stone letters, the words " The House of God." On entering we found a large congregation assembled.

the majority of which were young females. There was a pulpit, reading-desks, and pews, as in an Established Church; and the minister in a white surplice read most of the prayers of the Church of England. After psalms sung by the congregation out of the authorised version, a sermon was preached, which wholly evaded all reference to Joanna Southcott's peculiar doctrines, and might have been preached without offence in any other church or chapel of the land. The only remarkable things we saw here, was a series of large oil paintings on canvass, without frames, hung round the walls of the interior. These contained many strange and unintelligible scenes and groups, but one more prominent than the rest represented a ship with ten or twelve masts just arrived in a river from a sea-voyage, where she was safely moored by several hawsers fastened to a rock; and winged angels with white robes and flowing hair were going up the rigging in large numbers to furl the sails. This we were told represented the Voyage of Life, which ended by the ship's arrival in the river of Eternity, where she was moored to the Rock of Ages.

It appeared, on inquiry, that this, as well as all the other pictures, were painted by a youth who was both deaf and dumb: but who was the only person

VOL. I. R to whom Joanna Southcott would communicate her holy visions, and these were the pictorial representations of the same. They appeared to me ingeniously unintelligible, and framed upon the principle of the hieroglyphical prophetic pictures attached to Moore's Almanack, which are so beautifully vague that they may easily be interpreted after the event, as indicating every occurrence that could or might occur in the interval.

Our visit would have been most unsatisfactory, but that we made inquiry of the person who officiated as clerk, who readily answered all our questions, and from him we learnt, among others, the following particulars: Joanna herself was admittedly a most illiterate woman, but, as he believed, purposely chosen by the Almighty on that account, " that the weak thhigs of the world might confound the strong." He believed that she was pregnant, by immaculate conception, with the promised Sliiloh, for whom a most gorgeous cradle had been already prepared by a subscription among her followers. Her disciples were not confined to the common people, but numbered learned divines of the church, officers of the law, of the navy and army, and many medical men; they were thought to number at least 100,000, and her power was deemed so great that high prices were paid for seals prepared under her direction, the preservation of which in the coffin, when deceased, woukl ensure the possessor admission into heaven! The sale of these passports was admitted to be a large source of revenue. It was added that their value would be entirely destroyed if, from want of faith, the boxes in which they were sealed up were opened on earth; but those who bought them out of mere curiosity had no scruple to do this, and found a very ordinary kind of seal, sometimes in resin, sometimes in wax, with some doggerel poetiy recommending the possessor as a fit inhabitant of paradise! Since that period the bubble has burst, though there are still said to be some scattered remnants of her followers, who are distinguished by the outward costume of broad-brimmed, or what are now called ' wideawake hats," of a grey or brown colour, drab coats without collars or buttons, and a long and untrimmed beard; while their professed belief is, that though "the holy Joanna" for so they call her died without giving birth to the promised Shiloli, she is only withdrawn from the earth for a season, and will return, when mankind have more faith, to complete her mission! All this, when explained, astonished the Portuguese gentlemen, who, coupling the tyranny of impressment with the triumph of superstition, said they doubted whether England was as free a country, or the English so intelligent a people, as they boasted themselves to be.

A few days after this, an opportunity presented itself of our seeing the most popular prize-fighter of the day, young Gully, who had just beaten the champion of England, Gregson, in a terribly bloody encounter, and was to show himself at his own house to his admirers, as soon as the cuts and bruises he had received in the contest were sufficientlj healed. At that period Gully kept a small public-house, under the sign of the Plough, in Carey Street, Lincoln's Inn Fields, and thither we repaired on the first day of his exhibition. In him we saw a tall handsome young man, of about twenty-one years of age, his head fearfully battered, many cuts in his face, and both eyes recovering from intense blackness, but full of gaiety and spirits at his late triumph; he wore a little white apron before him, after the manner of landlords, and served his visitors with whatever drink they required; while his young wife, an exceedingly pretty woman, though of the St. Giles's style of beauty, assisted, in the most smiling and gracious manner, her victorious husband and his visitors. The rounds of the battle were detailed to us with great minuteness, and the only thing my Portuguese friends seemed to regret was that they were not spectators of so exciting a scene.

And here I must anticipate the order of events for the purpose of mentioning another occasion on which I met Mr. Gullj, at an interval of many years, but under such a change of circumstances to us both, as neither could then have dreamt of. In the year 1832, or thereabouts, the young Lord Milton, heir to the Earldom of Fitzwilliam, came of age, and, according to the custom of that princely family, a grand entertainment was given at their seat of Wortley House, near Rotherhara, in Yorkshire. It had been the usage on all previous occasions to invite to such entertainments all the notabilities of this the largest and wealthiest county in England, and especially all the members for the three ridings of the county, with all the members for the boroughs within their limits; and as it is characteristic of aristocratic life and manners to adhere as much as possible to ancient precedents, this usage was continued in the present instance, though the recent Reform Bill had brought a large number of new members into Parliament, who would haixlly have been invited to Wentworth House as private individuals. As I was at that time one of the members for the newly enfranchised borough of Sheffield, I received an invitation as matter of course, and went with my colleague on the evening appointed to share in the Fitzwilliam hospitalities. The scene was one of the most splendid I had ever witnessed. The spacious mansion was one blaze of light, the park itself through which it was approached was brilliantly illuminated, and there were more than five hundred carriages that had already set down their company, though it was yet only ten o'clock, and the arrivals continued incessantly till midnight, the guests dispersing only at five in the morning.

At the head of the staircase on entering the grand saloon, stood Earl Fitzwilliam to receive his guests, to each of whom he had something kind or complimentary to say; and as I had the pleasure of being personally known to his lordship before this visit, my reception was very cordial and gracious. There were already about two thousand persons assembled in their gayest apparel; with a blaze of diamonds and jewellery, especially on some of the elderly ladies, Avhose natural beauty having departed, was sought to be replaced by artificial attractions, in which rouge, false hair, and other auxiliaries were used, to harmonise with an openness of neck and bosom that was anything but appropriate. Among the groups, however, that passed from room to room in the general promenade, there was one that at- tracted universal attention. It was formed of three persons the central one, a fine, manly, athletic, yet well formed and graceful figure, and resting on either arm two of the loveliest women of all the assembled multitude, about eighteen and twenty years of age, dressed in plain green velvet, without a single ornament or jewel of any kind, but with such exquisite figures, beautiful features, blooming complexions, bright eyes, and rich and abundant hair, as might make either of them a worthy representative of the Venus of Cnidus, of Medicis, or of Canova. They were so little known that the question was perpetually whispered, "But who are they? who can they be? " They received as much attention from Earl Fitz-william as any other of the guests, and this only heightened the curiosity to know from whence they came, as they were evidently " unknown to the county gentry." At length it was discovered that they were Mr. Gully, the ci-devant prize-fighter, and his two daughters! He w as then member for Pontefract, had acquired a large fortune, and most honourably it was believed, on the turf, being an excellent judge of horses, had purchased a large estate, and was living in a style of great elegance at Hare Park, near Pontefract, respected by all his neighbours. w "ch a contrast as this scene presented to that of Mr, Gullj at the Plough pubhc-house in Carey street, Lincohi's Inn Fields, five-and-twenty years before, or to myself working as a compositor in the Clarendon Printing Office at Oxford, and living in a garret at a rent of eighteen-pence a week, appeared to me sufficiently striking to justify this departure from the natural order of the narrative, and the anticipation of events as 1 have described them.

About this period I became a member of the Royal Naval Lodge of Free and Accepted Masons, which then held its usual sittino; s at a hotel near Burr Street. Its master was one of the most celebrated masons of the day, being, I believe, one of the King's printei's, in the office of Strahan or Hansard, and best known as the author of a very popular work entitled " Preston's Illustrations of Masonry." I had long-desired to penetrate the mystery of this institution. Indeed, whatever was difficult of acquisition, or mysterious or forbidden, had always a very powerful charm for me, and I rejoiced when I fovind that I was deemed eligible for adjnission. The " honour of the craft," as it is called, forbids my making any further disclosures on the subject than this, that I was very agreeably disappointed; that the ceremonies of the initiation were interesting and agreeable; that the strictly masonic duties of "working in the lodge" were of a highly intellectual, figurative, and even poetical character; and that the social relaxation which succeeded the performance of duty was innocent and pleasurable; while the charitable object to which its funds were devoted, for the aid of the distressed brotherhood, gave it an additional recommendation. 1 was accordingly an enthusiastic disciple, a constant attendant, and soon worked my way from the "entered apprentice" to the "fellow-craftsman," and from that to the "master mason."

Voyage to Virginia, in America, in tlie sliip Rising States. Long and stormy passage in the autumn of tbe year. Entry of the Chesapeake and arrival at Norfolk. Acquaintance with American naval officers. Comparison between the naval services of England and America. Agreeable society in some of the families on shore. Many drawbacks from slavery and its accompaniments. Excursion to the Dismal Swamp. Poetic legend. Impressions of Moore's poems just then published. Detention at Norfolk. Non-intercourse with England. Amateur theatrical performance for the benefit of seamen. Departure for England. Lines addressed to me on parting. Crew of the Rising States. Old Testament names. Escape of a Virginia Nightingale. Lines to its companion. Safe arrival in England, and happy reception.

During my second stay in London, and before the Titus was ready for her next voyage, another brother of my wife's, Captain John Jennings, arrived from America, to which country he had gone in very early youth, and had become naturalised as a citizen of the United States. Having acquired some wealth, by fortunate voyages between the north-west coast of America by the Pacific and China, carrying furs from tlie former to Canton, and bringing from thence to New York silks, teas, and other Chinese produce, he was on the look-out for the purchase of some American vessel in London, with which to go to Norfolk, in Virginia, We now lived together, myself, my wife, and her two brothers, each commanders, at the boarding-house of Mrs. Mitchell, where half-a-dozen American captains and supercargoes also resided, it being quite an American rendezvous, in Burr Street, near the London Docks. This was the only street I had ever seen in London lined with a row of lofty trees on each side, at the edge of the pavement, forming an avenue of shade in the sunmer, like the trees of the Boulevards in Paris and other large French cities, and like nearly all the principal streets in New York and Philadelphia, a feature that made it especially agreeable to Americans.

An opportunity of effecting the purchase sought for, soon presented itself; and the ship Rising States, of Marblehead, commanded by Captain Adams, a master in the American navy, was accordingly transferred to Captain John Jennings, for 8,000., her burthen being about 400 tons. By a wise law of the United States, whenever a ship owned by any citizen of that republic, and registered in any American port, is sold in any foreign country, tlie owners and commanders are bound to find safe and gratuitous conveyance to their homes of all American subjects forming the officers and crew, to prevent their dispersion or distress. It was therefore arranged in the present case that Captain Adams, his officers and crew, should all remain on board to navigate the ship back to America, Captain Jennings going out as a passenger, to take the command in Virginia, and I accompanying him, doing duty with the chief officei', as his colleague or assistant, for the sake of practice and experience.

Our outward voyage, being in October and November, was very long and very stormy, with almost a constant succession of strong westerly gales, which at this season prevail in the northern portion of the Atlantic, so that we were nine weeks on our passage. During this period I read a large number of books, from Robertson's History of America, and the Abbe Raynal's works, including every thing relating to the conquest of Mexico and Peru, down to the lives of Washington, Patrick Henry, Thomas Jefferson, and the heroes and statesmen of the American revolution, with the speeches of Lord Chatham, Colonel Barre, Burke, and others in the British Parliament at that eventful epoch, winding up with Washington Irving's first published work, then just issued anonymously under the title of " Salmagundi, or the Whimwams of Launcelot Wagstaff," full of the most witty yet ludi- crous pictures of manners and society, especially in New York.

On reaching the Capes of Virginia, we sailed up that magnificent inlet of the sea, having the noble Chesapeake Bay on our right, and anchored off the town of Norfolk. It being in the winter, and the lands around the coast being generally low and covered with forests, the landscape was not inviting; and the town seemed to be an irregular assemblage of wooden houses, the only redeeming features of which were, that being painted white, with green verandahs and Venetian blinds, they had an air of brightness and cleanliness which was refreshing. But, on landing, the scene was much less agreeable, un-paved and dirty streets, with mud and snow mixed to a depth of ten or twelve inches, innumerable pigs and half-clad negroes and n:; ulattoes shivering with the cold, common-looking white men, dirty and coarsely dressed, and groups of half-intoxicated and beggarly-looking Indians, and their squaws, with their almost naked redskinned bodies, painted faces, feathered head-gear, and bows and arrows, made up a most uninviting picture.

Our first acquaintances were among the naval officers; there being five large and handsome frigates here in full sailing trim, anchored in Hampton Roads and ready for sea, of which the President, the United States, and the Constitution were three. Of the last of these, the sailing-master was a Mr. Gallagher of Baltimore, whom I had known in England, as chief officer of an American trader; and by him Captain Jennings and myself were introduced successively to Commodore Decatur, one of their most popular naval heroes, who was subsequently killed in a duel; Commodore Porter, who in the Essex frigate played so distinguished a part in the Pacific; and Commodore Barron, who was in great disrepute for having received the fire of an English ship of war, and being in so unprepared a condition as to be unable immediately to return it. The society of these officers, and frequent invitations to visit them in their respective ships, were extremely agreeable.

In the English service the officer of a ship of war would look down with contempt on the captain and officers of a merchant vessel, and never condescend to associate with them but as their superiors. Their pretension is, that trading for profit is not so honourable as fighting for it, and that fortunes made from the plunder of unoffending owners of merchant ships belonging to an enemy's country, during war, are more nobly acquired than by honest and legitimate commerce, which increases the wealth of the world instead of destroying it. They affect also a supreme disdain for all those whose lives are devoted to pursuits of gain; though their scruples arc easily silenced when they are themselves the receivers of pay, prize-money, gun-money, head-money, and freight of treasure on mercantile account.

The officers of the American navy have no such nice distinctions as these. Being frequently brought up in the early part of their career in merchant vessels, where they acquire their first lessons in seamanship, the society of officers in the mercantile marine is deemed quite equal to that of officers of the fighting marine; and feelings of mutual good will and respect exist between them.

All the frigates that we visited here were in splendid condition, the ships of the most beautiful forms, of greater tonnage, more guns, and heavier weight of metal, than even the first-class English frigates. The crews, being all volunteers for a limited period (impressment never having been tolerated by the Americans), were really picked men, as there were always more candidates than can be received: and though it was alleged that there were many among them of English, Scotch, and Irish birth, besides Danes, Swedes, and Prussians, they had all become naturalised as citizens of the United States, and considered themselves to be Americans. I should say that these frigates' crews of 500 men each, were equal, in smart seamanship, knowledge, and prompt fulfilment of duty, to the 600 or 700 which form the crews of English seventy-fours, taking into account the many inferior hands which such heterogeneous assemblages generally contain.

By degrees we became acquainted with several agreeable families on shore, with whom we passed many pleasant evenings after the duties of the day were done. Among these was one deserving especial notice. Mr. Hunter, the manager of one of the Norfolk banks, was an Irish gentleman who had made America his home for the last twenty years, he being then about fifty. By his first wife he had a large family of children, now all grown up, of which the son was a master shipwright, and superintended the repairs of our vessel, and the daughters, from twelve to twenty, were among the handsomest and most accomplished young ladies of Virginia. But these were all eclipsed by his second wife, a lady of about thirty, of Irish parents, but born in the West Indies, and beyond all question the most beautiful, most intelligent, and altogether the most enchanting woman that I had seen since leaving England: and her devotion to her husband so won on the affections of his children, that it was impossible to imagine a more happy or harmonious family than they formed.

The drawbacks to the pleasures of male society, however, were very great. Gentlemen of every rank and class chewed tobacco, and were rarely seen without a cigar in the mouth (tobacco being the great staple of Virginia, and in the early days of its settlement used as a currency, the price of wives even being often fixed at so many hogsheads of this noxious and offensive weed). At every visit, before breakfast and before dinner even, as well as in the afternoon and evening, sangaree and peach-brandy toddy were handed round to all the guests. Slaves were every where abundant, lying about the outhouses and passages, as indolent as dirty, and as little cared for as the hogs whom they made their companions; and any sentiment of pity for their condition, or expression of a hope for their ultimate emancipation, only excited a stare of astonishment, a smile of incredulity, or a frown of disapprobation.

During our stay here, we had to put the ship under the operation of being " hove out," that is, first made entirely empty, and then, by a leverage from the shore on her lower masts, brought completely on her beam-ends, or side, so as to lift her keel out of the

VOL. I. S water, for some repairs required for it, in consequence of our having struck the ground in our entrance near the rocky island and fort which guards the passage through the Capes of Virginia, called " The Rip-Raps." It is a tedious and dangerous operation, requiring the greatest vigilance to see that the strain of the tackles is uniform, and just sufficient for the purpose and no more, as an inch or two more than enough would cause the ship to roll over, when she would soon founder and be difficult to recover.

We made an excursion from Norfolk to the Dismal Swamp, which is within a few miles of the town, and certainly nothing could be imagined more dreary than the whole region of marshes, jungle, and dense forest which it presented. We read Moore's impressive ballad bearing this title, on the spot, written by him at Norfolk, and embodying the true spirit of such a scene and such a legend as he describes.

I was accompanied in this visit by an enthusiastic young German, about my own age, Mr. Giese, who had come out to join a mercantile house from Bremen, and whom I met again twenty years afterwards (in 1839), returned with a fortune, and settled at Baltimore, as well as Mr. Gallagher, whom I had first known at Falmouth as mate of an American trader, in 1806; then here at Norfolk as master of the Con- stitution, American frigate, in 1809; and, lastly, at New York, as a commodore of the American Navy, in 1839, commanding the North Carolina, of 80 guns, being the port-admiral, as he would be called in England, and having a fine family and a large estate near Wilmington, where we spent many agreeable days.

Among the books that excited most attention in Norfolk during this period, and formed the most frequent topic of conversation next to Washington Irving's " Salmagundi," was the recently published work of Thomas Moore, entitled " Odes and Epistles." In this charming volume, after the exquisite amatory odes to Nea, written in Bermuda, his Epistles, written from different parts of America to his aristocratic friends and patrons in England, contained some of the most pungent satires and severest censures ever yet uttered against the mixed institutions of the Republic. There is one written to Lord Viscount Forbes from Washington, the severity of which consists in its truth, which made it the more obnoxious to the slave-holding whites of Virginia; Moore having seen the same contrasts in Norfolk, and lamented them in a beautiful epistle from that city to his sister Kate in England. The lines that gave such dire offence, and rankled in the hearts of the Virginians, were these: ' ' Who can, with patience, for a moment see The medley mass of pride and misery, Of whips and charters, manacles and rights, Of slaving blacks, and democratic whites, And all the pie-bald polity that reigns In free confusion o'er Columbia's plains? To think that Man thou just and gentle God! Should stand before Thee with a tyrant's rod O'er creatures like himself, with souls from Thee, Yet dare to boast of ' perfect liberty." Away! away! I'd rather hold my neck By doubtful tenure from a Sultan's beck, In climes where liberty has scarce been nam'd, Nor any right but that of ruling claim'd, Than thus to live, where bastard Freedom waves Her fustian flag in mockery over slaves; Where motley laws admitting no degree Betwixt the vilely slav'd and madly free Alike the bondage and the licence suit, The brute made ruler, and the man made brute."

Opinion was of course very much divided on such a book as this. The female portion of society (to many of whom Moore was personally known, as he had first landed at Norfolk on his voyage from Bermuda), adored tlie poet of Love, and most of them had Ins chief amatory poems by heart. The men hated and denounced him because of his frank exposure of the inconsistency of their political professions and practice; and the difference between the two sexes here might fairly enough be said to resemble that which he describes as a belief in Bermuda, that after death all the men would become mules, and all the women turtle-doves.

Our detention at Norfolk was prolonged by the issue of certain orders of council from the British Government, which stopped all commerce between England and the United States, pending some dispute, I think about the right of search and impressment of English seamen found in American vessels, on which the British insisted, but which the Americans, to their honour, firmly resisted. This was called the " Non-Intercourse Act," and its effect was to throw out of employ a large number of seamen, and reduce their families to great distress. With a view to their relief, I proposed the performance of some drama at the theatre, by amateurs, and such professionals as would give their services gratuitously, the receipts to be appropriated to the commencement of a fund for the relief of the wives and children of the unemployed seamen. It was speedily adopted, and the play of " She Stoops to Conquer" was put under rehearsal, and performed to a crowded house, at double the usual prices. I was pressed to appear myself among the amateurs on the stage, but doubting my histrionic powers, I declined, and contented myself with giving my humble quota of aid, by taking the part of first flute in a very respectable orchestra. More than two thousand dollars were raised by the performance; and the fund was subsequently augmented by private and public subscription, so that we were well pleased with the result.

At length the restrictions on intercourse with England were removed by the settlement of the dispute that led to their imposition; and, having taken in our full cargo of tobacco, we prepared to sail for London. Our parting with friends was painful to both; but we each indulged a hope of meeting again, and realised the sentiment of Dibdin in one of his sea-songs,

"The hope of return takes the sting from Adieu!"

Mr. and Mrs. Hunter, being both Irish, and all the members of the family enthusiastic in their love of ' The Emerald Isle," the songs relating to Ireland and the Irish were those most frequently sung by them; and among these none awakened more feeling, perhaps, than the well-known " Exile of Erin." I was therefore agreeably surprised to find the following lines, embodying the wishes and feelings of this amiable circle, written by one of their number, placed in my hands at the moment of my leaving the family mansion to embark, adapted to the favourite air above named.

'Twas the last parting wish, breathed with heartfelt devotion,

By the friend who reluctantly bade us adieu, That we oft, while he wandered afar on the ocean.

Would recal the past scenes which together we knew. And sometimes, amid the gay circle of pleasure, Would silently steal a fond moment of leisure, While Memory unlocked the recess of her treasure.

To remember the Friend who is gone far away.

Then say, shall the wish which he sigh'd while expressing As if sad forebodings his fancy hung o'er, Shall the wish that he breathed, all its ardour repressing, Be doomed to oblivion, and thought of no more? Oh! no, while the bright orb of day shall be beaming, While Nature, with light, life, and love is still teeming, Vliile the heart's purple torrent in health shall be streaming, We'll remember the Friend who is gone far away.

To her faithful arms from whom Destiny tore him, To tlie infant that smiled on their union of love, To the friends of his bosom in safety restore him,

Ye spirits that wait on the mandates of Jove: Yet there, while their full cup of joy is o'erflowing, And with mutual delight their fond bosoms are glowing. Let him steal but a moment of Nature's endowing. To remember the Friends whom he left far away.

Should Fate, o'er the footsteps of mortals presiding.

Direct him again to Virginia's loved shore. The ardour of friendship, its warmth ne'er subsiding,

Shall welcome him still to the porch of our door. But oh! should this wish of our hearts happen never, Neither distance nor time our affections can sever, Nor e'en Destiny break the firm pledge, that, for ever We'll remember each other, when far, far away.

Our homeward voyage was not remarkable for any striking incident or disaster, and was on the whole both speedy and agreeable; though being at the close of winter we had our full share of dark nights and tempestuous weather. The crew of the Rising States, who were all from Marblehead, in Massachusetts, remained attached to the ship during all our period of detention. They were almost all related to each other by blood or intermarriage, all descended from the Puritan fathers who founded New England, and bore chiefly Scriptural names from the Old Testament, the frequent use of which, coupled with an ejaculation or an oath, seemed sometimes profane and sometimes ludicrous. They were in general excellent seamen, never shrinking from their duty, though sometimes a little democratically inclined to consider themselves quite as good as their officers, requiring to be led rather than driven; and sometimes they tried the patience of the officers so far as to bring out an oath now and then, involuntarily. For instance, the summons being given " All hands reef topsails, ahoy!" some of the more alert would be on the yard and out at the weather-earing before the more tardy were in the shrouds, when the boatswain would be heard vociferating at the top of his voice, almost drowned by the flapping of the canvass and the roar of the winds, "I say, you Habakkuk! you are tarnation slow in your movements; and you, Zerub-babel! unless you bear a hand, and show yourself smart, I shall mast-head both you and Master Heze-kiah, for going through lubber's hole instead of over the futtock shrouds." This last was a youth of about twenty, but remarkably diminutive in size, and, being thin as well as short, he abridged his labour by going up through the lubber's hole into the top, instead of up the futtock shrouds, as is usual with seamen. For this, when he came down on deck, a large heavy man, named Jedediah, reproached him, though there was more seamanship, it might be said, in Hezekiah's little finger than in Jedediah's whole bodj; so that all the crew commended him for his spirited and true reply, when he said, "I'll tell you what, my fine fellow, an inch of a small seaman is worth a foot of a large lubber any day in the week, and especially on a stormy one." Jedediah was carefully silent after this.

During my stay in Norfolk, I had received, as presents from the ladies of Mr Hunter's family, two beautiful Virginia nightingales, of rich ruby plumage, fine forms, and the most delicious notes imaei-nable, from whence they derive their name. They were carefully caged and intended as presents to my dear wife; but unfortunately, from the carelessness of the steward in feeding them, one escaped from the cage and was drowned in the sea; the other I succeeded in bringing safe to England, where it was much admired, but died in the first winter, from the severity of the climate. The escape of the one was very nearly followed by the loss of the other, who, seeing his companion at liberty, very naturally desired to accompany him in his flight; and had we been amidst tlieir native Virginian forests, I should have placed no obstruction to such an escape for both. But we were some hundreds of miles from any land, and I therefore retained the second bird against its will, after many struggles on its part to elude my grasp. This incident drew from me the following lines, addressed to the little captive:

Oh! cease, sweet bird, that fluttering fear. Nor deem the hand of danger near,

While I have thee in charge: Tliy plumage shall be free from harm. Thy food as pure, thy nest as warm,

As when thou wert at large.

Poor captive! could thy unconscious mind But know for whom thou art designed,

Thoud'st long to be her slave; Nor e'er in plaintive notes deplore To leave thy own loved native shore.

And cross th' Atlantic wave.

When once her kindness thou shalt prove, Thy little heart will bound with love.

And grateful kiss the chain That makes thee, in captivity, More happy far than ranging free

Among the feathered train.

Her fostering hand tliy wants shall feed, And every comfort thou canst need

Will be her morning care: And when at eve thy song shall close, Fly to her bosom for repose,

And fondly nestle there.

We reached England after a passage of about four weeks, calling at Falmouth for orders, and then proceeding to London, where I was delighted to rejoin my domestic circle and recount over the events of our absence.

First appointment as Captain of a West Indiaman. Departure for the Island of New Providence. Feeling of responsibility greatly increased. Regulations of discipline for officers and crew. Sailed with' a fleet of 300 sail from the Downs. Anecdote of a passenger's notions of geography. Circular whirlwind or white squall encountered. Midnight alarm, "The Devil is in the main-top." Capture of a magnificent Osprey, or Sea Eagle. Escape of the prize, and deep regret at our loss. Safe arrival in the beautiful harbour of Nassau.

I AYAS now considered perfectly qualified for a command; and in the course of a few weeks after our return from America, I received an appointment as captain of the Surrey, West-Indiaman, belonging to the firm of Gillespie and Stevens, in the Old Jewry. Our destination was the port of Nassau, in the Island of New Providence in the Bahamas, with a general cargo of manufactures adapted chiefly for the coast of Florida and the Spanish Main, as the Central American republics had not yet sprung into existence. The ship was well found, her crew able and sufficient, her accommodations excellent, her sailing qualities established, and everything promised a favourable voyage.

We left Gravesend with a fair wind, and on reaching the Downs anchored in the midst of a large fleet waiting for convoy 300 sail at least, some bound for the Mediterranean, others for the West Indies, and others for South America. In the nisht, while lying at single anchor, and hemmed in by clusters of vessels on all sides, it began to blow a heavy gale from the southward. Yards and top-masts were struck, cable veered out to seventy and eighty fathoms, yet ships were dragging their anchors and running foul of each other in all directions. I began, for the first time in life, to feel the full weight of responsibility. As chief officer, it was sufficient for me to discharge my duty, obey orders, or see those of my commander carried into execution, and leave the responsibility with him. But here I could not transfer this from my own shoulders to those of a superior; and I was at first dejected at the thought. But after a moment's consideration it only stimulated me to greater efforts, and all passed off" safely and satisfactorily.

There was one great advantage and pleasure, however, which I derived from my new position. It was that of being able to make the discipline of the crew more conformable to mj own notions than was practicable when acting under another. When the gale subsided, therefore, and the yards and top-masts were sent aloft, and all made ready for sea, I mustered the crew on the quarter deck, and expressed my wishes as to the regulations I desired to have observed for the safety of the ship and cargo, and the comfort of all on board, and among them were these: 1. To abstain from drinking spirits, as it was the source of nearly all the accidents, quarrels, and breaches of discipline that occurred at sea; and never benefited but always injured men in proportion to its excess.

2. To suppress all rising murmurs or feelings of dissatisfaction at their first birth, as they only gained strength by indulgence.

3. To abstain from oaths or coarse lano-uage to each other, as an ill word often provoked a blow; and the harmony in which men should live who were shut up in so confined a space, and could never escape from each other for many months at least, ought to be preserved as much as possible; and nothing could effect this so much as kind words and mutual good will and assistance.

4. To preserve cleanliness in their berths, their persons, and tlieir clothes, as favourable to health, good temper, and order: for which purpose one washing-day, free from all other duty, would be granted in the middle of each week, to wash tlieir own clothes, besides the daily washing of decks in the morning, and the cleaning out the berths when the hammocks were brought on deck for airing.

5. To attend divine service on Sundays in the forenoon, whenever the weather admitted, each man to present himself clean-shaved, washed and combed, and with his best apparel, the afternoon and evening being at their own disposal for writing letters, reading, or conversation.

6. On Saturday night, devoted at sea to the memories of wives and sweethearts, a dance to be allowed on the main deck, with songs and stories in the forecastle, it being assumed that there was neither man nor boy on board, who had not either a wife or a sweetheart; as a seaman, without an object of affection left behind him on shore, would be deficient in one of the most prolific sources of sympathy and enthusiasm, and could never be expected to perform his duty so well as one who looked forward to receive, at the end of his voyage, the reward of reciprocal affection from his betrothed or his bride.

And, lastly, I promised to keep a faithful register of the conduct of every one on board during the voyage; and at the termination of it, to give to those who most nearly conformed to the regulations prescribed, who were most approved by the officers for the faithful discharge of their duty, and most liked by the crew for their general good-nature and agreeable qualities, some handsome presents for their wives and sweethearts, as prizes for good conduct, which could not fail to make their meeting additionally agreeable, a promise that was received with three hearty cheers, such as seamen alone can give.

We sailed with the convoy from the Downs, with a fine north-east wind, and rolled away down channel with at least 300 sail of vessels, formino- three dis-tinct fleets, with a line-of-battle ship, two frigates, and four sloops of war, as convoy for the whole: and it was an animating and agreeable spectacle to witness so much order, so many fine vessels, such frequent interchange of signals, such vigilance in the sloops of war, scouring the horizon on all sides on the look-out for French privateers, and such careful crowding round the poop-light of the commodore, as night drew near, for safety. The Mediterranean fleet left us soon after clearino; the channel, steerinft southward, and the South American fleet a few days VOL. I. T afterwards, steering south-west, while, as the remnant bound for the West Indies, w e continued on our way.

Among the passengers we had a Jew, a Mr. Solomons, who, though not more than thirty, was wealthy enough to have purchased and laid in nearly half our cargo, some 25,000. at least. He was handsome, gaily and even fantastically dressed, with a bright green coat and polished gilt buttons, a light bufl' Avaistcoat, white corduroy breeches, yellow top hunting boots, a white hat, with green underlining, and the crown surrounded by black crape. While steering westward on our course, we one morning met a pretty large fleet of vessels coming eastward in the opposite direction, when Mr. Solomons, having surveyed them with the telescope, exclaimed, "Ah! ah! the Baltic fleet, I judge, by the cut of their hulls and sails!" A passenger, standing by, observed, "Why, Sir, you must be rather in arrear with your geography. The Baltic is behind us, to the eastward, and not before us; and this fleet cannot be from the Baltic, unless they have circumnavigated the globe." Mr. Solomons, not in the least embarrassed, coolly replied, " Yes, yes! 'Tis true enough my geography is, I dare say, at fault: the truth is, the only geography I ever studied was the geography of the dollar, and I think I know that as well as most men."

As an explanation or apology for this deficiency in his education, he related to us some of the events of his life. He was born in Whitechapel, London, where his father was a poor but industrious maker of black-lead pencils. The harsh treatment of his children induced his son to run away from him at the age of twelve, when he found his way in an emigrant ship from London to New York. There he entered into the service of a planter from the southern states, who had come up to the north to look for hands; and though at first employed by him in almost a menial capacity, he rose to be overseer of the plantation; and at the death of his master, who left no wife, family, or relations, he became master of the whole estate, slaves and all, whether by will or undisputed possession, I do not remember. He immediately sold off everything, realising about 10,000., came to England, purchased a cargo of manufactures suited for the West Lidies and Spanish Main, went to New Providence, opened a store there, traded successfully with the Spanish Americans around the Gulf of Mexico, and in a few years increased his capital-to 50,000., about half of which was in Providence in his store, and the other half forming part of our present cargo. Success had not made him haughty or arrogant; and though a man of no reading, he had seen much of the world, was naturally clever and shrewd, always good-humoured, and an agreeable companion.

Nothing remarkable occurred on this voyage except the following ludicrous incident. When Avithin about 100 miles of the coast of Florida, and just on the outer edo-e of the Gulf Stream, with a moderate breeze, and top-gallant sails set, we were visited about midnight by what is called " a white squall," that is, a sudden and violent gust of wind, which comes without the least warning of cloud or other premonitory symptom. In this case it was a perfectly circular whirlwind, as it caught us on the weather bow and lee quarter at the same time, and literally spun the ship round like a top or a tee-to-tum, though not of course with the same rapidity, the resistance of the water preventing this; but our rotatory motioh occasioned such a whirlpool in the sea, that I really feared we should be swallowed up in the vortex, which was like the

Maelstrom of Norway, or Charybdis in Sicily. The novelty of the danger imposed a profound silence, and " every man held his breath for a while," but at length it passed away, and we were happy at our deliverance.

The crew, however (at least that portion of them which formed the watch below), had hardly got comfortably into tlieir hammocks, before a newer and still more remarkable form of danger was discovered. One of the maintop-men of the watch on deck, who had stationed himself in the top, to be ready for whatever might be required there, and had rolled himself up in one of the top-gallant studding sails, called out with a lusty voice, "On deck, there! the Devil's in the main-top. Send up some hands to seize him! " As I was still on deck myself, I at first thought the man must be drunk; but he had never been addicted to drinking, and then I thought it must be a hoax; so I called out, "Main-top, there! none of your jokes, if you please, but mind your duty." The man, recognising my voice, replied, "It's no joke. Captain, I assure you; but the real Devil, as sure as this ship's the Surrey; so send the hands up, or I shall be carried off by him." At the same time we heard in the top a flapping of wings, a hoarse screaming or screeching, and could see, through the dim light of a moonless atmosphere, the sail in which the man was enveloped rising and falling, and he stoutly combating what we thought must be a phantom, but which turned out to be a solid reality.

In the meantime the boatswain's mate, without orders, had gone to the fore-hatchway, and shouted out, after piping with his call, "All hands to catch the Devil, ahoy! tumble up, there; tumble up, my hearties!" In a few minutes all hands were on deck; and on the main- shrouds on both sides, about a dozen men hastened to the rescue of their shipmate from the claws of Satan, and the capture of the Prince of Darkness himself if possible. On their reaching the main-toj), one man was struck so forcibly by one of the wings of the unknown assailant, that he fell on deck, and was much hurt bv the fall; another was almost blinded by a similar stroke on his face; and all that could be made out for some minutes was, that there was a great feathered monster, with claws, beak, and wings, combating with all his might the original occupant of the top, Avho, though bleeding at several points, stood his ground manfully. At length, by the aid of the studding-sail, in which they enveloped the monster, and the studding-sail sheets, Avith which they lashed his legs together, they secured him for the remainder of the night, and all again retired to rest.

At daylightj intense curiosity was manifested to be present at the uncovering of the mysterious creature; so that all hands were again on deck, when he was lowered down from the top, enveloped in the canvass which had secured him, and turned out to be a mag- nificent osprej, or sea eagle. It stood at least five feet liigli, and its extreme breadth from the tips of its expanded wings were at least eight feet. It had a noble head, beautiful eyes, with several rings of different bright colours encircling the pupil, a strong hooked beak, thick and strong legs, large talons or claws, a richly speckled brown back of feathers, and wdiite breast and bellj. Deeming it a prize worthy of preservation, and presentation to some ornithological collection, I wished to secure it for the remainder of the voyage, and while the carpenter was preparing a cage or house for it, it was fastened by the leg with a strong rattling-line to the ring-bolt of the spanker boom, just abaft the tiller, with a range of about three fathoms of line for the freedom of his movements. His first exploit was to pounce upon a stray duck who had wandered from her coop, into which he transfixed his talons, and devoured it alive, with apparent satisfaction. We subsequently fed it with the offal of poultry used for the table, and such supplies of fish and animal food as we could command, of which it ate voraciously. On the third day after its capture, and when we were near to New Providence, we were caught in a sudden squall, and it became necessary to take in the spanker, when one of the sailors approaching the bird too closely, as he was engaged in hauling in the boom sheet, the eagle plunged his strong beak into the naked calf of the man's leg, his trousers being turned up, as the deck was full of vrater from the heavy squall of rain, and drew out of it a solid mass of flesh of several ounces, so as to disable the man probably for life; and the sailor, naturally enraged at this attack, took out his knife, cut the lanyard by which the bird was secured, and it flew aloft into the air with exulting screams of triumph.

Our first care was to dress the wound of the unfortunate seaman with styptics and bandages to prevent loss of blood, and to keep him in a state of repose and low diet to prevent fever, till we reached the port, when he was transferred to the hospital, and sufficiently cured to return home with us, but lame, and unfit for duty aloft. The bird Itself kept hovering over our vessel, as if meditating some revenge, or being unwilling to leave us till within sight of land. It frequently, therefore, alighted on our main-royal truck, and there, as the ship's motion required, balanced itself by its outspreading wings, and presented a most remarkable object, like the eagle surmounting an old Roman standard, or crowning a military trophy raised to celebrate a victory on the field of battle. As it flew off" and poised itself in air, the rope by which it had been fastened on board still being round its leg, waved to and fro like a pendant or a streamer, and added to the singular appearance. Several of the men and officers petitioned hard to be allowed to shoot it while on the wing, but 1 would not give permission for this, as I should have been really sorry to see it drop dead or wounded on deck or in the ocean. Following its natural habits, it soared often so high as to be beyond our sight; when suddenly it would drop down with closed wings, like a heavy lump of lead, and just as it approached the surface of the water, pounce its talons into a living fish near the surface, spread out its wings, floating or sailing along through the air, and devouring the delicious morsel with avidity. I remembered the passage in " Coriolanus," in which Shakspeare, with that universality of knowledge which distinguished him above all other poets, says, speaking of the great Roman,

"I think he'll be to Rome, As is the osprey to the fish, who takes it By sovereignty of nature."

Whether it exercises, by the strength of its eye, which was in this instance of most dazzling power and beauty, a species of fascination on fish near the sur- face, as serpents of various kinds are said to exercise on birds, and as the Great Serpent, for whom our sailors at first took this osprey, exercised on our mother Eve, I cannot say; but the manner in which it grasped its prej from the water and bore it unresistingly aloft to be devoured, did reallv seem to be, as Shakspeare expresses it, exercised " by sovereignty of nature," tliough it is hai'dly necessary on that account to accept literally the comment which Dr. Johnson offers on this passage, when he says, " that it is reported that when the osprey hovers in the air, all the fish in the water near him turn up their bellies, and lie still for him to seize which he pleases!"

At length our outward voyage was terminated by our safe arrival in the harbour of Nassau, where the beautiful transparency of the water enabled us to see our anchor distinctly, on a white limestone bottom: though just before entering the port, the ocean is intensely blue, from its immense depth the island rising almost perpendicularly like a wall from the lowermost depths of the sea.

First entertainment at a military mess-room. Agreeable society among the civil authorities. Dinners, balls, and suppers in constant succession. Singular septennial celebration of a marriage. Trade of the Bahamas with the Spanish Main. Manner of conducting the smuggling or contraband. Description of the parties engaged in this traffic. Division of profits between smugglers, priests, and revenue officers. Reminiscences of the old English buccaneers. Portrait of one of the last remaining specimens. Wreckers, their character, occupation, and gains.

Our stay in New Providence was peculiarly agreeable. Having brought out a young military officer among the passengers, I was invited to the regimental mess, and there made some acceptable acquaintances, thouo-h I fell terriblv below their standard in the supposed requisite capacity of a thorough-bred gentleman to carry off his two bottles of wine, besides cold rum and water and shrub-punch at and after dinner. As if the natural appetite for these strong drinks was not powerful enough, " devilled fowl and turkey" were introduced after the second bottle, highly peppered with cayenne to excite thirst, and many entered on a new bout after this heating repast. And yet T was assured that this was the ordinary daily life of the military officers in the West Indies; so that I could no long-er wonder at the fearful raor-tality prevailing among them, without attributing it to the climate, which, in the Bahamas at least, I should think as salubrious as midoubtedly it is as agreeable as any in the world.

Another of our passengers was connected with the principal clergyman of the island, the Reverend Mr. Stephens, whose beautiful and accomplished daughter, Barbara, was a perfect Desdemona, in her love of listening to tales of adventure by sea and land, and as amiable and modest as she was truly lovely In person and mind. This brought me Into another and a more congenial circle. of acquaintance than the military. Our ship was consigned to a worthy merchant, Mr. Thompson, a Scotch gentleman, who was also Treasurer of the island, and had a most agreeable wife, but no family. As I was received at his house at all times, and often slept there when I remained on shore, I met here In succession nearly all the official as well as mercantile notabilities of the island. I became acquainted also with the numerous and hospitable family of Mr. Dyer, who was then Judge of the Admiralty Court of the Island, and whom I often visited afterwards in London, where, on his return from the West Indies, he for many years filled the office of Police Magistrate in the Court at Marlborough Street. And, lastly, I had the pleasure of being frequently and cordially received by the Governor, Mr. Vesey Munnings, who, on my leaving Nassau, gave me a letter of introduction to his brother, then a barrister of Gray's Inn, of my visit to whom I shall speak hereafter. Captain Douglas, of the Navy, who commanded a sloop of war in the harbour, and whom I had frequently met at the principal houses of the island, so entirely put aside the hauteur and prejudices of his rank and profession, as to interchange visits with me on board our respective ships, and proved himself a cordial friend as well as a most lively and agreeable acquaintance.

The official and business occupations of the heads of families being very light, the evenings were always given up to entertainment; so that during the month we remained in harbour, I never passed a single evening alone. Dinners, balls, and evening parties succeeded each other daily, and all were kept up with the greatest spirit. The female portion of the society were generally young and handsome, with an entire absence of the aged and the juvenile, who are generally sent to England, and the dancing was sustained with more animation under a heat of 96 of Fahrenheit, than in Englmd at 60.

One of the entertainments I attended was as singular as it was pleasant. It was the third celebration of a wedding, by a major in the army, to the same wife, to whom he had been married twenty-one years; but as be had almost a Mosaic veneration for the number seven, and deemed the marriage ceremony, white gloves and ribbons, bride cakes, and its other auxiliaries, sufficiently agreeable to bear occasional repetition, he was actually re-married at each septennial period; feeing the clergyman for going througli the full marriage service again; sending out his card, linked to that of his wife bv a silver cord in a true lover's knot; both playing over again the pleasant parts of bride and bridegroom, as if the marriage had taken place for the first time. As no one was offended by this whim, but many were hospitably entertained, it was regarded as an innocent eccentricity, in which all might partake without censure.

As the island of New Providence itself, and indeed the whole group of the Bahamas, had but a very small population, they afforded no very extensive mart for the consumption of British manufactures. This deficiency was amply compensated, however, by the extensive trade which it carried on with the coast of

Florida, and with tlie Spaniards of Cuba, and tlie Spanish Main, including Yucatan, the Belize, Honduras, Nicaragua, Costa Rica, Veragna, New Granada, and Venezuela, including the Caraccas and Cumana to the very mouths of the Orontes. All Central and South America, with slight exceptions, were then under the dominion of Spain (1809), and as the same absurd and suicidal import duties on all foreign goods of 33 per cent., which were exacted in the mother country, were imposed also in her colonies, the whole of the trade was contraband, neither the Spaniards nor any other of the nations of Europe having yet discovered the fact, palpable enough to all their subjects, that high duties were sure to encourage smuggling, and that the only way to secure the duties being legitimately paid into the customhouses, as part of the revenue of the country, was to make them so reasonably light, that most traders would prefer paying them to bearing the penalties of seizure, fine, and imprisonment, which would be the unsuccessful smu o-ler's doom.

This contraband trade was carried on in vessels of light draught of water, great length, and capable of immense speed by large lateen sails of light cotton, whenever there was wind enough to fill them, and by twenty or twenty-four oars or sweeps, when it was calm. Several of these swift craft entered Nassau during our stay there; and Mr. Solomons' portion of the cargo was all sold to their crews on the ship's deck, without being landed or passed through the English custom-house at all, there being no import duty payable on British manufactures brought to the island; so that these were handed over the side as fast as the bargains were concluded, and i e money paid for them on delivery. The crews of these smuggling vessels consisted of a captain, three or four subordinate officers, and from twenty to thirty men all very dark, some from the bronzing of the sun only, and others with a redder tinge from the admixture of Indian blood. All were dressed in light garments of white cotton, with gay coloured caps and sashes, forming the most picturesque groups, and all spoke Spanish intelligibly. The chief personages of the equipage were, however, two Roman Catholic priests, who wore their brown cloaks, with hood and cowl, some with white cord girdles, and others with a large black cross hanging round the neck, and chap-lets of beads in their hands.

These priests and the captain of each vessel transacted the whole business of examining the samples of the goods, fixing the price, and paying the money; and the mode of doing business was this: Small pattern-books, containing samples of the contents of each box or bale, were examined by the smugglers, and the approved ones marked; no box or bale, however, being opened to see whether their contents corresponded with the samples shown, so that the whole package had to be accepted or rejected entire. The next step was to exhibit the English invoice, and add 25 per cent, to the gross amount of it (though it was generally believed that duplicate invoices were made out in England for this purpose at 25 per cent, above the real cost, making the whole actual profit therefore 50 per cent.). The money was then paid in gold doubloons and silver dollars, bags and boxes of which were brought up by the smugglers for this purpose from their own coasts, and the invoice being then delivered over to the purchaser, the transaction was closed; there being no books kept on either side, and neither bills nor receipts exchanged. As soon as the smuggling craft had completed her lading, she left for her destination; and it was said that on their reaching the coast, they would make signals, which would be well understood by their co-partners on shore. The custom-house officers could only be prevented from doing their duty by being made participators in the gains; and the usual scale for the subdivision of the profits of the VOL. I. U voyage, whatever tliej might be, were as follows: One fifth to the captain and officers of the vessel; one fifth to the priests; one fifth to the custom-house officers on shore, and two fifths to the crew. The goods were all sold off, for ready money, to inland smugglers, within a few hours after landing; and the priests, who had given their blessing to the enterprise at its first starting, terminated their duties by giving absolution to all concerned at its close.

We were assured, by those familiar with the countries named, that this practice of smuggling and using contraband commodities prevailed among all ranks in Spanish America, as it undoubtedly did in Spain itself, and from the same cause. No wonder, therefore, that both the mother country and the colonies should become so impoverished by a constantly decreasing revenue, thus obliging them to have recourse to forced exaction of taxes and loans from their already exhausted subjects, which in the end produced rebellion and separation of the transatlantic possessions of Spain, and thus inflicted poverty and humiliation as the natui'al consequences of the mis-government under wdiich they had so long been oppressed.

While at Nassau I was thrown into the company of more than one of the old buccaneers, as w ell as some of the wreckers, as they are called; and most original characters they were. In complexion, from constant exposure to the sea atmosphere and the sun, they had reddish-brown skins, approaching almost to that of the North American Indians, jet black hair changed to iron-grey, hanging in curls over their necks and shoulders, loose sailors' costume, open and hairy bosoms, and large virgin gold ear-rings, lengthening the lower lobe of the ear by their massive weight. One of these men boasted that he had taken his from the ears of an image of the Holy Virgin in a Roman Catholic church, which he and his comrades had plundered on the coast of Peru. Another, being sensible of his own deficiencies, as he could neither read nor write, had his two sons educated in England, one at Oxford, who now held a living in the Established Church, and another at Eton, who was now a post-captain in the Navy; while his three daughters were educated at one of the first establishments near London, and were all three married to men of fortune or title. Though the children had frequently entreated their father to leave New Providence and settle in England, as he had ample means of so doing in great comfort, he had constantly declined complying with their wishes, habit having rendered his present way of life and present companions (many of them comrades in his buccaneering enterprises) so much more agreeable than any new modes of hfe he could adopt, or any new friendships he could form, that he was afraid to make the change. They were not received into the best society here, which indeed would have been irksome to them, but they had a sufficiently large circle of acquaintance among the tradesmen and middle classes; and their frequent dinners and suppers, with an abundant supply of sangaree and cold punch for morning visitors, and old Jamaica rum and water for their evening carousals, formed attractions which brought around them a large circle of friends.

The wreckers were deemed a class below these, though many of them were even more wealthy. These men kept fast schooners of the Bermuda and Baltimore build and rig, which cruised among the rocky islets or keys of the Bahama group, and threaded their intricate channels in search of vessels needing pilotage or supplies; and also to rescue whatever could be saved from wrecks in this dangerous navigation. It was universally believed here, however, that they caused more wrecks than they prevented; sometimes by showing lights at night whidi deceived ships into a presumed safety, by steering their course towards them; at others by appearing to indicate a safe channel, and thus inducing vessels to follow in their track. In all cases, however, they carried with them large supplies of rum, so that if they fell in with a wreck which by proper exertions might he saved, it was their usual practice to give the officers and seamen free access to their spirit casks, the result of which invariably was, that both officers and men became helplessly drunk, the wreck was completed, and the sober wreckers then made their harvest by plundering the vessel of all that was worth removal, and dividing the spoil in fixed proportions according to rank and duty, as in privateers and ships of war in cases of capture and prize-money.

Homeward voyage from tlie Bahama Islands. Rapid sailing. American models. Clipper ships. Absurdity of the ancient rules for measuring tonnage. Cause of the general ugliness of old English vessels. Anecdote of a slow-sailing ship of Bristol. Entry into the British Channel in midwinter. Running fight with a French privateer off Dunge-ness. Drifted on the French coast. Fired at from the batteries. Lost a cable and anchor on a wreck at the Goodwin Sands. Driven into the North Sea. Heavy gales and lono- niofhts. Deliberation as to runnino; into the Texel and becoming prisoners. Breaking of the gale, and safe run for England. Lines written on the occasion to the air " All's Well."

Our homeward voyage from the Bahamas was a continued succession of storms, being in the dead of winter the latter end of November and all December. We had a fine passage up the Gulf Stream to the Banks of Newfoundland, and from thence strong westerly gales, before wdiich it was sometimes impossible to show an inch of canvass. As we were but lightly laden in point of weight, though with a full cargo of cotton and other products of the Bahamas, we ran during one twenty-four hours a distance of 304 nautical miles under bare poles a rate of thirteen knots throughout, a speed then thought marvellous for a mercantile vessel, and only attained by the fastest ships of war; but the improvements in naval architecture since that time, chiefly stimulated by American models, and aided by legislative improvements in the mode of measuring for tonnage, has caused this rate of speed to be exceeded by the clipper ships of Aberdeen, Sunderland, and London, engaged in the China trade, as well as by the " Flying Clouds " and other fleet vessels of the Americans sailing round Cape Horn to their newly incorporated State of California.

As an instance of the absurdity of our old shipping laws, and the hindrances they opposed to improvement in the beauty of forms or increase of speed in our merchant vessels, it may be stated that the rule for determining the amount of a ship's tonnage was to multiply the length by the breadth, and add the depth of the hold, the total of these three elements forming the basis of calculation for the tonnage required. It is clear that any addition to the length or breadth, these being multiplymg numbers, would make considerable addition to the tonnage, while increased depth of hold, this being an additive number only, would not effect any great augment- ation. Now, as the dues paid by ships on entering port or leaving it were calculated by their measurement tonnage, and not by what amount of cargo they could actually carry, the problem among ship-owners who wished to evade the payment or lessen the amount of these duties, was, how to construct a vessel that should carry the largest amount of cargo with the smallest measurement tonnage for duty. The ship-builders soon solved this by constructing ships of small dimensions in length and breadth, and large dimensions in depth proportions which utterly destroyed the beauty of form, and equally impeded the sailing of vessels, as well as increasing their liability to take the ground, from their increased draught of water. Hence it often happened that ships built for specific purposes where great speed was required, and which were therefore long and broad, but shallow, measured 500 tons chargeable with duty, yet would not carry 300 tons of cargo; while others, built for capacity rather than speed, would measure 300 tons for duty, and carry 500 tons of cargo. A ludicrous instance of an extreme case occurred at Bristol, where a ship was built of such little length and breadth, and such great depth of hold, that while she measured only 200 tons, she carried 800 tons of cargo. She was sent to the West Indies to load with sugar and rum; and having only a very light cargo on her outward passage, she realised, before the wind with all canvass spread, about five miles an hour, this being her greatest speed. On her return voyage, however, when deeply laden, and drawing thirty feet of water (a vessel of 200 tons of the present day drawing little more than ten), and sailing with a fleet under convoy, she could never be moved faster than three miles an hour under the most favourable circumstances. As the rate of a fleet must always be regulated by the speed of the slowest, in order to keep them all together, the commodore, seeing this " floating warehouse," as she was appropriately called, always lagging astern while the whole fleet had to shorten sail for her coming up, ordered some of the faster vessels to take her successively in tow; but these, after parting many hawsers in the vain attempt, were only kept back, without advancing their tow by half a mile an hour. The commodore himself then took her in tow, and under a heavy press of sail, gave the lumbering hull another half-mile or so of speed; but at length considering that it was unjust to the rest of the fleet to retard their progress longer for the sake of this one, he left her to her fate; and it was ascertained that she did not reach England till five weeks after the arrival of the convoy with which she started.

This absurd legislation, now happily altered, was the sole cause of the great inferiority of English merchant vessels in beauty of form and speed, not only to our own ships of war, but even to American traders, who laboured under no such restrictions: but now that these have been removed (though, like all other improvements, it was stoutly resisted by those who oppose all innovations), we have as beautiful and fast merchant vessels as any country in the world, of which the Thames and the Mersey present magnificent specimens of every size: while the Chinese (the most thorough conservatives of mankind) still adhere to their junks, of which Noah's ark must have been the prototype.

It was towards the end of December when we entered the British Channel. The nights were lono; and dark, and the days so thick and foggy with heavy south-west gales, that we neither saw the Scilly, the Longships, the Lizard, or any other lights, till reaching Dungeness, groping and feeling our way up Channel by the lead, though it was sometimes dangerous to heave the ship to the wind for that purpose; and as the gale still continued, we ran in under the lee of the spit of sand which forms the promontory of Dungeness, to anchor there till daylight. Vie had scarcely veered out cable, and got the sails furled, however, before a large lugger, her decks crowded with men, ran alongside and attempted to board us; being, in short, a French privateer, with which the upper part of the Channel swarmed at this season of the year, when they could run out from Calais or Boulogne after dark, be over on the English coast before midnight, and seize vessels unprepared before any of the English cruisers could perceive the capture or come to the rescue.

Aware of this danger, we were fully prepared to encounter it, having our six guns nine pounders loaded, shotted, and primed, matches lighted below (as gun-locks for cannon were not then introduced), small arms and boarding-pikes all ready; our only deficiency being in men, as our whole crew numbered only thirty, while the lugger had a tier of ten guns on each side, and, as far as we could judge from the crowd, at least two hundred men. As she shot by us, having missed her helm, there was not a moment to lose, so that we gave her a broadside of round, grape, and canister at once, and cutting the cable, (for there was no time to weigh the anchor) set the topsails only, and steered into the offing, where she followed us. We had here a hard strucr2; le: there was so much sea on, that the lee guns were perfectly useless, and the weather ones could hardly be de- pressed sufficiently for effect; and this was still more the case with our antagonist, as his vessel was more crank, and lay over considerably more than ours, when lying athwart the wind and sea. Her great object was to board us, as then the overwhelming superiority of her numbers would have made us an easy prey; so she threw her grappling irons into our rigging and chains, and, but for the vigilance of our men in cutting the lanyards of them with axes ready at hand, we should have closed and been captured. As it was, the guns were discharged on either side when the ship was steady enough to make them tell, volleys of small arms were reciprocally interchanged, and a desultory fight of this kind was kept up for an hour in a pitch dark night, with a heavy rolling sea, close-reefed topsails only set, and the ship's head at every point of the compass in turn, like two pugilists watching each other's movements, and walking round each other in the ring.

As privateers, however, generally seek prizes that offer no resistance, their object being purely plunder, and not honours or fame, our antagonist at last sheered off, leaving us a few wounded, but none mortally, our sails and rigging cut up, our best bower anchor left behind at Dangeness, and the whole crew worn out with the fatigue of a long night's fighting and watching, so that we saw her sheer off with great satisfaction.

As no land or lights were now in sight, our next duty was to ascertain our exact position, and this could only be done by soundings; for no account had been taken, or indeed was practicable, of the various courses and distances steered since leaving our anchorage. The soundings, both as to depth of water and quality of the bottom, of which a portion was brought up by the tallow affixed to the bottom of the sounding lead, indicated our vicinity to Dover; and the wind being strong from the north, we hauled up E. N. E. to round the South Foreland, and steer into the Downs. Just as day broke, however, the look-oiit at the mast-head exclaimed, "I and on the lee-bow! " We thought this impossible, as we expected to make it on the weather-bow; but it was too true. The conflict of the night had driven or drawn us insensibly towards the French coast, just opposite Dover, and the promontory on our lee-bow was Cape Gris-nez. This was Christmas-day, and a most uncomfortable one it was. We were obliged to claw off the shore as well as we could. The second reef was let out of the topsails, the fore and main course set, the jib and spanker hoisted; every yard was braced sharp to the wind, every bow-line hauled out, pre- venter braces and back-stays up, two men and an officer at the wheel, the weather-leeches of the sails lifting and the lee scuppers in the water,-svhile every moment I expected to hear the masts spring, or the tacks and sheets give way. But the vessel behaved nobly, and looked up to within four points and a half of the wind, while we edged along so close to the rocks off Cape Grisnez, that a biscuit might have been thrown on shore, and the rebound of the waves in receding from the coast helped us off like a strong tide under our lee, and brought us into deep water. It was a most anxious half-hour, the rounding this ugly cape. We saw several batteries on shore, but as the occupants of them must have expected every minute to see us dashed to pieces on the rocks, they took no pains to impede our progress, for there was not way enough on the ship to be certain of her coming round in stays, and not room enough to ware, so that our only hope lay in hugging the wind under a press of sail. As soon, however, as we had escaped this danger, we had a gun from the battery over our head to summon us to show our colours. We hoisted the English flag, which was followed by other guns in succession; but, though two shot passed through our rio; o; ino; and sails, and did some slight damasre in that way, no serious injury was effected, and we were soon beyond the limits of their range.

Our troubles, however, were not yet at an end. The gale from the northward increased in violence as the day advanced, and as this was dead in our teeth for getting into the Downs, we had to make short tacks under close-reefed topsails and courses throughout the day; and when night came, as it was pitch dark, we stood on to the north-east, and came to an anchor under the lee of the Goodwin Sands, where we lay in tolerably smooth water, with sixty fathoms of cable out, till midnight. The ship was then perceived to be drifting to leeward, either by the anchor coming home, or the cable being parted: and all hands being called to make sail, as soon as we had got way upon her, the capstan was manned to heave in the cable, when its end arrived at the hawse-holes, chafed and torn in rags, by having fallen on some buried wreck, of which there are many about this region, and thus jagged and parted. As the wind had gradually gone round from north to north-west, and at last westerly, our position was even less favourable than before for reaching the mouth of the Thames. We had, therefore, nothing for it, but to stand away to the northward into the German Ocean, still under close-reefed topsails, and making almost as much lee-way as head-waj, so as to be continually drifting neai'cr and nearer to the shore under our lee; and there was neither a lull nor the slightest shift of wind to enable us to take advantage of them to escape from the threatening danger. The straining of the hull, from the ship's labouring hard in a short and chopping sea, caused several leaks to spring, so that it was as much as all hands could do, in short spells at the pump, to keep the vessel free. Three weary nights, each of sixteen hours long, (the sun setting at four and rising at eight,) and three short days of only eight hours each, passed in this anxious state, reduced us all to our last legs, and we were as dejected in mind as we were exhausted in body. When we reached the 53rd degree of north latitude, we were close in shore, off the Helder and the Texel, and our soundings reduced to ten fathoms, with the low land right under our lee, and the breakers on the shore visible from the deck. As there seemed no hope of escape from being wrecked on a lee shore, the question was raised among the officers, whether it would not be better at once to run into the Dutch port of the Helder and give ourselves up as prisoners, (for Holland was then under France, and at war with England,) and thus save our lives by a voluntary surrender of our liberty. It was a nice point to determine, and it was necessary to consult the crew before the question could be finally determined. At daybreak, therefore, the hands were all summoned on the quarterdeck; the proposition, and the reasons for it, were submitted to them, and all seemed to acquiesce in its necessity. I cannot say that I joined heartily in the resolution; and I recommended, therefore, a perseverance till noon, the period when changes of wind most frequently occur, as, if there were no abatement of the gale by that time, we should still have four hours of light before us, and a single hour would be sufficient to reach the Helder in safety. The respite was acquiesced in, most fortunately for us all; for, in less than an hour after our conference, the wind began to moderate, so that we were able to shake out a second reef, set top-gallant sails, and look up to north-west by compass. The gale was evidently broken; and in another hour the wind veered round to south-east, the very opposite point of the compass; so that by ten o'clock, we were enabled to crowd all sail, with the wind a-beam on the larboard tack, and stand right across for the Lowe-stoff light by Yarmouth.

As soon as all sail was set, and the decks cleared up, eight bells were struck, and the welcome cry

VOL. I. X

"All's Well!" never sounded more agreeably in the ears of any weary seaman than it did in my own, as it was in perfect harmony with that relief from all apprehension of danger which, but a few hours before, weighed heavily upon the hearts of all on board, but on none of course more heavily than on the heart of their commander.

In the tranquil joy of the leisure now afforded, remembering that the celebrated air of " All's Well," the duet sung by Braham in the operetta of the British Fleet, was a great favourite with my wife, I wrote the following lines, adapted to that air, expressive of the feelings which recent scenes had so naturally inspired:

AIR "ALL'S WELL."

When crowded high is every sail, And proud top-gan'sails court the gale, When every cautious reef unbends, And high each royal-yard ascends; As o'er the waves We foam along, Kcmembrance wakes Her magic song: And while before the breeze we steer, In plaintive notes, distinct and clear, Tliy parting accents on mine ear Still lingering dwell;

"all's well.". 307

When, torn from all that life holds dear,

We wept, embraced, and sighed, Farewell!

Farewell! Adieu, my life! my love! Farewell!

When, o'er the surface of the deep In glassy calm its murmurs sleep, And not a breath of Zephyr's train Disturbs its still and tranquil reign;

When billow s cease Their sullen roar,

And Ocean feels

Their rage no more; While Cynthia, with her silver ra3's In dalliance on his bosom plays, Then fondly on her orb I gaze.

While Memory's spell Awakes the scenes of happier days, Ere, Love, to thee, I bade Farewell!

Farewell! A Ions: and oh! a sad Farewell.

And e'en when Winter's angriest storms, The face of the Great Deep deforms, And every wave's impending gloom Pi-epares some weary seaman's tomb; When forked fires,

At midnight dark. Gleam wildly round Our shattered bark; X

E'en then I walk the dangerous deck, 'Mid scenes of tempest, death, and wreck, And hang in fancy o'er thy neck,

Whose rising swell Subsides at chilling horror's check, As thus I bid a last Farewell!

Farewell! In Heaven we'll meet on Earth, Farewell!

But see! the welcome dawn appears. The storm abates the dark scud clears, 1 hands aloft!" fast breaks the gale " Cross all the yards spread every sail." The summons shrill

The crew obey. And joyous hail

The brightening day. Oh! thus I think, while time shall flee Some dawn of hope I yet may see, To waft me home again with thee In joy to dwell; And there, from every sorrow free, No more to hear the sound, Farewell!

Farewell! Oh! haste, blest hour! till then Farewell!

About midnight we made the Lowestoff Light, and continued on to Orfoi'dness, where we anchored under the stern of a collier from the North, whom we liailed, and who promised to send us a pilot on board as soon as tlio weather slioule moderate, for It still blew a hard gale. Instead of so doing, however, the collier weighed her anchor, and stood away for the Thames. We determined to follow in her wake, as the safest plan we could pursue; for all our officers and men, as well as myself, however well acquainted with the navigation of those passages by which the Thames is entered by all ships arriving from the western world, or up the British Channel, were entirely ignorant of those by which the Thames is entered from the east and north, never having once passed through them. In attempting to weigh our anchor, however, which was the heavy sheet anchor, as our best bower was lost off Dungeness, and the small bower amid the wreck of the Goodwin Sands, the men were so reduced in strength, by continued labour, sleepless nights, long hours at the pumps, and other duties, as to be unable to raise it from the ground; so that there was no alternative but to cut the cable and leave our only anchor behind. By this time, however, the collier was out of sight a-head, and our only course was now to steer boldly up the channel of the Swin, and make the best use of our eyes for the buoys and beacons above water, with the constant heaving of the lead for the depths below. Two men were stationed s, s look-outs on tlie fore- topmast crosstrees, and two on tlie forecastle, while there was an officer at each gangway in the waist, and myself on the qnarter-deck. I do not know that I ever passed a more anxious time, but it was only bv such vigilance and such precautions that we could hope to succeed. As we approached the sand-bank of the Mouse, we intended to pass to leeward of its beacon, according to the sailing directions, which indicated that as the right channel; but the beacon had been washed away in the late gales, and a couple of cables' length to leeward of its usual position there stood a tall ship's mast, entirely devoid of rigging, with the wood-work of the platform of the top still remaining attached to it, and making it therefore look exactly like the beacon displaced. The helm was put hard a-weather to go under its lee, in the belief that it was the beacon; nor did we perceive the difference till very near to it, wdien it became necessary to luif round, and brace sharp up to the wind again, to keep to windward of it, where the right channel was; as, if we had continued five minutes longer on our course, we should inevitably have struck on the sand, and shared the same fate as the unhappy vessel whose solitary mast had thus led us asti'ay.

In this manner, without a pilot, and with not a man on board who had ever navi: i; ated this intricate channel before, we groped and felt our way up to Gravesendj where, having no anchor now left, we hove-to off the town, soon got a river pilot and a couple of kedges and hawsers on board, and in two tides reached the West India Docks the pilot dc-clarino; his belief that ours was the first instance in which a ship had ever been brought safely through the Swin without some one on board previously acquainted with its difficult navigation.

Association with captains, merchants, and ship-owners. State of society and manners among these classes. Softening and refining influences of female society. Practices of shiji-owners versus underwriters. Interest of both parties in increase of shipwrecks. Illustrations of the working of this in practice. Resignation of my command of the Surrey, and reasons why. Appointment to the command of a new ship, the William. Preparations for a voyage to the Mediterranean. French society in London contrasted with English.

First dinner with lawyers in chambers at Gray's Inn. Shipment of the crew. Crimps and their odious practices. Procurement of a Mediterranean pass. Humiliating policy.

Anecdote of summary justice on a Wapping lawyer.

Being now regularly admitted among the class of captains in tlie merchant service, I became a daily frequenter of Lloyds, and the Jamaica and Jerusalem coffee-houses, where the captains and ship-brokers iisually congregate at certain hours of the day, and of the Royal Exchange, from three to four o'clock, where merchants and ship-owners daily assemble, and where ships are chartered, cargoes bought and sold, and hundreds of thousands of pounds 'change hands " as the phrase is in the course of a single hour. I regret to say, however, that I found the portion of time necessarily devoted to such places of rendezvous hang very heavily on my hands. Though taking a more than usual degree of pride in the equipment, discipline, and smart appearance of the ships under my command, I could not bring myself to feel the same degree of interest in the rise and fall of freights, the fluctuations in the markets, the tricks had recourse to, in order to obtain goods and passengers, and the false allurements held out to obtain seamen for the crews, which were of every day occurrence. Nearly all those with whom I was thus brought into close familiar intercourse were men who seemed to possess no knowledge of or taste for literature in the most ordinary sense, and whose reading was confined entirely to tlie newspaper, the shipping list, and the prices current of the day. In the opportunities I enjoyed of dining with merchants and ship-owners, there was great hospitality, as far as an abundant supply of every requisite for the table, and an assortment of the best wines were concerned; but the chief enjoyment of both hosts and guests seemed to lie in the excessive indulgence of the appetite of hunger and thirst, commendations on the exquisite quality of the viands and wines, and anecdotes of successful bargains and transactions on 'Change and in the counting house; but never, on any occasion, the slightest allusion to any new work of literature, any recent discovery in science, any noble production in art, or any reference whatever to any topic of historical, antiquarian, poetical, philanthropic, or religious interest. The result, therefore, of my first experience of mercantile society was a conviction that the daily practice of " buying as cheap and selling as dear as possible" had a tendency to increase selfishness and worldlv-mindedness, to contract rather than expand the finer feelings of the heart; and that there was a great fallacy in the popular sentiment of " the elevating character of the occupation of the British merchant" arisino- from a want of knowledo-e of their habits and manners, or a want of candour in describing them.

In parties where ladies were present the cases of which, however, were much fewer than what were called " gentlemen's parties," from which ladies were intentionally excluded a great improvement was visible. New books, new music, new operas, new poems, furnished topics of conversation with them; and they appeared but too happy to find among the male guests, persons of kindred tastes to enter with earnestness into such discussions. From my fondness for all these subjects, and the extent to which I had employed my leisure in rcadiiig, I found myself always a welcome addition to what w as called " the ladies' circle; " and strange to say, this very fact excited considerable jealousy among several of my contemporaries, fellow captains, who regarded me as an unworthy colleague, because I preferred the enjoyments of music and female society to joining them in what they held to be the superior felicity of cold brandy and water, and a genuine Havannah cigar.

I speak here of the state of things as they existed in 1811- upwards of forty years ago since which, no doubt, many improvements have taken place, as well as in the principles and practices recognised as legitimate and honourable at that time of day, some of which deserve mention as indications of the spirit and temper of the times.

An illustration of the mode in which some shipowners obtained, through pliant commanders, compensations to what they were not justly entitled, is worthy of narration here. The Surrey, as previously mentioned, had anchored under the lee of the Goodwin Sands and lost an anchor and cable there, by their friction on a sunken wreck. It was thouirht necessary to haul the ship into a dry dock to examine her bottom, in order to see whether she had herself received any damage from this circumstance. With the exception of a small portion of the fore-foot being wrenched from the bolts, there was none needing repair. But the copper was observed to be honej-combed and much worn. In the coppering of ships' bottoms, it should be observed, that there were then two descriptions of sheets or plates used; one warranted to last good for seven years, being of superior weight and thickness, and the other warranted only for five years, being lighter and thinner. The copper of the Surrey was of the latter description, and had been already in use the full period of its warranted service. Now, if it could be shown that this decayed or honey-combed state of the copper was caused by abrasion on the Goodwin Sands, an entirely new suit of copper-sheathing for the ship would have Ijcen supplied by the underwriters, as comino; under the damao-es ao-ainst which the ship was insured. But if, on the other hand, it was shown to be merely the result of age, or natural wear and tear, the expenses of such new coppering would devolve upon the owners.

I was accordingly asked, and really expected to state in a formal protest for this purpose, that the copper had been thus injured by our having been on shore on the Goodwin Sands, and that the friction of the ship's bottom on the shoal had been the sole caus j.

This I refused to do; when I was told tliat, liowever good a seaman I might be, I did not know my duty to the owners in whose service I was; and that for so young a captain thus to impair his prospects by such a refusal as this, was, to say the least of it, a proof that I was wholly unacquainted with business. I was willing to submit to this reproach, and persevering in my refusal, gave such offence as to make any other service more agreeable to me than one which expected such accommodatino- conduct as this.

On inquiring among other commanders of my acquaintance, I found that this case was, to them at least, not at all so novel and surprising as it appeared to me. I learnt also, for the first time, that it was a general belief, among the old and experienced captains, that both underwriters and owners had an actual pecuniary interest in the total loss of their ships, a fact I was slow to believe, but respecting which I found very few to doubt. By the classification of ships for insurance at Lloyd's, it was the custom to have the first and best classed as A1, and these remained either five or seven years on that class, depending on their peculiar construction and equipment. At the expiration of that time, they would require a thorough and expensive repair, and then fall into the second class, when the rate of insurance on them would be increased, while their chances of getting freight or passengers would be diminished. If, however, such vessels were lost within the period for which their classification held good, the underwriters were bound to furnish an entirely new ship and equipments in all respects equal to the one lost, or the value of the same in money. It was clearly, therefore, much more to the interest of the owner that his vessel should be lost before she had run beyond her full term of first class, as in that case he would have a new one to supply her place than to run her into the second class, incur the heavy expense of a thorough repair, and find his vessel after all less eligible for freight or passengers, his only two sources of gain. Instead, therefore, of ships being built so strong as to remain safe for ten, or even twenty years, which would be quite practicable, vessels were purposely constructed to last for five years, or six, as their probable loss might occur before they were worn out, and they would cost therefore much less in their construction.

It would not always be easy to get captains, unless they were largely interested as owners also, to effect such losses, as it is not generally easy to ensure the complete wreck of a vessel without endangering the lives of the officers and crew. Many would be afraid to ask such a favour of any captain, lest tliey should be refused, and many would be too honourable to have recourse to such a mode of gam; besides which, a certain combination of circumstances would be requisite to make the loss of a ship excusable: and unless it could be made to appear unavoidable, it might be disputed, as far as the liabilities of the underwriters were concerned; though, generally speaking, they found it their interest to pay their engagements without much dispute, as a reputation for litigipusness would lessen their popularity and decrease their business.

The interest of the underwriter in the occasional and frequent loss of ships is sufficiently evident from the fact that the more frequent such losses are, the higher the rates of premium rise, and that if it were possible to reduce such losses to a minimum, underwriting as a business would cease to be profitable at all. On the same principle, therefore, that insurance offices against fire find their business increase, and premiums more readily paid after a large fire on shore; so, in heavy losses at sea, a similar effect takes place among insurers against sea risks.

The Government, too, have a pecuniary interest in the loss of merchant ships; because all its duty-paid materials of timber, iron, hemp, and stores of various kinds go to the bottom, and new supplies of all these duty-paid materials are required to replace them, which adds to the revenue: while all the merchants and manufacturers, who supply the cargoes, if they insure them to their full value, and make the insurance cover the assumed profit also, which is often the case, have an equal interest in the loss, because the insurance covers the whole, and new supplies are required to furnish the stocks thus removed from the market and sent down to Neptune's domain.

Every now and then cases of such wilful losses of ships are detected, and the parties who perpetrate the crime are proceeded against by the proper authorities and punished, with fine, imprisonment, and transportation. The annals of the Court of King's Bench furnish many such cases; but for every one detected and brought to justice, there are perhaps eight or ten that escape undiscovered, and those who are caught are only considered more unfortunate than those that escape.

The truth is, that the eager race after fortune, in which so many competitors are engaged, causes men to become less and less scrupulous in proportion as they act in large numbers, and are surrounded by contagious examples; and " the honour of the British merchant," proverbial as it is, is not always proof against strong temptation.

taKE COMMAND OF THE " AVILLIAM." 321

Having resigned the command of the Surrey, from the impossibility of my complying with the conditions expected of me, in reference to the proposition about new coppering the vessel, as before narrated, I had an offer made me to command the William, then destined for a voyage to the Mediterranean, which I eagerly embraced, as I had long felt a strong desire to visit that classic remon. I accordino-ly laid in a large stock of books relating to every country lying within the Straits of Gibraltar, including Europe, Africa, and Asia, as far as tlie eastern extremity of the Euxine or Black Sea, having more than a hundred volumes of history, biography, travels, and poetry, from Herodotus to Brydone, and from Homer to Lord Byron, who had just begun to appear on the literary stage. I had a few weeks to spend in London before our day of sailing, and these were passed most agreeably.

The owners of the ship now placed under my command were Messrs. Goujon and Gernon, two French merchants, one from Marseilles, the other from Bordeaux, their office being in Langbourne Chambers, Fenchiirch Street. As these gentlemen were both well educated and men of taste, which is not always the case with English shipowners, their society was unusually agreeable; and my frequent

VOL. I. Y visits to their respective residences one at Penton-ville and the other at Clapham furnished me abundant pleasure, bringing me as it did into contact with French society among their guests, in which I felt great delight, from their liveliness and vivacity, and their freedom from the dull and heavy port-wine drinking of English merchants generally.

The ship's broker was Peter Hoskin, Esq., whose office was in Mincing Lane, but who lived in a nice country house at Eltham, where I also passed many agreeable hours with his accomplished sister and himself; and a young friend of liis, Mr. Knibbs, then, I believe, a broker on the Stock Exchange, but one of the most polished and intellectual, as well as one of the most fascinating and agreeable, companions I liad vet met with in London. This brought me into a new class of society; but I remember the shock I received at an exhibition which I had least expected, at one of the dinners of the circle to which I was invited. Among other literary men present, was the Rev. Mr. Maurice, Assistant Librarian of the British Museum, chiefly known to the world as the author of a splendid and elaborate work in quarto, on the INIythology of the Hindoos, which tiien enjoyed the highest reputation; but the subsequent researches of more learned and accurate

Oriental scholars since his day have detected in it many errors and fallacies. As the party consisted wholly of gentlemen, there was no restraint in the xise of wine, or the topics of conversation; and I was surprised to find, that in the depth of their potations, these literati, of whom I had ignorantly expected an exhibition of the temperance of Seneca and the wisdom of Socrates, exceeded the regimental mess of the West Indies, and thought three bottles of strong port wine per man a very moderate allowance quoting Pitt, Fox, and Sheridan as six-bottle men in tlieir day and generation. The conversation was coarse and obscene to a degree that no naval or military man would tolerate; and I longed for the hour of rising to escape from such an atmosphere. The termination of the entertainment was in harmony with its general character. The reverend and learned Orientalist of the British Museum became insensibly drunk, by taking glasses of brandy at intervals between his port wine, and at length fell helpless and insensible underneath the table. His grey hairs, his literary reputation, and his reverend character made this one of the most painful scenes I had witnessed for some time; but the rest of the party regarded it with indifference. His servant was called, and by liis aid the apparently lifeless body was carried down stairs, put into a liackney coach, and driven to his lodgings: this being, as I was afterwards assured, the almost uniform concludinc: scene, whenever the reverend and learned gentleman dined out. Such was life in London, in some circles at least, between forty and fifty years since.

Having been invited to dinner by Mr. Munnings, of Gray's Inn, to whom I presented my letter of introduction from his brother the governor of New Providence, I waited on him at his chambers, on a Saturday evening at six o'clock, and there joined a party of about twenty, mostly barristers, who had been invited to meet me, and to each of whom I was presented, with manv more eulofries than I thoufjht I deserved, but which arose from the high commendations which the governor had bestowed on me in liis letter. Tliis was the first time in my life that I had ever been in the presence of so many learned men, and I accordingly expected very grave conversation, and discussions on important questions of jurisprudence, politics, and moral philosophy; overlooking the fact that as these form the staple of their consultations and professional labours, they were the less likely to enter into their convivial assemblages. The truth is, that I heard more anecdotes, jokes, and puns from these legal gentlemen than I had ever lieartl before in any party within the same space of time; and the fears with which I was haunted, on first taking my seat at the table, that I should be quite unequal to sustain my part in the conversation of so learned a body, soon gave way to the confidence inspired by the mediocrity of the remarks of many who were rather more eagerly listened to than their superiors. The prominent character of the party was a complete abandonment of all care, professional or otherwise, and a determination to enjoy themselves to the full. The only wines drank were port and Madeira the former predominating; and I was somewhat surprised that young and old for there were men of twenty-five and men of sixty in the party seemed about equal in the capacity to carry oft' an amazing quantity of both without falling under the table, like the reverend Orientalist before described, or manifesting in any very marked manner the signs of intoxication. There was no retirement from the table, for coffee or other refreshments, till midnight, when we separated; but the butler seemed to need no reminding of his duty, for the empty decanters were taken away and their places supplied by full ones as fast as was necessary, without any orders for their being replenished. I should think that on the average each guest drank at least two bottles of port or Madeira, some as many as three; and I had great difficulty in resisting the importunities of my right and left hand neighbours in passing the bottle, to do so without filling my glass, to the great astonishment of several, who said they thought sea captains more than a match for lawyers in their capacity for drinking; while my own wonder was, that men who had to think so much, could drink so hard as they did; but this was explained by their saying that Sunday intervened to carry off the effect of Saturday liight's indulgence. I had seen many-Saturday nights at sea where two glasses of grog instead of one were the indulgence allowed for drinking to '"sweethearts and wives " but this Saturday night on shore far exceeded, from its long duration as well as excess, anything I had either witnessed or expected.

As the time was now approaching in which our preparations for sea had to be completed by the shipment of the crew (for the river work of fitting out and taking in the cargo was performed by dock labourers), this disgusting task had to be performed in person. At this period the wages of seamen ran high, from the scarcity of hands, as all English sailors that could be found were impressed for the ships of war: and it was mostly, and sometimes entirely, from foreign seamen that an English captain could collect his men. Instead, however, of these coming on board the vessels fitting for sea, and offering their services, as is usnal when men are abundant, they had to be hunted after in the vile dens of crimps, along the shores and alleys of Wapping, Rotherhithe, and the banks of the Thames. These crimps were a set of abandoned traffickers in a sort of white slave trade, as bad as that amono; the negroes on the coast of Africa; and their constant practice was this: As soon as a ship arrived from abroad, the crimps came on board, in the river or in the docks, and as the seamen were then always without money till their wages should be paid, they were easily tempted to go ashore with such crimp as Avould allure them by a small sum of money in hand for immediate indulgence, and the promise of a home and accommodation of a superior kind, on credit till their wages should be paid; and as it was the custom to discharge the crew immediately on the ship's being secured in her berth in the river or in the docks, each crimp walked off with as many men as he could persuade to accompany him to his own abode. This was a common lodging-house, in which as many as twenty seamen could be received at once: and here the first indulgence of the kidnapped victims began bj a drinking bout, the materials for wliich were supplied bj the house, a supper and a dance followed, the females being all prostitutes, out of which each seaman had a wife assigned to him for the period of his stay. In the course of about a week, or sometimes less, the unhappy prisoner being all this time kept in a state of intoxication something short of being dead drunk, just to enable him to join in the debaucheries prepared for him, a score was run up against him, not only sufficient to absorb all the wages due to him for his past voyage, but also to trench upon his advance for the coming one.

At this stage of the proceedings, the crimp was willing to allow his victim to enter for a new ship; and in order to-obtain men, the captains were obliged to visit these dens, select their men, pay up the score due to the crimp, take the seaman's order on his owner for the wages due, and then see him safe on board with his chest and hammock, with rarely or ever any other kind of outfit or provision for his future voyage. On the day fixed for sailing from Gravesend, the crew were mustered, perhaps half of them only by this time sober, when they signed their articles of agreement to perform the voyage out and home for a fixed rate of wages (able seamen being then at 5l. a month), and two months advance were paid to tliem, half of wliicli, and sometimes all, would be claimed by a crimp; and the other half, when so much remained, bo expended in such few necessaries as so small a sura could command. The captain was regarded as a lucky man, who could muster all his crew perfectly sober on reaching the Downs.

It was my recollection of the miseries inflicted on seamen by this state of things, that made me so earnest an advocate for the establishment of Sailors' Homes, which I recommended for England in the Parliamentary Report of the Select Committee on Shipwrecks, of which I was appointed chairman in 1834, and which Report was made the basis of many improvements for the seaman's benefit; while in America I had the satisfaction of beini; instrumental to the formation of such Sailors' Homes in all the chief ports of the United States, from Boston to New Orleans, and was the means of raising, at the various public meetings held on this subject, at least twenty thousand dollars for the purpose of their ei'ection and maintenance. Happily they are now abundant in England also; but the friends of seamen should never relax their efforts till there is at least one such Home established in every port.

Another duty devolved on me as a commander.

vvliich, though of a totally different nature from that of shipping the crew, was equally revolting to my feelings. This was a visit to the Admiralty in Whitehall, for the purpose of procuring what was called a " Mediterranean Pass." For a long series of years the Deys of Algiers had carried on a system of piracy or buccaneering against all Christian vessels, deeming them lawful prizes, to whatever nation they belonged; and, appropriating to themselves the plunder of their cargoes, they made slaves of all the passengers and crews. If there were any young or handsome females among the former, they vere taken into the harem of the Dey, or of the principal officer of the ship effecting the capture; if there were others not young enough or handsome enough for such a purpose, they were kept for ransom, and all the rest were put to work as slaves often in chains on such undertakings and in such modes as the Dey might direct. That such a state of things should be tamely submitted to by the weaker Governments of Spain, Sardinia, Italy, and Sicily might not excite much surprise; but that so powerful a maritime nation as Great Britain should allow such a practice to exist for a single day, is really as much a matter of reproach as it is of wonder; but so it was. And the great Government of England most disgracefully pur- chased the exemption of its merchant vessels from liability to such atrocious treatment, bj paying an annual subsidy to these lawless Moorish robbers. Nay, still more, it was said to be then the practice, and had been so for several years, for the English Government to build in one of the royal dockyards, and equip and arm with brass guns, a corvette for the Algerines, one of which was presented to the Dey every year, as part of the annual tribute paid to these barbarians; and that such vessels were actually employed by them against the weak and defenceless Christian ships of the several countries named! Be this as it might, this at least is certain, that every merchant ship bound for the Mediterranean was considered liable to become a prize to an Algerine cruiser unless provided with a Mediterranean pass; and this was furnished by the British Admiralty, on payment of a certain fee by the owners of the ship requiring it. I went to the Admiralty for mine, and there received a parchment document, cut out from a large book, by an undulating line like an indenture, or a banker's check, so that the document and its counterpart might correspond; and this certifying the vessel carrying it to be British property, and commanded by a British subject, would cause all

Algerine cruisers to respect it, and let the vessel go free.

Execrable as such a practice seemed to me, and I never failed to denounce it whenever it was spoken of, there were not wanting persons to defend it, on grounds as atrocious as the practice itself, namely, that whereas bj this system the carrying trade of the Spaniards, Sardinians, Sicilians, and Italians, in the Mediterranean, was greatly impeded and restricted, tlie maritime commerce of England was thereby increased; and that in a mercantile point of view it was w ell worth the while of the British Government to maintain this state of things by paying the annual tribute to insure her own ships from capture and pillage! a doctrine to which I could never subscribe. The only treatment which such barbarians deserved was the visit of a hostile fleet to demand the freedom of all the slaves then in captivity, and guarantees for the future abandonment of their piracy against all nations, or the complete destruction of all their ships, artillery, ammunition, and arms, so as to render them incapable of continuing so indefensible a practice.

Not long after this, the Americans so thought and so acted; for when some outrage was committed by the Bey of Tunis against one of the merchant ships of the United States, instead of offering to buy their forbearance by an annual tribute, the President of the young Republic (Maddison, I believe) sent a squadron under Commodore Decatur, to lay their town in ashes unless immediate and ample reparation were made for the injury inflicted: and the haughty Bey was compelled to surrender.

Wliether it was the influence of this example, or the improved state of public opinion and morality, that led to a similar treatment, by the British, of the Dey of Algiers, I know not; but not long after this. Lord Exmouth's expedition against the stronghold of the freebooter was planned and executed; and from that date Algerine slavery and Algerine piracy both ceased, and will never more be permitted to rear their heads aajain.

Notwithstanding these drawbacks, I promised myself more pleasure from my voyage to the Mediterranean than from any other I had yet performed; and was eager to get the ship ready for sea.

As soon as this was accomplished, the vessel dropped down to Gravesend, while I remained in town to complete tlie final arrangements with the owners and Customhouse authorities, and then joined the ship there. On going aboard I found an unusual degree of noise and bustle among the crew, and on inquiring into tlie cause, I learnt the following facts. As the seamen were to be paid their two months' wages in advance on the day after my joining, and before the ship sailed for the Downs, some pettifogging lawyer from Wapping, of the class called "land sharks," as they make seamen their chief prey, had come down by one of the Gravesend smacks, got on board unseen by the officer of the deck, and joined the seamen in the forecastle. Entering freely into their habits, he drank and smoked with them, having broug; ht with him some rum and tobacco as treats to the men, and wished to persuade some of them that after sionino; their articles of agreement for the voyage, and receiving their two months' wages in advance, if they chose to run that is, leave the ship, and take their money with them the captain would have no legal means of punishing them, and he would undertake their defence. Several of the men having corroborated this statement, I determined in the present case to take the law into ray own hands, and risk the consequences. I accordingly ordered the boatswain to pipe "All hands on deck!" at which summons all the crew came up from the forecastle, leaving only the Wapping lawyer there; as he, having heard of my arrival, was unwilling to appear. I then went to the fore-hatchway myself, accompanied bj two boatswain's mates, and bade them go below and start np any skulkers tliey should find there; liaving previously arranged the crew in a double line on both sides of the deck, to be prepared to make the lawyer " run the gauntlet," each of the men being furnished w ith a small piece of rope called " rattling-stuff," for the purpose. The boatswain's mates descended into the forecastle, and did their duty with great zest and efficienc They laid it on upon the back of the lawyer so lustily with the rope described, that as he came up the hatchway he w as enveloped in a cloud of his own powder; it being the custom among professional men of that day not merely to powder their heads profusely, but to powder their black coats half way down the back, as indicative of their gentility; and as he attempted to make for the gangway, in order to get into one of the boats alongside, he had to run the gauntlet between the rows of the seamen, each of whom " peppered his jacket well," as they called it. On going over the ship's side he said to me, "Ah! Sir, you shall hear more of this matter. I shall bring an action of assault against you, which will cost you more than you expect." I accordingly wrote to the owners, stating what I had done, and instructing them, if necessary, to defend the action; but their solicitor, whom they consulted, bade me " apprehend no evil, as the wretch of an attorney, who was a disgrace to his profession, would not dare to carry his threat into execution; for Lord Ellen-borough, wdio was then Chief Justice, on a statement of the case, would be sure to strike such a man off the rolls, and expel him with ignominy from the bddv."

The matter being thus definitively settled, the crew were paid their advance, without any desertions: and in our passage to the Downs, and thence to Portsmouth for final orders, from which port our voyage would have to commence, we had the satisfaction of seeing them all disciplined into good order and perfectly fit for duty; while my own expectations of pleasure from the voyage grew higher and higher every day, as the most interesting period of my life was now about to begin.

Anticipations and' preparations for the Mediterranean.-De-j arture from Portsmouth. Farewell lines. Voyage along the coasts of Spain and Portugal. Cape St. Vincent. Victory of Sir John Jervis. Sagres the early seat of Portuguese enterprise. The Lusiad of Camoens, and his romantic history. Straits of Gibraltar. Tariffii and Trafalgar. Description of the bay and town of Gibraltar. Immense strength of its rock-hewn batteries. Variety of character and costume in its inhabitants. Brief sketch of the sieges of Gibraltar. Redeeming traits of humanity to prisoners. Lady Mary Wortley Montague on War. Franklin's Apologue on the same subject.

The prospect of the rich field before me in our intended voyage up the Mediterranean, induced me to pass from the ordinary " Ship's Log," which had hitherto been the chief record of the events of my maritime life, to the keeping a more full and complete " Journal," not merely of events, but of thoughts and opinions suggested by them, as well as of historical and poetical reminiscences arising out of the scenes by which, in such a voyage, the traveller is sure to be surrounded. It is from this Journal therefore, still preserved in all its integrity amidst a VOL. I. Z 338 DEPARTURE FROM roRTSMOUTH.

thousand accidents by flood and field, that tlie ma-tei"ials for the remaining Story of my Life will bo chiefly drawn, with such abridgments and corrections as experience may suggest, in order to bring the lai'gest amount of interest within the smallest compass of space.

It was in the month of June, 1811, that I commenced this first voyage to the Mediterranean from Portsmouth, under the most favourable auspices that could well be conceived, full of hope, yet not without some touch of despondency, wdiich, parting from those we love most dearly in the world, can never fail to inspire. As the wind, though light, was favourable for going down Channel, it was determined to pass through the Needles; and the charge of the ship being in the hands of the pilot till we had cleared that narrow passage, I had comparative leisure and freedom from responsibility. The crew were busy in the performance of their duty, though several of them had friends on board desirous of continuing with them as long as possible, " to see them well off"," as they expressed it, and then going ashore with the pilot when he delivered up his charge. I availed myself, therefore, of this leisure to write the following farewell lines to my wife in

London, wliich were taken on shore by the pilot to be forwarded to her by the post.
AIR "THE ANCHOR'S WEIGHED."

The ships unmoored, fresh breezes fill

The sails, to waft me, Love, away; And hark! tlie boatswain's whistle shrill. Pipes to the bustling crew " Belay I" But oh! while mirth their laughing temples crown, As in the sparkling bowl their cares they drown, I pensive sit, and sing, in sighs, to thee, The anchor's weighed! Farewell! Remember me.

Tho' many a league of trackless tide

Between us, Dearest, soon will roll. Nor time nor distance can divide Thy lovely image from my soul: Yet oh! believe the hour at last will come To waft me back to happiness and home; Till then, let Fairy Hope our guardian be, The anchor's weigh'd Farewell! Remember me.

As months of absence steal along. Thy praise shall be my dear employ,

And oh! may this, my simple song," Sometimes inspire thy heart with joy, z

Yes! ever when thy tongue shall breathe this lay, Believe tliat thus, tho' banished far away, I often dream of home, and sing to thee, The anchor's weighed Farewell! Remember me.

Our run from the Land's End of England to the Cape Finisterre of Spain, was remarkably rapid and agreeable; and from thence to the Rock of Lisbon, which we sighted two days afterwards, as pleasant as could be desired. As the northerly breeze now left us, however, and the wind veered round to the opposite point of the compass, we had to beat to windward instead of going free, and hauling in towards the land we had a near view of the group of islands off the entrance to the Tagus, called the Burlino-as. They were said to be used as a convict settlement of the Portuguese, and their sterility and aridity made their aspect very forbidding. They may be approached with safety, as they have bold shores and deep water all around them.

As we stood along the coast of Portugal, with a slant of wind from the westward, the face of the country presented more agreeable landscapes, diversified by villages and summer retreats, as well as by a superb palace of considerable extent, exhibiting a long range of buildings adorned with spires and domes. It was seated on the brow of a hill com- manding a complete view of the entrance to Lisbon, and advantageously placed to receive the refreshing coolness of the sea-breeze. The extent and magnificence of this pile induced us to suppose it of royal or ecclesiastical foundation, as nothing short of the funds of the State or the Church could be adequate to the erection and support of so extensive and superb a building.

At noon we were nearly abreast of the Rock of Lisbon, whose rugged summit towers above the hills tliat surround it, and projects with boldness into the sea, presenting a strong rocky cape, which braves the fury of the western ocean apparently unharmed; for though the waves of the Atlantic beat incessantly against it, there are no traces of any great encroachment or destruction along its base.

On the eighth day after our leaving Portsmouth, we approached close to Cape St. Vincent, the promontory which terminates the western coast of Portugal towards the south; and off which the great victory was obtained by the English fleet under Admiral Sir John Jervis, over the Spaniards, in 1797, the prizes of which I had the opportunity of seeing brought into the Tagus when returning from my own captivity in Spain; for which the gallant admiral was lionourecl with a peerage, under the title of Earl St. Vincent. The cape is steep and rocky; and some of the adjacent cliffs present a striking appearance of oblique strata, which may be seen distinctly in the separate layers or veins. Immediately on the summit of the Cape are a nnmber of well-built houses, and an edifice resembling a castle.

A little to the southward of this, stand the town and fortifications of Sagres, on the ramparts of which we could distinctly see the sentinels and guards. These were built by that illustrious patron of naval enterprise, Henry Duke de Viseo, in the reign of Alphonzo the Third, about the year 1250. It was called " The Sainted Cape," in consequence of the bones of St. Vincent having been buried there, though they were afterwards conveyed to Lisbon by Alphonzo the First. The Portuguese poet, Ca-moens, in the third book of his Lusiad, thus adverts to this event:

"But holy rites the pious king preferred: The martyr's bones on Vincent's Cape interred, (His sainted name the Cape shall ever bear) To Lisbon's walls he brought with votive care."

The mountainous scenery of the background, behind tlie Cape, indistinctly appearing through the blue haze of distance, was beautifully picturesque.

Though Portugal, as a kingdom, appears now to be sunk so low in the scale, its early history is full of interest, and it may without presumption be considered the parent of conunercial enterprise and the nurse of maritime discovery; for the Portuguese were the first to effect the passage ronnd the Cape of Good Hope, and to plant their flag in India, wliere they have left behind them, in the vast number of descendants from their early settlers amono-the half-caste Christians of India, proofs of zeal and success in the propagation of the Gospel among the heathens of the East.

It was a source of great pleasure to me to read Mickle's translation of the noble poem of Camoens, "Os Lusiados," so near the scene of his nativity and death, both of which took place at Lisbon; and it was at the same time a cause of much pain to reflect on the contempt and neglect with which a man of such genius was treated by his contemporaries. Camoens was born in Lisbon about the year 1520. His father, who commanded a Portuguese vessel, was wrecked on the coast of Africa and perished there with the greater part of his fortune. The son's education was completed by his mother in the University of Coim- bra. Soon after tlds, wliile living in retirement at Santarcm, he began his epic poem on the discovery of India, and he continued it during his military operations in Africa. In an action with the Moors off Gibraltar he lost his right eye, when among tlie foremost in boarding the enemy. After several years' service in Africa he returned to Lisbon, and on leav-incr it for India was heard to exclaim, in the menu-mental words of the Roman Scipio Africanus, "In-grata Patria! non possidebis ossa mea!"

Though Camoens began his great poem in Europe, the m-eater iiortion of it was written either in the tented life of a soldier in Africa, or in the more boisterous turmoil of a sailor's life on tlie ocean. The ship in which he sailed for India was wrecked on the coast of China, and all he had on board, except the manuscript of his poem, was lost. This precious relic he saved by holding it in one of his hands while he swam to the shore with the other, in the same manner as Julius Cgesar is said to have saved his " Commentaries" when he swam from the shore to his vessel in the harbour of Alexandria. When the Lusiad was at length printed, the work was dedicated to the reigning King of Portugal, who allowed the poet a small pension. But this was cut off by his successor to the throne, and Camoens was thus reduced to poverty and want. It is recorded that an old black servant of the poet, a native of Java, who had grown grey-headed in the service of his master, literally begged in the streets of Lisbon to support the life of Camoens, whom he had also been instrumental in saving from shipwreck. This was the fate of one who had deservedly acquired the title of the " Iusi-tanian Homer," in whom the first judges of literary merit have declared that the genius of Sophocles, Pindar, Virgil, and Ovid were united; and wdio, when resting from the bolder flights of epic strains, could tune his harp to gentler lays of love, as Moore in his epistle to Lord Strangford, written oflp the Azores, lias testified in these lines:

"Dear Strangford! at this hour perhaps
Some youthful lover (not so blest As they who in their ladies' laps
May cradle every wish to rest) Warbles, to touch his dear one's soul,
Those madrigals of breath divine, Which Camoens' harp from rapture stole,
And gave all glowing warm to thine."

The town of Sagres, on Cape St. Vincent, was one of the earliest points of departure for the early navigators of Portugal. It was founded by the Duke of Viseo soon after his conquest of Ceuta in Africa, and it is said tliat the grand view of the Ocean which presented itself to him as he looked westward and southward, from the summit of the Cape, gave him the first idea of planting his town of Sagres on the Pro-montorium Sacrum of the Romans. Here his arsenals and dockyards were constructed; under his auspices the mariner's compass was here first introduced, and the methods of determining the latitude and longitude at sea first taught to the young aspirants for maritime distinction. The sea astrolabe, a nautical instrument, which derived its name from the ancillary sphere invented by Hippar-clius at Alexandria, was improved and introduced into the Portuguese service. Skilful mariners from all countries were encouraged to settle at Sagres, and a public school and observatory were there established by the Duke. It was impossible, therefore, to pass a scene of so much historical and maritime interest without feeling the highest veneration for those whose names are associated with its foundation and progress. At sunset we lost sight of Cape St. Vincent, and on the following morning we approached the Straits of Gibraltar. By standing in shore during the night, we were near the Spanish coast in the morning, and there closed in with a large fleet that w as then entering the Straits under a heavy press of sail. At noon, the breeze freshening from the westward, we opened the bokl Rock of Gibraltar, and stood in for tlie Bay. At Tariflfa we observed tlie new lighthouse just erected by the Spaniards on its point; and on passing the renowned site of Trafalgar, every one on board seemed to be impressed with solemn emotions on viewing a sea so recently dyed with the blood of their fellow seamen, and many voices audibly repeated the last signal of the victorious and dying Nelson, "England expects every man to do his duty," a signal which will be a watchword of the navy as long as England shall have a single ship afloat.

As the commodore of the fleet of which we now formed a part, passed Europa Point, the extreme southern promontory, an exchange of salutes took place between the ship and the garrison, and the loud echo of the Rock increased by its reverberations the force of the sound, while several vessels of the fleet took this opportunity of scaling their guns, which, with the presence of a large fleet under crowded canvass entering the Bay at the same time, formed a most interesting maritime picture.

As I cast my eyes upon the cloud-capped mountains that bounded our southern view, I had some difficulty in realising the fact that I was now on the borders of Africa. Every league of our future pro- gress would onlj bear me farther and farther off, however, from tliose I liad so recently left in dear and happy England, which I could address with the greatest truth in the expressive language of Goldsmith:

"Where'er I roam, whatever realms I see, My heart, untravelled, fondly turns to thee; Still ever homeward turns, with ceaseless pain, And drags at each remove a lengthened chain,"

Gibraltar has been so often described, and is so well known from its memorable siege by the Spaniards, and their defeat by the intrepid General Elliott, that it will be unnecessary to say much of its history; but some description of the Rock and town, and some record of the impressions made by a first visit to it, may not be unworthy of record.

The bay, in which we anchored, is safe and commodious; and though it has the Spanish towns of San Roque on the north side, and Algeziras on the west, it is so well commanded by the foi'tifications that overlook it, as to make it perfectly secure for British vessels, even in time of war. The inner harbour is formed by two moles projecting into the sea, making an artificial dock or basin. These moles are well planted with heavy cannon, and, like all the fortifications of the Rock, tljcy are bomb-proof. Tiio landing place is a spacious wharf, at the end of which is the Town-gate, where sentries are posted to examine all who pass, and to prevent all persons from communicating with the town who are not provided with pratique, or a licence from the health-office to land.

The town of Gibraltar, which is about a mile long, and a quarter of a mile broad, is built along the western foot of a steep and abrupt mountain, anciently called Calpe, which, with Mount Abyla on the African shoi'e (now called Ape's Hill) formed the famous pillars of Hercules. This abrupt and mountainous mass, which is about two miles lono-, and one broad, and called with great propriety the "Rock" of Gibraltar, is computed to be 1,400 feet above the level of the sea, and rises so steeply from its base to its summit, as to make it perpendicular in many parts, particularly on the northern and eastern sides. It appears at a little distance to be a bare and rugged surface of stone, incapable of the least vegetation; but on a nearer examination a few trees and gardens, the work of toil and expense, arc to be seen. On the western face, which is the only side that can be ascended, and which faces towards the Bay, there are roads cut zig-zag for going up to the summit, wliicli would be inaccessible in a straight line. On the extreme heights are two signal posts and watch towers, with a small battery to each, to give alarm in case of danger; and in every part of the Rock that is at all accessible to human tread, large caverns have been hewn out and port-holes opened through the sides, forming subterranean batteries, the height of which above the plain below would protect them against the fire of an enemy, while the same elevation would enable them to pour down destruction on the heads of their assailants.

The principal portion of these excavated batteries and galleries is on the northern cliff of the Rock, looking across the low sandy isthmus, which connects it with or separates it from Spain; and whicli isthmus is usually called the Neutral Ground. Any force attempting to approach Gibraltar by this isthmus, would be blown to atoms by the thousand cannon that are said to line the perforated rock in that direction; so that nothing but treachery within the garrison could ever make Gibraltar the prey of any enemy by land; and of its strength to defend itself against any amount of force by sea the memorable defence of General Elliott furnishes sufficient proof.

In passing through the town of Gibraltar, it is impossible not to be struck with the medlev of charac- tors seen among its permanent and temporary inhabitants. The English residents, in addition to the troops in garrison, which are always a fluctuating number, are supposed to be about 2000, and the foreigners or visitors about 5000, though these numbers also vary much from year to year. The houses are in general well built, partaking partly of the English and partly of the Spanish style of architecture, well adapted to the situation and climate. The public buildings appeared to be substantial, and the streets, though narrow, were well paved, and much cleaner than those of Lisbon.

The languages most frequently heard in Gibraltar are English and Spanish; but in this respect it is really a modern Babel, as its inhabitants and visitors include persons of nearly every nation, kindred, and tongue: English, French, Spanish, Portuguese, Italians, Turks, Greeks, Moors, Arabs, and Jews, with intermediate classes and divisions even of these; so that if a traveller wished to see in the shortest time and narrowest space the greatest number of specimens of the human race, he could hardly choose a better spot than Gibraltar for this purpose. The English and French dress much the same as in their respective homes. The Spaniards assume an air of grandeur amidst their poverty, that is sometimes ludicrous.

The persons of distinction among them are attended hy all the parade that they can command; while the clergy, in their monastic and ecclesiastical habits of humility, seem to look on the laity as an inferior race of beings.

The Spanish ladies of Gibraltar were the most interesting of all the various personages that formed the moving panorama of a morning or an evening walk through the town. They are remarkable for the most elegant figures, and a majestic gait, in which they are said to excel the women of every part of the globe. Their complexion is a rich brunette, with regular features, small rosy lips, and beautifully white teeth. They dress universally in black, with a scarf or hood thrown over the head, which covers the ears and neck, and falls gracefully over the shoulders. It is difficult to describe it exactly; but its effect is picturesque and striking. There are indeed many allurements in the beauties of an Andalusian woman, and something irresistible in eyes full of fire and expression, sparkling from beneath fine arched brows, shaded by dark and glossy tresses, and occasionally eclipsed by the seemingly accidental intervention of an elegant fan, the graceful exercise of which displays an arm that serves but to rivet admiration more firmly. These ladies are, however, so carefully at- tended hy female guardiiins, tliat silent homage is all that can be safelj paid to them.

The lower orders of Spaniards here are chiefly Andalusian peasants, who bring in supplies of various kinds to the garrison and town. They still continue the costume of the days of Cervantes, and resemble exactly the peasants of the old Spanish paintings of Murillo, Zurbaran, Velasquez, and others. They wear high and short-quartered shoes of light brown leather, tied with a rose-knot of some gay-coloured ribbon; cotton or silk stockings, often in rags: velvet or leather breeches, the knees and front finely worked with braid; round and hollow silver fillagree buttons, hanging by a slight chain; and long open slashes cut round the thigh, showing a white lining beneath the outer velvet; calico shirts open at the neck, and sometimes turned down over the neck and shoulders, with a frilled collar like the English court dress in the time of the first Charles; a velvet jacket, also worked with braid, with silver fillagree buttons and slashes round the arms; with a black velvet cap and feather, ornamented with silk tassels, not unlike a college cap with the flat portion removed. I was at first surprised to see persons of so low a rank in life dress so expensively, as a suit of this description must cost from 20l. to 30.; but I was told that they were

VOI-. I. A A cliiefly made by the females of the family at home, and that a single suit lasted for many years, which I could well believe from the threadbare condition of many that I saw.

The Portuguese and Italians dress as in their own countries; the Turks with ample sweeping robes and large full turbans, exhibiting a variety of the brightest colours harmoniously blending, and costly scymitars, pistols, and yatagans. The Greeks wear the Albanian dress, with wliite petticoat-trousers, gold-embroidered velvet jackets, gay sashes for the waist, and small red caps for the head. The Moors, many of whom are negroes, and the Arabs from the great Desert of

Sahara, wear the haick, a white serge cloak, with a hood for the head, having neither shirts, turbans, or shoes; and the Armenians, and Barbary Jews from

Morocco, Algiers, Tunis, and even Tripoli and Egypt, have all their several peculiarities of dress by which they are easily distinguished; making altogether the most varied and motley assemblage of human beings, differing in physiognomy, complexion, and dress, from each other, and furnishing a fine school of study for the ethnologist and the cosmopolite.

Gibraltar was first visited by the Moors, who crossed over from Africa here in the invasion of Spain, In A. D. 710, by the General Tarik, from wliom the Rock was called Gebl-el-Tarlk, or the Mountain of Tarik, of which the name Gibraltar is a corruption. It was conquered further hy the Spaniards on the expulsion of the Moors by Ferdinand and Isabella, and remained in their possession till 1704, when it was taken bj the English under Admirals Sir George Rooke and Sir Cloudesley Shovel, its capture being effected by two English captains, Hicks and Jumper, with two boats' crews! a most daring and unprecedented exploit. By the treaty of peace between Spain and Great Britain, it was formally ceded by Philip of Spain to Queen Anne of England, together with Minorca. In 1 727 it was besieged by the Spaniards under the direction of a general of great repute the Conde de la Torres with 20,000 men, who were repulsed by the Earl of Portniore, the English governor, and Admiral Sir Charles Wager. In 1779 it was again invested by the Spaniards, and the English garrison reduced to great distress by the blockade which kept out their supplies of provisions, when Admiral Rodney was sent to its relief, and, after capturing eleven sail of the linetrom the Spaniards off" Cape St. Vincent, he repaired to Gibraltar and rescued it from the impending danger. The grand attack on this envied possession of the English was made a few years afterwards, when all the resources of Spain were collected for its destruction. Many batteries of the largest guns were advanced across the isthmus from Spain, with mortars of the greatest dimensions; and the historians of the siege say, that it seemed as if the Rock must have been overwhelmed with the torrents of fire that were continually disgorged upon it, as the cannonade continued dav and ninht almost incessantly for three weeks, in every day of which 100,000 lbs. of gunpowder were used, and from 4,000 to 5,000 shot and shells were discharged into the town. It then slackened, but was not entirely intermitted for one whole day for upwards of twelve months! The sufferings of the besieged, from death, wounds, and famine, present a horrible picture. Mothers and children, it is stated, clasped in each other's arms, were so completely torn to pieces, tliat it seemed more like an annihilation of their shattered fragments than a dispersion of them! General Elliott, however, defended the place with an intrepidity, coolness, and perseverance, of which history furnishes few similar examples; and though the combined fleets of France and Spain assembled in the Bay of Gibraltar included fifty sail of the line, with a host of floating batteries containing 154 pieces of heavy cannon, besides 300 mortars and howitzers, and a land force of 100,000 men to attack it from the shore, their efforts were wliollj unavailing, and they were obliged to abandon the attempt in despair. The spot is still pointed out where the Queen of Spain and her court sat on one of the hills commanding a view of the Bay, sufficiently removed from danger to view the conflict, and thousands of spectators surrounded her on this conspicuous eminence.

One redeeming feature of this wholesale destrnction of human life is recorded; namely, that the generous humanity of the victors equalled their valour; and that immense efforts were made by the conquerors to save the lives of those who were floating about in the Bay from the vessels that had been sunk and destroyed, many hundreds of whom were thus rescued from a watery grave. This exercise of humanity towards such bitter enemies under such circumstances of recent exasperation and pending danger, conferred more true honour on those who so distiniruished themselves than the victory they had won; and in some measure lessened the impression of sorrow at the madness of mankind in thus slauohterino; each other like demons or fiends, in such wholesale butcheries as these. Since this memorable period Gibraltar has never been attacked, and it is now deemed impregnable against any force.

It is impossible to remember such passages of our history and not to be reminded of the sensible observations of Lady Mary Wortley Montague, in one of her letters to Pope, written after her passage over the fields of Carlowitz, which had been the recent scene of a bloody battle between Prince Eugene and the Turks. " Nothing," says this enlightened and charming writer, " seems to be a plainer proof of the irrationality of mankind (whatever fine claims we pretend to reason), than the rage with which they contest for a small plot of ground, when such vast parts of fruitful earth lie quite uncultivated and uninhabited. It is true, custom has given it its sanction; but can there be a greater demonstration of a want of reason, than a custom being so firmly established so plainly contrary to the interests of mankind in o-eneral? " And in another of her letters to her daughter, the Countess of Bute, when ingeniously comparing the age of the world and the progress of mankind to the stages that mark the periods of human existence, she says, "I imagine we are now arrived at the aoe of fifteen: I cannot think we are older, when I recollect the many)alpable follies which are still almost universally persisted in. I place that of loar as senseless as the boxing of school-boys; and whenever we come to man's estate.

(perhaps a tliousand years hence), I do not doubt it will appear as ridiculous as the pranks of unlucky lads."

The American philosopher and statesman, Franklin, places the subject in perhaps a still more striking point of view; and the period which he selected for his illustration of the wickedness and folly of war, was just about this of the siege of Gibraltar, namely, the contest between the fleets of Lord Rodney and the Count de Grasse in the West Indies. The substance of the apologue under which he presents his view of the subject is this: A mortal transported from earth to heaven, after having for some time enjoyed its beauties and delights, asked one of the angels to take him on a journey through the realms of space, to visit some of the planets, including the earth. The angel consenting to this wish, and both being furnished with wings and the power of immense rapidity of flight, they set out together for this purpose. After visiting several of the planetary orbs in succession, the angel at length conducted his visitor towards the earth, and they arrived just over the West India islands, where two large and powerful fleets were approaching each other; the one was English, commanded by Lord Rodney, the other

French, commanded by the Count de Grasse. As they drew near, the admiral's ship of the English fleet hoisted a red flag, which was answered by the French admiral hoisting a white one. Not a living being in either ship had ever seen the face of any creature in the other. No unfriendly act, or word, or look had ever been exchanged between them, nor was there the least ill-will from any one individual to any other, for the crews were entirely unluiown to each other. Nevertheless, with their flags flying, the ships drew nearer and nearer, till at length they opened their batteries on both sides, and soon the masts, sails, and rigging of each were cut to pieces, as the din of battle arose throuoh the curling clouds of smoke, mingled with the groans of the dying. The sides of the ships ran over with torrents of blood, the dead were cast into the deep, and the whole sea around them became crimsoned with fiore. At sight and hearing of so horrible a scene, the visitor exclaimed to the angel "I desired you to conduct me to the earth, but you have brought me to hell; " to which the angel replied, "Oh! no, devils are far more wise than men; they never war ao-inst each other, any more than tigers or wolves. When they fight, it is at least against another race than their own; man being the only creature that seems to take a delight and that without provocation in revellino; in the blood of his own kind."

This was written by me in my Journal forty-two years ago (1812); and now, while transcribing it from thence for the press (1854), the frightful details of the siege of Sebastopol, and the battles of the Alma, Balaclava, and Inkerman, are filling every English heart with horror; yet one or two solitary voices alone call out for its cessation, while millions demand only more reinforcements to continue the work till Russia shall be humbled to the dust, and her ambition of conquest destroyed. This being the demand of France, who robbed Turkey of her African dominions by force of arms! and of England, who overthrew the Mohammedan empire of India, and has conquered from its native princes and people an empire containing a hundred and fifty millions of people, and a revenue of twenty millions sterling! How true is it that nations have one standard of justice for themselves and another for the rest of mankind!

Departure from Gibraltar for Malta. Mountains of Europe and Africa. Ancient lake. Constant currents inward from the Atlantic Equal supply from the Euxine and from large rivers. Theories of evaporation and under currents Opposite coasts of Spain and Numidia. Classical reminiscences. Hippo Regius. Carthage. Anecdote of a naval captain's caprices. Impress of officers and seamen, and their restitution. Arrival at Malta. Harbour of St. Paul. Imposing entrance of the port of La Valetta Stay at Malta. Brief notices of the island. Remarkable instance of cruelty and superstition. British influence on native character and society. Manners of private life and entertainments.

The business of the ship having been completed, we prepared to sail, and left Gibraltar for Malta, with a fleet under convoy of the Cyane, a twentj-eight-gun frigate, in the beginning of July, when the climate, though warm, was inexpressibly delightful to the feelings. The narrow passage by which the transit from the Atlantic to the Mediterranean is effected is not more in some parts than five leagues across; and though Europe and Africa are thus brought face to face, as it were, there is sufficient general resemblance between the mountains, the valleys, and the coasts on either side, to justify or confirm the belief or tradition that these two continents were once united, that the Mediterranean was then a closed lake, the barrier having at some remote period of history been broken through, and the low lands so completely submerged as to leave only the mountains to form its present boundaries.

The first peculiarity which arrests the attention of a navigator on enterino; the Mediterranean, is the constant settino; of the current inward through the Straits, without any visible outlet for such a constant accumulation of water; more especially as it is well known that the Euxine or Black Sea, with all its mighty rivers of the Don, the Dniester, and the Danube, pours a constant stream into the Bosphorus and Sea of Marmora, and thence by the Archipelago of Greece into the INIediterranean also; in addition to which, the Nile of Africa, the Po of Italy, and the Rhone of France, to say nothing of smaller streams, all pour their waters into the same great reservoir. The celebrated Dr. Halley, in the Transactions of the Royal Society, endeavoured to prove that the evaporation continually arising from the surface of the Mediterranean was sufficient to account for the loss of all the water poured into it from these various sources, and that a large portion of this evaporation being blown southward by the Etesian winds, up the valley of the Nile, and across Africa, till it came in contact with the chain of Atlas and the Mountains of the Moon, not far from the equator, produced those heavy rains which fed the annual inundations of the Nile, and brought back the water thus taken from it to its original place again.

Nautical men generally, however, maintain that there is an under current of water running outward from the Mediterranean to the Atlantic, which restores the balance; and this is confirmed by many facts of ships being sunk in certain positions within the Straits, and their hulls being afterwards found considerably to the westward: while experiments tried by sounding lines and other contrivances for ascertaining the existence of under currents, all tend to confirm this theory, which may now be considered established. So rapid is the upper current, however, settino; in from the Atlantic to the Mediterranean, as to flow at the rate of four and five miles an hour, and to make it difficult for any but the very fastest ships of war to beat to windward against it; so that while passages into the Straits are best made in mid-channel, where the force of the current is strongest, outward-bound ships effect their passage best by keeping close in shore and availing themselves of the eddies which there set towards the Atlantic, though at a much feebler rate.

As we had the wind from the eastward, we had to beat across the Straits, but having the in-setting current under our lee, we made good progress, and the standino; from shore to shore, thouiih leno-thenino- the voyage while it lasted, increased the interest, as we passed from beneath the snow-clad summits of the Sierra Nevada, rising; over Granada and the Alham-bra, which were quite visible as we neared the coast about Malaga, and then stood over to the arid shores of the ancient Mauritania and Numidia. In the course of our transit we passed many Spanish and Portuguese vessels, all of the most inferior kind in build, equipment, and still more, if possible, in evolutions or handling by their crews, in which they seem to stand at the very lowest)oint of the scale, and immeasurably below the English, though they were once so greatly their superiors. In contrasting the present naval superiority of Great Britain to both Spain and Portugal, we cannot but be forcibly struck with the vicissitudes of human affairs. Thomson, the English poet, has a pleasing and accurate allusion to the early superioritj of the latter kingdom espe-ciallj, in the following lines:

"Then, from ancient gloom emerged
The rising world of Trade! the genius then
Of Navigation, that in hopeles sloth
Had slumbered in the vast Atlantic deep
For idle ages, starting, heard, at last,

The Lusitanian Prince, who, heaven-inspired,
To love of useful glory roused mankind,
And in unbounded Commerce mixed the world!"

Even when Camoens wrote the Lusiacl, about the reign of our Eighth Henry, of so little importance did England appear in the scale of maritime nations, that the poet, in his description of Europe, omits all mention of England; while in the episode respecting the Twelve English Knights, which Veloso introduces to cheer his companions of the mid-watch, Camoens merely notices England as being always covered with snow.

La na grande Inglaterra, que de neve
Boreal semper abunda."

On the African shore we passed along the tract of land in which were established the maritime colonies of Hippo Regius, to the westward of Carthage, which was once filled with monuments of Roman art and luxuiy, but of which few or no traces now remain. Crossing over again, while beating up against an easterly wind, we neared the Spanish coast, Avithin sight of the snowy mountains of Granada half enveloped in clouds, and soon after passed Cape de Gatte, one of the most striking headlands or promontories on this side of the sea.

Contiiming our onward way, as winds and circumstances admitted, we soon passed the islands of Majorca and Minorca, the latter remarkable for one of the finest harbours in the woi'ld, and now both belonging to Spain, and on the 15tli of July we made the island of Sardinia, in sight of which we remained several days, detained by calms and contrary winds, being sometimes within half a cable's length of the shore. It presents a succession of high rugged mountains, with immense masses of rock projecting on all sides, the intervening spaces being filled up with a light coloured hetith or grass. Even the low lands present an aspect of general sterility, except in a few sloping plains that approach the sea. It is said, however, to have many fertile valleys in the interior, and the mountains are reported to be inhabited by almost savage aboriginal tribes. The soil of the island produces corn, the vine, and a variety of excellent fruits, and the smaller islets which skirt its coasts furnish good cattle, turtle, and game. There are also mines of some value, which were anciently worked to advantage, but these have fallen into neglect, under a careless government and an indolent people.

Standing ao-ain to the southward, with lio-ht airs from the east, which impeded our progress in that direction, we came within sight of that portion of the African coast on which the Carthage of antiquity stood, and of which the destruction is so complete, that there are barely remains enough of its wreck to enable travellers to trace its site.

It was here that one morning at day-light I was suddenly revised from my cot by the whistling sound of a cannon ball cutting the air within a few yards of our stern, and jumping instantly on deck, I found it was a shot from the Commodore of the fleet, with a special signal to us to tack and regain our position. In the course of the night, from the want of proper vigilance on the part of the officer of the watch, we had fallen a little to leeward, and this was the authoritative missive by which we were reprovcd for the negligence. We obeyed the signal of course, tacked immediately, and stood on till we passed under the stern of the Cxjane, which led the convoy. There we wcre ordered to back the main-topsail and pre- pare to receive a boat from the Commodore. This done, a lieutenant, midshipman, and cutter's crew came alongside, and as soon as the officer came on deck he ordered the crew to be mustered. All hands were piped up for this purpose; when, to our surprise and mortification, he selected the second mate, the carpenter, and six of the finest men and ablest seamen of the crew, and ordered them into the cutter, with their chests and hammocks, as the Cyane was short-handed, and His Majesty had need of their services. The men were all most reluctant to go, and would have resisted, but the cutter's crew were all armed with pistols and cutlasses, as an ordinary press-gang, and resistance would have been useless. I told the officer, we should enter a protest against the Commodore in our log, and that his commander would hear from me again on the subject; at which he laughed heartily, as though it were the most absurd thing on earth to hope for redress against any injury inflicted by a man-of-war.

The signal being displayed to make sail, we proceeded on our course; but as soon as the cutter was gone, I went to my cabin, and wrote a letter to the Commodore, in which I endeavoured to point out the injustice of his conduct; saying that if his ship wanted hands, nothing would have been more easy

VOL. I. B B than to press a single seaman from each vessel in the fleet, by which his strength would be considerably-increased, while no one would have been materially Aveakened; but that by taking eight of our very best men, he had placed us in such a position that for Avant of them we might possibly be unable to fulfil the proper duties of the ship in case of danger; and that if wrecked or taken by pirates, in consequence of this loss, the protest which I had entered in the ship's log-book, of which I enclosed him a copy, would be used by the underwriters as the ground of an action at law against him for damages, and he might be made to pay the whole value of the ship and cargo. I added, further, an appeal to his own sense of justice and honour, and (somewhat pedantically I admit) quoted for his consideration a passage of Cicero, to the effect, " that the true magnanimity of men in authority was as advantageously displayed in clemency towards involuntary offences, as in severity towards wilful and premeditated crime;" and I closed my letter by asking the Commodore to permit me to wait upon him personally, or to return me at least a portion of the men he had impressed from my crew.

This letter was sent on board the frigate by the hands of my chief officer, Mr. Brock, in our own boat.

in a short interval of calm which enabled him to reach the ship. On coming alongside, he was permitted to come on deck, where he was met by the Commodore himself, to whom he presented the letter; after reading which the angry commander tore it into pieces, and throwing them over the lee-quarter, said to the bearer: " You may return to your ship, Sir, and tell your master, there is no answer."

This was very mortifying; but perseverance in a good cause is the duty of all, and waiting my opportunity, some three days after this it fell calm again when, being pretty near the frigate, a station I had always endeavoured to keep, I had my own boat manned, and went to pay the Commodore an uninvited visit. He perceived our approach with his spy-glass from the cabin-window, and hastened on deck, where in a few minutes hands were sent into all the tops to set the royals and light studding-sails to catch any air that might be floating aloft; and while the heavy canvas of the courses and topsails clung idly and immoveably to the mast, the thinner canvas of the loftier sails swelled out every now and then with evidence of an upper breeze, by which the frigate crept through the water at the rate of from three to four knots, and made our pull in a hot July sun all the more fatiguing to reach her. At length we got alongside, and I was soon on the quarter deck, where I reported myself to the officer of the watch who came to the gangway to meet me, as " Captain Buckingham of the ship William, desiring to speak with the Commodore." This announcement drew a crowd of young officers, lieutenants, masters' mates, and midshipmen around me, anxious, it would seem, to see a man who had the " audacity" (for that was the term used) to think of remonstrating with a Commodore; and such a one too as their commander, who was reputed throughout the fleet to be a Tartar. At length the Commodore himself appeared from his cabin, saluting me ironically, by lifting high from his head the cocked hat, then universally worn on duty, and making a low bow, as if he were about to addi'ess a superior. He then surveyed me from head to foot, as if he would penetrate my very inmost parts by his dark eagle-eyes; and after a minute or two of profound silence he exclaimed, "And so, Sir, you thought to knock me down, first with the threat of a lawsuit by Lloyds' underwriters, and next by a sentence of Cicero, a dead old Roman. Now, Lloyds and Cicero be damned. Sir, and you too with them. I know my duty as Commodore of this fleet, and have half a mind to send you below to join your old shipmates," I replied, "As you please. Sir; I can only say, if you do, I abandon my ship to your charge, and you will be held responsible for the consequences." The calmness and self-possession with which this was said, evidently produced an impression of its sincerity. No further words were addressed to me by the Commodore; but turning to the officer of the deck, he said, "Send the fellow back again, and make all sail." I accordingly returned to my boat, regained my ship, and in three hours after this, my second mate and carpenter, and four out of the six pressed men, were returned to me by the officer who first took them out. Such were the despotic caprices of naval men in those times, now happily numbered among the things that are passed. And yet this very commander stood high in the opinion of the service as a " smart officer," who could always be depended on; and whose courage was no doubt unimpeachable, however weak his discretion.

A freshening breeze from the westward was a wel-come relief after our long detention by light airs and calms, and we profited by the change to crowd all sail direct for Malta. In approaching this island from the west, we passed close to the smaller island of Gozo, within half a mile of the shore, as the water is everywhere deep around the whole group. This was the island in which Telemachus and INIcntor were said to have been wrecked and sumptuously entertained by Calypso; and it was with increased pleasure I read, for the third time, the exquisite romance of Telemachus, so full of wisdom as well as beauty, as we coasted along the shores rendered for ever interesting by the association with poetry and philosophy combined. It must be admitted, however, that we saw nothing of the grotto of the goddess in our progress, nor did we observe those verdant banks eternally covered with flowers, nor those lofty trees for ever in bloom, that lost their heads in the clouds, and afforded a sacred shade to the baths of herself and her companions. These may have existed in ancient days, or have been the creations of the poet's fancy: at least they are not to be seen at present.

Drawing nearer to the chief port of Malta, we passed also the creek called " The harbour of St. Paul," in which it is believed that the great apostle of the Gentiles was wrecked, in his memorable voyage from Cesarea to Rome, where he was afoino- to appeal to Caesar against the unjust sentence of the colonial governor of Judea, as related in the Acts of the Apostles. The spot seems well adapted for the circumstances of which it is believed to have been the scene; and though there have been some critics who contend that the island of " Melita," for

SO it is called in the Greek of the New Testament, was at the entrance of the Adriatic Sea, the evidences are greatly in favour of Malta being the island indicated, where the centurion and the crew were saved, as well as Paul, from the destruction with which they were threatened, and where the barbarians were astonished at seeing the viper fall harmless from the apostle's hand, as it crept from the wood prepared for the fire, and which made them regard him as a god.

At length, about sunset, we were abreast of the opening to the harbour of Valetta, and entered it soon after. Nothing can be conceived more imposing than the scene presented to the navigator who for the first time sees this magnificent port. Though the entrance is extremely narrow (a great advantage to its strength of defence), tlie depth of water is everywhere sufticient for the largest slii)s of war that float: and the fortifications and batteries that guard the entrance on either hand, where the guns rise tier over tier in countless numbers, seem to threaten instant annihilation to any enemy that should dare to approach it. As you go further up the harbour, the public and private buildings of the ciry add greatly to the effect, and produce an impression of strength, durability, and opulence, which few island settlements can boast. Lateral harbours, in creeks leading from the main harbour into the land, afford shelter for smaller craft and vessels under repair; and, as an island fortress, a splendid naval station, and an imposing city, I had never yet seen anything equal to Malta as a whole.

After securing the ship at her moorings, I went on shore to see the merchant to Avhom we were consigned, and remained at Malta about a fortnia; ht transactino- the business required, taking note of Avhat was most remarkable, and recording my impressions at the time.

The period I passed in Malta was one continued round of hospitality from its merchants and their families, to whom I became known during my short stay there; and scarce a day passed without an excursion into the country, or an evening party in town; and in my intercourse with the most intelligent of these, added to such observations as I had an opportunity of making personally among the general mass of the inhabitants, I gathered up the information which is here presented in a condensed form.

The island of Malta is about 50 miles in circumference, its extreme length being 17, and its greatest breadth 9 miles. It is one mass of white limestone rock; and, from the appearance of its cliffs on the soutliern side towards Africa, there arc reasons to believe that it once formed a part of that great continent, though distant now from tlic nearest part of it 198 miles. Its aborimnal inhabitants seem more African than European in their physiognomy and complexion, and the indigenous language spoken by them is a barbarous mixture of Phoenician and Arabic; so that they are probably a mixed race of Carthaginians and Moors, subsequently still more varied by admixture with other races, particularly with Greeks and Italians.

The principal city is Valetta, which crowns the peninsula that separates the principal harbour from the quarantine ground,—the houses rising so steeply from the water's edge to the suinmit, as to present a series of flat-roofed terraces, each overlooking the one below it. Thus the side streets ascending from the harbour to the upper part of the city are literally flights of steps, with a platform at each cross street going in a lateral direction, these being the only level streets in the town. The public buildings and principal private residences are on the crest of the hill, and here the streets are broad and well paved, though most of the others are narrow; but as all of them are built of the white limestone of the island, and the fortifications are of the same structure, there is every- wliere an air of solidity and durability which strikingly contrasts with the slender wooden buildings of most of our colonies, the West India islands especially. There is another town, called Civita Vecchia, or the old city, in the interior, which is still the seat of the Archbishop's see, and has several monasteries, nunneries, and churches; but as there is no trade or commerce there, the grass grows in the streets, and the place has the silence of death. All the other settlements in Malta are mere villages, called casals, the houses of which are built of stone, as the cheapest material at hand; and the grounds around them cultivated with cotton of two sorts, white and brown, some grain, and the vegetables and fruits most marketable in the cities, and most conducive to their own subsistence.

The most remarkable, and at the same time the most encouraging, fact connected with the history and agriculture of Malta is this: that at an early period of its history, it was a barren rock, without soil and without production, till the Knights of St. John of Jerusalem, to whom the island was ceded by Charles the Fifth on their being driven out from the Holy Land and Cyprus, procured supplies of soil from Sicily, overlaid a large portion of the surface of the rock, and so increased its productive powders.

that it now sustains a larger population on a given area than almost any spot in the world, being about 600 inhabitants to the square mile; the average of what is by many considered to be " over-peopled" Ireland, containing 250 persons to the square mile.

During our stay at Malta we visited several times the palace or country residence of the Governor, and enjoyed many agreeable walks in its delightful gardens, partaking freely of the fruits with which it abounds, especially the grapes, and the dark blood-red orange peculiar to the island, and of exquisite freshness and flavour.

We visited also most of the churches, and especially that of St. John, the principal cathedral, admiring the richness of its decorations, and especially the portraits of the grand masters, from the earliest to the last of the order, executed in a mosaic so fine as not to be distinguishable from oil paintings on canvass, except in certain angles of light from the sun. The whole pavement of the church is a series of gorgeous tomb slabs executed in mosaic of bright coloured marbles, and covering the remains of the knights of the order interred below. We were told that the gates which separated the chancel from the nave, at the time of the knights, were of solid bar silver; and that when Napoleon Bonaparte on his way to Egypt, captured the island, finding his funds run short, he had these gates removed, melted down, and coined into dollars on the spot, to recruit his finances, which act of sacrilege, as it was deemed, excited the utmost horror and indig-nation in all classes. In consequence of this, conspiracies were formed, among laymen as well as priests, to inflict signal vengeance on the officers who superintended this work of desecration. Four of these conspirators, we were assured by persons living at Malta at the time, entered into a vow to feast on the heart of a certain French officer, who had made himself peculiarly obnoxious by his activity in thus despoiling the church of its chief treasure. The officer was accordingly waylaid, murdered, and his heart torn from his body. It was then cut into small pieces while yet warm, and served up, with the blood still reeking, to these infuriated cannibals. They had actually seated themselves round this bowl of human flesh and blood, and were about to devour its contents, when one of the party suddenly remembered that it was Friday, and that as good Catholics they could not, Avithout offending the rules of Holy Church, taste flesh-meat on that day. This was an insuperable obstacle. No scruples as to the murder and the cannibalism of the act had ever interposed themselves, or, if they had, they were easily conquered; but this scruple as to the sin of eating flesh on a fast-day was sufficient to stay even their bloody banquet. The dish was accordingly put by for the day; and, revolting as is the fact, we were assured that they met together after mass on the following Sunday, and literally fulfilled their vow of feasting on the heart of their victim!

It is hoped and believed that the influence and example of the British Government, to which Malta is now subject, the presence of so many of the civil and military officers necessary for its administration and protection, the constantly increasing number of English merchants, visitors, and residents, will help to soften these ferocious traits of superstition; and that the blending of English and Italian society and manners may have the effect of greatly improving the tone of thought and feeling amono; the INIaltese themselves, though they will always perhaps preserve some distinctive traits of character.

In the dinner and evening parties which I had the pleasure to attend during my stay here, I found a happy mixture of English reserve and decorum, French vivacity and politeness, and Italian softness and languor, so tempering each other as to make a much more agreeable whole thon either of them separately. The three languages were generally understood, though Italian was more current than French, and French better known than English. The dinner parties were less formal, less heavy, and occupied much less time than at home, though chiefly given by the English. The evening receptions were in the French style, with no other refreshment than coffee, lemonade, and ices, but most agreeable and brilliant conversation; and the balls, notwithstanding the heat of the climate, as animated as those I had seen in the West Indies, and enjoyed more thoroughly than in London.

Departure from Malta for the Archipelago. First sight of the shores of Greece. The Morea. Island of Cerigo or Cythera. The birth of Venus. Pirates of Greeks and renegades of all nations. Islands of Falconera and Milo. Surrounding scenery. The " Shipwreck " of Falconer. Similarity of feeling. Enter the harbour of Milo for a pilot. Greek visitors. Hatred of Turks. Attachment to Russia. Excursion to the town of Milo on the mountain. Patriarchal state of society and manners. Incident between an English lady and a Greek mother. Expensiveness of female costume. Family garments. First acquisition for forming an antiquarian taste. Voyage through the iegean Sea. Crowded impressions. Explanation of motives for future brevity of description.

My anticipations of pleasure from our voyage through the Greek Archipelago to Smyrna, grew higher and higher as the period of our departure approached; and in the intervals of leisure I could command, I read all the books I had with me on the East, and conversed with every one I met with from that classic region, on its present state and condition.

All our preparations for sea being completed, we sailed from Malta on the 25th of July; and being favoured with a fine breeze throughout the night, we had lost sight of the island at daybreak on the fol- lowing morning, when we discovered a polacca-rigged vessel ahead. As piracies were of frequent occurrence in this sea, committed both by Greek and Austrian corsairs, whenever there was a sufficient disparity of force to ensure them against resistance, we w ere on our guard against any sudden attack, and prepared our ship for action, by calling all hands to quarters, loosing the guns, and having matches lighted. As we crowded all sail, we overhauled the polacca about noon; and running close alongside her to windward, just to show that wc were sufficiently well armed and manned not to fall an easy prize to any marauder, we passed on without molestation; and continuing still under a heavy press of sail, we left her so rapidly, that at sunset she was nearly hull down astern.

On the following morning, having had a fine run during the night, the rising sun displayed to our view the lofty hills of Greece, his morning beams shedding on their blue ridges the richest varietv of tints. It was the land between Cape Drosso and Cape Matapan, the southernmost promontory of the modern Morea, and the soil of the ancient Sparta. It is impossible to describe the sensations I felt on beholding, for the first time, these venerable shores. Throughout the whole of the day, as we steered along its capes and bays, I was in a state of excited enthusiasm; and, Avliile viewing those now silent and barren mountains, transported myself in imagination to every spot renowned in Grecian history, burning with impatience to tread its classic ground; but struck, like Byron, with the deathlike stillness and entire absence of all animation which seemed everywhere to prevail, and which led to his beautiful and touching apostrophe and comparison in the opening of the Giaour, beginning

"He who hath bent him o'er the dead Ere the first day of death has fled,"
and ending

"Such is the aspect of this shore. 'Tis Greece! but hving Greece no more; So coldly sweet, so deadly fair, We start for soul is wanting there. Chme of the unforgotten brave! Whose land, from plain to mountain cave. Was Freedom's home, or Glory's grave; Shrine of the Mighty! can it be That this is all remains of thee!"

At six P. M. we hauled round the cape, which is a bluff, ragged point, and the Gulf of Bagene or Co-lokythia, deriving both its names from two small

VOL. I. c c towns situated within it. A heavy thunderstorm gathering, we took in all the light sails, and single reefed the topsails. It burst, however, without occasioning us any serious injury, and w as followed by a serene sky and steady bj'eeze, when we sliook out oiir reefs, made all sail, and stood on for the channel of CeriitO. Durino; the whole of the nisjlit we lay becalmed between the two islands of Cervi and Cerigo, the latter being the ancient Cythera, the fabled birthplace of Venus from the foam of the sea; and a great number of most suspicious looking craft Avere nearer to us than we thought desirable. The wdiole of this and the neio-hbourino; coast of Greece was at this time infested by a race of pirates, boastins; their descent from the ancient Lacedre-monians, and who acknowledge no law" but that of the strongest. In calm weather these pirates come off in fast-sailing or swift-rowing craft, and plunder indiscriminately all vessels incapable of defending themselves against aggression; taking care, however, to ascertain, if possible, the extent of their powers of resistance beforehand, and then, if necessary, to overwhelm them by numbers. A knowledge of this circumstance induced us to be on our guard; and having all our guns ready, matches lighted, and boarding-pikes and muskets on deck, tlie whole of tlie crew, officers, and passengers, remained on deck the entire night, ready for any emergency. Our state of preparation alone saved us, as three or four smaller vessels, less carefully provided against attack, were carried off and towed into the creeks of the coast before our eyes, and without its being in our power, in the profound calm, to render them the slightest assistance.

Amid this scene of tranquil beauty, as far as the grand features of Nature composed the picture, I enjoyed, notwithstanding the momentaiy expectation of a battle, the full force of those poetic associations which the mere hills and rocks, the glassy sea, and the balmy air around us were calculated to bring vividly to my remembrance. Among the poems which I read with increased delight, upon the spot itself, was the beautiful ode of Moore, entitled " The Fall of Hebe," which contains a luxurious description of Venus, under the name of Cytherea, laying her head upon the lap of Lyjbus:

"All must be luxury where Lyteus smiles, His locks divine Were crowned With a bright meteor brait

Wliicli, like an ever-springing wreath of vine,

Shot into brilliant leafy shapes, And o'er his brow in lambent tendrils played; While mid the foliage hung.

Like livid grapes, A thousand clustering blooms of light. Culled from the gardens of the galaxy! Upon his bosom Cytherea's head Lay lovely, as when first tl: e Syrens sung

Her beauty's dawn, And all the curtains of the deep undrawn Revealed her sleeping in her azure bed."

After a slow progress, from light and variable winds, which, in any other part of the world would have been tedious, but was here onlj a prolongation of scenes and associations of the most agreeable kind, we came in sight of Falconera, Mile, and its surrounding islands, intending to call at the latter, as is usual, for a pilot It was from the island of Falconera that the marine poet Falconer, in his inimitable " Shipwreck," took that animated survey of the classic regions by which his ship, the Britannia, was then surrounded, and from whence he so skilfully and accurately enumerates all the characteristic traits: Athens, Corinth, and Sparta; Thermopyla3, Arcadia, Ithaca, Argos, and Mycena?; Dclos, Lemnos, and Troy, to Delphos and Parnassus, with all the promi- nent points connected with the mythology, history, and poetry undyingly connected with each. I had read his beautiful and touching work again and again, and always with increased pleasure; but never with such intense enjoyment as while sailing through the Greek Archipelago, with the very places he so graphically describes passing successively before my eyes. To enjoy this the more fully, as soon as the sails were trimmed, I repaired to the maintop, and there, alone, and absorbed with the subject, enjoyed it free from any interruption; for there was not a creature on board who could have the least sympathy in my pleasures, in which my condition was just like that of the poet himself, who, speaking of his shipmates who formed the crew of the Britannia, says: ' Did they,

Unskilled in Grecian or in Roman lore, Unconscious pass each fame-encircled shore? They did for, blasted in the barren shade, Here, all too soon, the buds of learning fiide: Sad Ocean's genius in untimely hour Withers the bloom of every springing flower; Here Fancy droops, while sullen cloud and storm The generous climate of the soul deform."

At length we reached the harbour of Milo, just in time to find shelter from a sudden and violent north- cast gale; and finding good anchorage in a commo dious harbour, we remained here till the gale abated.

In the course of an hour we received a visit from a Greek, the brother of the British vice-consul, these posts being most injudiciously filled, throughout the Levant, not by Englishmen, but by Greeks, Armenians, and other foreigners, who, having no particular regard for the interests or honoui- of the nations they professedly represent, are generally indifferent to both, especially if their own interests clash with either. This gentleman was accompanied by a Greek priest, by the chief secretary, and by his son, a handsome and intelligent youth of fifteen, who afterwards became a pilot, and was the individual who was killed alongside the English admiral's ship by the first shot that commenced the battle of Navarino, under Sir Edward Codrington, some years afterwards. They all spoke Italian, so that we needed no interpreter, as I had been for some time familiar with that tono'ue.

Among my books in the cabin, was a copy of " Eton's Survey of the Turkish Empire," in English. The work was well known to my Greek visitor, and, taking it down and opening it, he found, what he had seen appended to other copies of the same work, a version, in modern Greek, of the " Memorial pre- sentecl by the Greek Deputies to the Empress Catherine of Russia, imploring her to place her grandson over the Greek nation as their Emperor." This gave rise to an animated conversation on the tyranny of the Turks; and after reading the Memorial aloud to his companions, all of whom seemed to be greatly excited by its contents, he translated it into Italian for me, and endeavoured to enlist my sympathies in the cause of Greek Emancipation. He said that there was not a Greek under the Turkish rule who was not penetrated with the greatest hatred of their despotism; and that they all longed for the opportunity to show that they had courage enough to win their independence, and wisdom enough to maintain it. This was in 1812; and from that period on to the outbreak of their successful revolution, their love of liberty grew more and more intense. Of the use they have made of it, there will no doubt be many different opinions, but no Englishman who enjoys the fruits of our own " glorious revolution," can consistently blame the Greeks for achievino; theirs.

On the following morning, an invitation came from the patriarchal chief of Milo, to pay him and his family a visit; and as the gale from the northeast made it perfectly useless to leave the harbour till it abated, I gladly accepted the opportunity of seeing a new place and a new community. Leaving the ship in charge of the pilot, and accompanying the guide sent to escort us to the town, which stood on the highest pinnacle of the rocky island, and from below seemed wholly inaccessible, we landed at the watering-place, amid the ruins of ancient Greek baths and fragments of sculptured marble, and found here several asses saddled for our use. I mounted mine astride, according to the English mode, which excited shouts of laughter; and I soon discovered that the Greek mode of riding was very different; they sat sideways on the saddle, both feet hanging down the right side and resting in a grass-rope stirrup, the left arm being used for the bridle. I accordingly adopted this mode also; and as we advanced up the mountain I found its advantage, as we had frequently to travel in ruts, or cuttings in the rocks, so narrow that the animal's body could barely pass through, so that we had to hold our legs up, and throw them over the creature's neck. The distance was only two miles, and it took an hour and half to traverse it, the paths being such as no English horse would venture upon, and often on the edge of a precipice, with not three inches of margin to spare. I felt more terrified in some parts of the route than I had ever been hy danger of any kind at sea.

When we reached the foot of the town, we were obliged to ah'ght and walk up the remainder of the waj, the street being literally flights of steps, and the houses so placed that the roof of the lower one is just on a level with the foundation of the one above it. This position was chosen for safety against pirates. The mountain terminates in a sharp point, and around this the houses are built. The entrance to the town is through an arched gateway, which we ascended by a flight of steps; and we found the streets within this gate mere narrow passages, just allowing two persons to pass freely, and hewn out of the solid rock into steps, the angle of elevation being from 40 to 50, and the houses, about a hundred in number, all constructed of solid blocks of stone.

After being gazed at by all the women and children, and barked at by the dogs as strangers, we at length reached the chief's house, which was but a little larger than the others, and consisted only of two rooms on the same floor, but clean and orderly. We were received by him with great cordiality; he spoke English fluently, and entertained us with the best the island could afford. Though nearly a hundred years old, he appeared to have all the rosy health, vigour, and activity of an English fanner of sixty, or a shipmaster of fifty. He was the father of twenty-five children, and nearly all the male population of the town had sprung from his loins, the sons marrying wives from other islands, and the daughters getting husbands also from other towns. The name of this patriarch was Antonio Mitchello; he was born in this island in 1715, wanting therefore only three years to complete a century. He went to sea at nine years old, became a pilot for the Archipelago, and followed that profession till he was seventy, when he retired, and gave place to his sons. Though he had no appointment from the British Government, he was proud to call himself English consul, and rendered all the aid and hospitality his means allowed to ships of that nation.

At noon, a second party came up from the harbour, consisting of a naval commander, an English traveller, two merchant captaiiis, and two English ladies with an infant; and after these had been duly received and refreshed, we all accompanied the chief in paying visits to his descendants, stopping at every house almost for a few minutes, and taking either wine or sweetmeats at each. At one of these a scene occvirred which seemed at first alarming, but happily went off smoothly at last. The infant of one of the

English ladies had particularly excited the attention of all the Greek women, who strove to ovitvie each other in their expressions of tenderness towards it; and one of them, who was nursing a child of her own, as a mark of especial fondness, suckled the little stranger at her breast. The English lady, perceiving it, rushed from her chair, tore the infant from the bosom of the Greek, and, overcome with agitation, had scarcely time to reach her seat before she swooned away.

It is impossible to describe the surprise of the Greeks at such an unexpected incident. They silently looked at each other with the wild stare of astonishment, until surprise gave way to indignation, and they unanimously declared it to be an insult of the grossest kind. The Greek mother expostulated through the chief, who acted as her interpreter, and asked whether the English lady doubted the purity of her milk, or the chastity of her character; the former, she said, was " as unmixed as the rain of heaven," and the latter " as white as the snow of the mountain." These were her literal expressions. One of the English party then said that the English mother was in the act of weaning her infant, and wished to deprive it of the breast altogether, which was the only excuse that could be admitted; though, the infant being only four months old, many seemed to doubt the truth of this assertion. The good nature of the Greeks soon overcame all difficulties, however, and harmony was at length happily restored.

When we all dined together, later in the day, the English ladies revolted at the deg; radino; sio; ht of the Greek females all acting as waiters or servants; and their astonishment was at its height when they learnt that the wives and daughters never sat at table at the same time with the husband and brother, but always ate alone, and were content with whatever happened to be left by their lords and masters. This is a practice the Greeks must have borrowed from the Turks.

In the evening we all went to visit a bride and bridegroom who had been just married, and we were struck by the great predominance of female beauty of the true classic mould in the party, as well as with the sumptuousness of some of the dresses, many of which we were told were worth 200l. sterlincr each. These, however, are richly embroidered robes with gold and gems, which pass on from mother to daughter for several generations, each adding something to make them richer still. That worn by the chief's granddaughter was reckoned to be more than two centuries old.

Though Milo was at this time nominally under the

Turkish government, there was not a single Mohammedan in the island. Indeed it was said no Turk wovild venture on tlie experiment, as every Greek would think it an act of merit to kill him, in such detestation is the whole race held. Of government, indeed, thej could be said to have none, the chief hearing appeals in all disputed cases, and his decisions being never resisted. Every man seemed to be his own cultivator, builder, and mechanic; and as the community subsist almost entirely on the produce of the island, corn, sheep, goats, fish, poultry, and game, being abundant, with grapes, olives, melons, and other fruits, and cotton, wool, and skins for clothing, they have no need of foreign trade, and are as independent, and apparently as happy and contented except with their political degradation as possible; while the climate is delicious, and makes bare existence, with competency of food and raiment, pleasureable.

Milo was a flourishing republic some centuries before Christ, but has undergone all the vicissitudes of the Greek nation and people. In 1700 Tourne-fort describes it as containing 20,000 inhabitants. At present there is barely 1000, though the island is fifty miles in circumference, has many fertile plains and valleys, and one of the finest harbours in the world, being nearly circular, from twelve to fifteen miles round, with all depths of water from five to fiftj fathoms, excellent holding-ground, and capable of containing a thousand ships at once, being so completely land-locked and well sheltered, that, when anchored within, the entrance or outlet of the harbour cannot be perceived.

As we returned to embark in the evening from the watering-place where the natural springs and fragments of ancient Greek baths exist, my attention was arrested by a sparkling point, like a small piece of glass or crystal in a heap of dehns; and on taking it up I found it to be a genuine Athenian silver coin, about the circumference of an English sixpence, but four or five times as thick, with an owl in relief on the one side, and the word Athena, in Greek capitals, on the other. As this was the first acquisition I had ever made in the way of antiquities, it affoixled me a new pleasure, and helped to stimulate a taste as yet quite in embryo, but which, like most other passions or hobbies, as by some they are regarded, grows by what it feeds on, and increases with every new acquisition.

On the following morning, we sailed from Milo for Smyrna, and had a most delightful passage through the gean Sea, passing the numerous islands with wliich it is studded, as well as the coast of Attica, embracing Athens, Salamis, and Marathon; all so suggestive of history, poetry, philosophy, art, eloquence, and valour, as to become really oppressive from the multiplicity of thoughts and feelings which were crowded into so limited a space of time. We were favoured with lio-ht and variable airs durino- all the former part of this short passage, which enabled us thus to thread our way in so devious a course. But at length a strong northerly gale, the Etesian wind of the ancients, set in, and compelled us to shape our course to the eastward, which soon brought us over to the island of Samos and in the neighbourhood of Ephesus, spots as renowned as many of the others we had passed; the former the birthplace of Pythagoras, whose doctrines effected such changes among his contemporaries, and the second the site of the temple of the great Diana, whose image her worshippers believed had descended to them from heaven, and to whom Paul preached in the theatre against their idolatry, but whose eloquence was drowned in the tumult and the cry of ' Great is Diana of the Ephesians!"

Of all these memorable places which passed, as it were, in panoramic view before my eyes, at a period of my life when my mind and heart were full of poetry and love of the grand and the heroic, I wrote copious accounts in the Diarj which I had begun to keep with great regularity since I entered the Mediterranean Sea, and of which I still retain the originals; and I have the greatest difficulty in repressing the desire to introduce portions of these records here. But their omission wall afford a greater space to the personal narrative to which an Autobiography ought in strictness to be confined.

I have no doubt, however, that there will be many readersjwdio, when Icome to speak of Alexandria, Cairo, Memphis, Thebes, Jerusalem, Damascus, Baalbeck, Antioch, Nineveh, Babylon, Persepolis, and other renowned cities of antiquity, in which I remained a sufficient time to make researches of some extent, will regret the rapidity with which I shall pass over them: but the reason I have here assigned for brevity in all such parts, namely, to give the Story of my Life the more fully, will justify the omissions.

END OF THE FIEST VOLUME.

London:

A. and G. A. SrotxiswoodE,

New-street-Squaie.

A CATALOGUE

NEW WORKS IN GENERAL LITERATURE,

PUBLISHED BY

LONGMAN, BROWN, GREEN, and LONGMANS, 39, PATERNOSTER ROW, LONDON.

CLASSIFIED INDEX.

Agriculture and Rural Affairs.

Pages

Bavldon on Valuing: Rents, etc. " " 5

Ca'ird's Letters ou Agriculture " " i

Cecil's Stud Farm-. 7

Loudon's Encyclopaedia of Agriculture 1-1 ,, Self-Instruction for Farmers, etc. 14 ,, (Mrs.) Lady'scountrycompanion 14 Ixw's Elements of Agriculture- 15 ,, Domesticated Animals–. 14

Arts, Manufactures, and Architecture.

Bourne's Catechism of the Steam Engine 6 ,, On the Screw Propeller- 6

Brande's Dictionary of Science, etc. 6

Chevreul on Colour-.– 8

Cresy's Eucyclo. of Civil Eugineering 8

Eastlake ou Oil Painting-.- 8

Gwilt's Encyclopaedia of Architecture 9

Jameson's Sacred and Legendary Art 11 ,, Commonplace Book. 12

Louclon's Rural Architecture– 14

Moseley's Engineering and Architecture 14

Richardson's Art of Horsemanship- 19 . Steam Engine, by the Artisan Club. 6

Tate on Strength of Materials- 2'2

Ure's Dictionary of Arts, etc.- 24

Biography.

Bodenstedt and "Wagner's Schamyl 23

Brightwell's Memorials of Opie- 18

Bunsen's Hippolytus–. 7

Chesterton's Autobiography– 8

Clinton's (Fynes) Autobiography- g

Cockayne's Marshal Turenne– 23

Freeman's Life of Kirby— jo

Haydon's Autobiography, by Taylor lo

Holcroft's Memoirs— 23

Holland's (Lord) Memoirs– 10
Lardner's Cabinet Cyclopjedia. 13 Maunder's Biographical Treasury.-16
Memoir of the Duke of Wellington 23
Memoirs of James Montgomery- 16
Merivale's Memoirs of Cicero- 16
Russell's Memoirs of Moore– 17
Pages
Russell's Life of Lord William Russell 19
Southey's Life of Wesley– 21 ,, Life and Correspondence 21
Stephen's Ecclesiastical Biography 21
Taylor's Loyola—- 22 ,, Wesley 22
Townsend's Eminent Judges– 22
VVaterton's Autobiography and Essays 24
Books of General Utility.
Acton's INIodern Cookery Book– 5
Black's Treatise on Brewing— fi Cabinet Gazetteer–. 7,, Lawyer. 7
Gust's Invalid's Own Book Hints on Etiquette.–. Hudson's Executor's Guide
On Making Wills Lardner's Cabinet Cyclopjedia-Loudon's Self Instruction
Lady's Companion ,, (Mrs.) Amateur Gardener Maunder's Treasury of Knowledge
,, Biographical Treasury.
,, Scientific Treasury ,, Treasury of History ,, Natural History
Pocket and the Stud
Short Whist–. 20 Thomson's Interest Tables— 22 Traveller's Library—-23
Webster's Domestic Economy– 24 Willich's Popular Tables-.- 24
Wilmot's Abridgment of Blackstone's Commentaries–. 34
Botany and Gardening.
Conversations on Botany-. g
Hooker's British Flora.-.- 10 ,, Guide to Kew Gardens– 10
Pycroft's English Reading Recce's Medical Guide—Rich's Companion to Latin Dictionary Riddle's Latin Dictiouaries Richardson's Art of Horsemanship Roget's English Thesaurus Rowton's Debater
London: Friuted by M. Masok, Ivy Lane, Paternoster Row.
Liiidley's Introduction to Botany Theory of Horticulture Uoudon's Hirtufibritaiii-iicus (Rlrs. 1 Am. iteur (Jardener Self-Instruction for Gardeners,, Encyclopoedia of Trees Shrubs ,, Gardening ,, Plants nivers's Rose Amateur's Guide
Chronology.
Blair's Chronoloyflinl Tables-
Bunsen's Ancient Kt ypt–
Haydn's Beatson's Index–Nicolas's Chronology of History
Pages- 14
Pages
Commerce and Mercantile Aflairs.
Atkinson's Shipping Laws " " n
Francis On Life Assurance " ' ij
Loch's Sailor's Guide– ",, Lorimer's Letters to ayoungmaster Manner 14

M'Ouuoch'a Commerce and Navigation 15
Thomson's Interest Tables– 2-
Criticism, History, and Memoirs.
Austin's Germany— 5
Balfour's Sketches of Literature 5 3lair's Chrou. aud Historicaltables 6
Buuseu s Ancient Egypt- " 7 ,, Hippolytus ' ' " ' Z
Burton's History of Scotland " 7
Chalybaeus's Speculative Philosophy 8
Convbeare and Howson s St. Paul S
Eastlake's History of Oil Painting 8
Erskine's History of India- 9
Francis's Annals of Life Assurance 9
Gleig's Leipsic Campaign 3
Gurney's Historical Sketches- 9
Hamilton's Discussions in Philosophy, etc. 9
Haydon's Autobiosfraphv, by Taylor 10
Holland's (Lord) Foreign Reminiscences lo ,, Whig Party- 10
Jeffrey's (Lord) Contributions 12
Kemble's Anglo-Saxons in England 12
Larduer's Cabinet Cyclopeedia 13 Macaulay's Crit. and Hist. Essays–15 ,, History of England- 15 ,, Speeches— 15
Mackintosh's Miscellaneous Works 15 ,, History of England- 15
M'Culloch's Geographical Dictionary 15
Martiueaii's Church History– 16
Maunder's Treasury of History- 16
Memoir of the Duke of Wellington 23
Merivale's History of Rome– 16 ,, Roman Republic– 16
Milner's Church History– 16
Moore's (Thomas) Memoirs, etc.- 17 Mnre's Greek Literature—-17
Ranke's I'erdinand and Maximilian- 23
Rich's Companion to Latin Dictionary 19
Riddle's Latin Dictionaries– 19
Rogers's Essays from Edinburgh Review 19
Roget's English Thesaurus– 19
Russell's (I. ady Rachel) Letters- 19
Life of Lord William Russell 19
St, John's Indian Archipelago- 19
Schmitz's History of Greece– 20
Smith's Sacred Annals—Southey'sthe Doctor etc. Stephen's Ecclesiastical Biography ,, Lectures on French History Sydney Smith's Works—,, Select Works- ,, Lei tures on Moral Philosophy 21
Taylor's Loyola.— i.2 ,, Weslev—Thirtwall's History of Greece—Townsend's State Trials.—Turkey and Christendom—
Turner's Anglo-Saxons— ,, Middle Ao; es.— ,, Sacred History of the World- Zumpt's Latin Grammar—-

Geography and Atlases.

Butler's Geography and Atlases Cabinet Gazetteer—- Durrieu's Morocco—- Hall's Large Library Atlas Hui hes's Australian Colonies-Jesse's Russia and the War Johnston's (Jeneral Gazetteer M'Cuuoch's Geographical Dictionary ,, Russia and Turkey Milner's Baltic Sea.-.

Murray's Kncycloptedia of Geography Sharp's British Gazetteer Wheeler's Gsography of Herodotus

Juvenile Books.

Amy Herbert 20
Corner's Children's Sunday Book 8
Earl's Daughter (The)– 20
Experience of Life—- 20
Gertrude—. 20
Hewitt's Boy's Country Book- 11 (Mary) Children's Year 11
Katharine Ashton— 20
Lady Una and her Queendom- 12
Laneton Parsonage– 20
Mrs. Marcet's Conversations- 15 16
Margaret Percival— 20
Pycroft's English Reading- 19
Medicine and Surgery.

Bull's Hints to Mothers ,, Management of Children Copland 's Dictionary of Medicine-Gust's Invalid's Own Book Hollaiid's Mental Physiology-Latham On Diseases of the Heart Little on Treatment of Deformities Moore On Health, Disease, and Remedy Pereiraon Food and Diet Psychological Inquiries–Recce's Medical Guide—

Miscellaneous and General Literature.

Atkinson's Sheriff Law— 5
Austin's Sketches of German Life 5
Carlisle's Lectures and Addresses- 23
C'halybaeus's Speculative Philosophy 8
Defence of Eclipse of Faith– 9
Eclipse of Faith—- 8 Greg's Essays on Political and Social
TO Messrs. LONGMAN and Co."s CATALOGUE.
Pages
Haydn's Book of Dignities– 10
Hole's Essay on Mechanics' Institutions 10
Holland's Mental Physiology– 10
Hooker's Kew Guide— 10
Hewitt's Rural I-ife of England- 11 ,, Visits to Remarkable Places 11
Jameson's Commonpl'icc Book- 12
Jeffrey's (Lord) Contributions- 12 hast of the Old Squires— 18
Loudon's Lady's Country Companion H
Macaulay's Critical and Historical Essays 15 ,, Siieechcs— 15 Mackintosh's (Sir J.) Miscellaneous Works 15
Memoirs of a Maitre d'Armes- 23

Maitland's Church in the Catacombs lo
Pascal's Works, by Pearce– 18
Pycroft's Eng-lish'R-cading– 19
Rich's Companion to Latin Dictionary 19
Riddle's Latin Dictionaries– 19
Rowton's Debater—- 19
Seaward'fi Narrative of his Shipwreck 2
Sir Ro er De Coverley– 2l
Smith's (Rev. Sydney) Works- 21
Southey's Common-Place Books- 21 ,, The Doctor etc.– 23
Souvestre's Attic Philosopher- 23 ,, Confessions of a Working Man 23
Stephen's Essays—- 21
Stow's Traininy; System– 2l
Thomson'soutlineof the Laws of Thought 22
Townsend's State Trials— 22
Willich's Popular Tales— 24
Yonge's Eng lish Greek Lexicon- 24 ,, Latin Gradus— 2-1
Zumpt's Latin Grammar— 24
Natural History in General.
Catlow's Popular Conchology– 7
Kphemera and Young on the Salmon 9
Gosse's Natural History of Jamaica 9
Kemp's Natural History of Creation 23
Kirby and Spence's Kntomology- 12 r ee's Elements of Natural History 12
Maunder's Treasury of Natural History 16
Turton's Shellsof the British Islands 24
Yaterton's Essays on Natural History 24
Youatt's The Dog—- 24
The Horse 1-Volume Encyclopaedias and Dictionaries.
Blaine's Hural Sports— 6
Brande's Science, Literature, and Art 6
Copland's Dictionary of I Iedicine–8
Cresy's Civil Engineering– 8
Gwiit's Architecture— y
Johnston's Geographical Dictionary 12
Loudon's Agriculture— 14 ,, Rural Architecture- 14 ,, Gardening. 14 ,, Plants-. 14 ,, Trees and Shrubs– 14
M Cuuoch s Geographical Dictionary 15 ,, Dictionary of Commerce 15
Murray's En cvclopffdia of Geography 17
Sharp's British Gazetteer-. 20
Lire's Dictionary of Arts, etc.– 24
Webster'sdomestic Economy- 24
Religious and Moral Works-Amy Herbert—— 20
Atkinson on the Church— 5
Bioomfield'sgreek Tpstamentg- 6 , f Annotations on ditto- 6

Pages
Calvert's Wife's Manual- 7
Conybeare and Howson's St. Paul 8
Corner's Sunday Book– 8 lale s Domestic Liturgy- 8
V efence of Eclipse 0Faith- 9
Discipline—- 8
Earl's Daughter (The)– 20
Eclipse of Faith—- 3
Knglishman's Greek Concordance "9 ,, Hcb. and Cbald. Concord. g
Experience of Life (The)- 20
Gertrude— 20
Harrison's Light of the Forge 10
Hook's (Dr.) Lectureson Passion Week Jo
Home's Introduction to Scriptures jj ,, Abridgment of ditto "11 flulbert on Job– ' "
" H
Jameson's Sacred Fjcgendb- 11 I, Monastic Legends- " H ,, Legends of the Madonna
Jeremy Taylor's Works– " 12
Katharine Ashton— 20
Kippis's Hymns— 12
Lady Una nd her Queendom 12
Laneton Parsonage— "20
Letters to My Unknown Friends 12 ,, on Happiness– 12
Litton's Church of Christ- 14
Maitland's Church in the Catacombs 15
Margaret Percival– " " 20
Martineau's Church History- 16
Milner's Church of Christ- ig
Montgomery's Original Hymns 16
Moore On the Use of the Body 17 n,, Soul and Body "17 , 's Man and his Motives 1
Mormonism—— 3
Neale's Closing Scene– 18 ,, Resting Places of the Just 17
Riches that bring no Sorrow 17 ,, Risen from the Ranks- 17
Newman's (J. H.) Discourses- 18
Ranke's Ferdinand and Maximilian 23
Readings for Lent–. 20 , t Confirmation- 20 Rohinson's Lexicon to the Greek Testa- ment—- 19
Saints our Example– 20
Self-Denial. 20
Sermon on the Mount–. 0 .1,, illuminated 20
Sinclair's Journey of Life- 21
Smith's (Sydney) Moral Philosophy 21 ,, (G.) Sacred Annals- ' 21
Southey's Life of Wesley- 21
Stephen's (Sirj.) Ecclesiastical Biography 21
Taylor's I-oyola— 22 ,, Wesley— 22

Theologia Gerraanica- 22
Thumb Bible (The)– 22
Turner's Sacred History- 22
Poetry and the Drama.
Arnold's Poems—- 5
Aikin's (Dr.) Britishpoets– 6
Baiuie's (Joanna) Poetical VVorks- 5
Barter's Iliad of Homer— 5 ijode's Ballads from Herodotus- 6
Calvert's Wife's Manual– 7
Flowers and their Kindred Thoughts 18
Goldsmith's Poems, illustrated. 9
Kent's Aletheia 12
Kippis's Hymns—-
Pages
Linwood's Anthologia Oxoniensis 14
Macaulay's Lays of Ancient Rome 15
Moutgomery's Poetical Works 16 ,, Orininai Hymns 16
Moore's Poetical Works– 17 ,, Lallarookh– 17 ,, Irish Melodies– 17 ,, Songs and Ballads- 17
Shakspeare, By Bowdier–20 ,. s Sentiments and Similes 11
Southey's Poetical Works- 21 ,, British Poets– 21
Thomson's Seasons, illustrated 22
Thornton's Zohrab—- 22
Watts's Lyrics of the Heart- 24
Political Economy Statistics.
Banfield's Statistical Companiou- 6
Caird's Letters on Agriculture- 7
Francis on Life Assurance– 9 Greg's Essays on Political and Social
Science—- 9
Laing's Notes of a Traveller– 12 23
M'Cuiloch's Geographical Dictionary 15 ,, Dictionary of Commerce 15
London—- 23 ,, Statistics of the British Empire 15
Marcet's Political Kconomy– 16
Willich's Popular Tables— 24
The Sciences in General and
Mathematics.
Bourne's Catechism of the Steam Engine ,, on the Screw Propeller-Brande's Dictionary of Science, etc.
,, Lectures on Organic Chemistry
Cresy's Civil Engineering—Delabeche's Geology of Cornwall, etc.
f, 's Geological Observer-De la Rive's Electricity—-Faraday's Non-Metalhc Elements-Fuuom's Marvels of Science– Herschel's Outlines of Astronomy-Holland's Mental Physiology Humboldt's Aspects of Nature ,, Cosmos–
Hunt's Researches on Light—Lardner's Cabinet Cyclopaedia Marcel's (Mrs.) Conversations- 15 Moseley's Engineering and Architecture Owen's Lectures on Com-

parative Anatomy Our Coal Fields and our Coal Pits-Pesehel's Elements of Physics Phillips's Fossils of Cornwall, etc.

Mineralogy–.

yf Guide to Geology—Portlock's Geology of Londonderry Smee's Klectro-Metallurgy–Steam Engine, by the Artisan Club Tate on Strength of Materials Todd's Tables of Circles— 22

Wilson's Electricity and the Electric Telegraph–.– 23

Rural Sports."

Baker's Rifle and Hound in Ceyloo 6

Berkeley's Reminiscences– 6

Blaine's Dlctionaryof Sports- 6

Cecil's Stable Practice-. 8

Records of the Chase–. 7

Cecil's Stud Farm—

The Cricket Field—-

Ephemera on Angling— ,, 's Book of the Salmon

The Hunting Field-.-Loudon's Lady's Country Companion

Pocket and the Stud-

Practical Horsemanship—

Pulman's Fly-Fishing—

Richardson's Horsemanship.

St-John's Sporting Rambles–Stable Talk and Table Talk

Stonehenge on the Greyhound The Stud, for Practical Purposes

Veterinary Medicine, etc.

Cecil's Stable Practice—

Stud Farm—-

The Hunting Field—-Morton's Veterinary Pharmacy

Pocket and the Stud–.

Practical Horsemanship—

Richardson's Horsemanship–Stable Talk and Table Talk-The Stud for Practical Purposes

Youatt's The Dog—,, The Horse

Pages

Voyages and Travels.

Baker's Rifle and Hound in Ceylon Barrow's Continental Tour—Carlisle's Turkey and Greece—De Custiue's Russia.—

Eothen——,

Ferguson's Swiss Men and Mountains-Forester and Biddulph's Norway- Gironifere's Philippines—

Hill's Travels in Siberia—-

Hope's Brittany and the Bible—,, Chase in Brittany.-

Howitt's Art Student in Munich Hue's Tartary, Thibet, and China-Hughes's Australian Colonies–Humbley's Indian Journal.–Humboldt's Aspects of Nature Jameson's Canada–.-Jerrmann's Pictures from St. Petersburg Laing's Norway— ,, Notes of a

Traveller– 12 i Macintosh's Turkej and Black Sea-Oldmixon's Piccadilly to Peru–. Osborn's Arctic Journal—-

Peel's Nubian Desert-.–Pfeiffer's Voyage round the World-Power's New Zealand Sketches Richardson's Arctic Boat Voyage-Seaward's Narrative of his Siiipwreck-St. John's (H.) Indian Archipelago (J. A.) Isis

M There and Back again fhon. F.) Rambles—
Sutherland s Arctic Voyage Traveller's Library–
Werne's Africau Wanderings-
Works of Fiction.
Arnold's Oakfield
Lady Willoughby's Diary-.
Macdonald's villa Verocchio—Sir Roger De Coverley–. Southey'bthe Doctor etc.–,

NEW WORKS AND NEW EDITIONS
PUBLISHED BY
Messrs, LONGMAN, BROWN, GREEN, and LONGMANS,
PATEKNOSTER ROW, LONDON.
Miss Acton's Modern Cookery-

Book, Modern Cookery in all its Branches, reduced to a System of Easy Practice. For the use of Private Families, In a Series of Recipes, all of which have been strictly tested, and are iven with ihe most minute exactness. By Eliza Actox. New Edition; with various Additions Plates and Woodcuts. Fcp. Svo. price 7a. 6rf.

Alkin. Select Works of the

British Poets, from Ben Jonson to Beattie. With Biographical and Critical Prefaces by Dr. Aikin- Neweditiou, with Supplement by Ijucv Aikin; consisting; of additional Selections, from more receut Poets. Svo, price ISs,

Arnold. Poems- By Matthew
Arnold. 55.6.
Second Edition. Fcp. Svo. price

Arnold. Oakfield 5 or, Fellowship in the East. By W. D. Arnold, Lieutenant 58th Regiment, Beng al Native Infantry. The Second Edition, revised. 2 vols, post Svo. price 21.

Atkinson, CGJ Sheriif-Law; or, a Practical Treatise on the Offfice of Sheritf. Undersheriff, Bailiffs, etc.: Their Duties at the Election of Members of Parliament and Coroners, Assizes, and Sessions of the Peace: Writs of Trial; Writs of Inquiry; Compensation Notices; Interpleader; Writs; Warrants; Returns; Bills of Sale; Bonds of Indemnity, etc. By George Atkinson. Third Edition, revised. Svo. price 10s. 6d,

Atkinson, (G–) The Shipping

Laws of the British Empire: Consistingof Park or M rijie Aftsuranee, and Abbott on Shipping. Edited by George Atkinson, Serjeiiiit-at-Law. Svo. price loa. Grf.

Atkinson, (WJ The Church:

An Explanation of the Meaning contained in thebilile; shewing; the Ancient, Con tinued, and Prevailing Error of Man, the Substitution of Worship for Religion: and shewing that the Principles of all Right Individual Action and of General Government or the Government of all Nations are comprised in Revealed Religion. Bv William Atkinson. 2 vols. Svo. price 30s.

Austin- Germany from 1760 to 1814; Or, Sketches of German Life from the Decay of the Empire to the Expulsion of the French. By Mrs. Austin. Post Svo. price 13a.

Joanna Baillie's Dramatic and

Poetical Works, complete in One Volume: Comprising the Plays of the Passions, Miscellaneous Dramas, Metrical Legends, Fugitive Pieces, (several now first published), and Ahalya Baee. Second Edition, including a new Life of Joanna Baillie; with a Portrait, and a View of Bothwell Manse. Square crown Svo. 21s. cloth, or 42. bound in morocco.

Baker. The Rifle and the Hound in Ceylon. By S. W. Baker, Esq. With several Illustrations printed in Colours, and Engraviivg-s on Wood. 8vo. price 145.

Balfour. Sketches of English

Literature from the Fourteenth to the Present Century, By Clara Lucas Balfour. Ft'p. Svo. price Js

Barter- Homer's Iliad, translated almost literally into the Spenserian Stanza; with Notes. By W. G. T. Barter. Svo, price 18s.

Banfield. The Statistical Com- panioq for 1854: Exhibiting the raost Interesting Facts in Moral and Intellectual, Vital, ifconnmical, and Political Statistics, at Home and Abroad. Corrected to the Present Time: and including the Census of the British Population taken in 1851. Compiled from Official and other Authentic Sources, by T-C. Banfield, Esq- Fcp. Svo. price 65.

Bayldon's Art of Valuing Rents and Tillages, and Tenant's Right of Enter ing and Quitting Farms, explained by several Specimens of Valuations; with Remarks on the Cultivation pursued on Soils in different Situations. Adapted to the Use of Landlords, Land Agents, Appraisers, Farmers, and Tenants, New Kdition; corrected and revised by John Donaldson. Svo. 10s. Gd,

Berkeley. Reminiscences of a

Hunt man. By the Honourable Gkantley F. Berkeley. With four Etchings by John Leech (one coloured). Svo. price 14.

Black's Practical Treatise on

Brewing, based on Chemical and Economical Principles: With Formuhe for Public Brewers, and Instructions for Private Fami lies. New Edition, with Additions. Svo price 10. Gd.

Blaine's Encyclopsedia of Rural sports; or, a complete Account, Historical, Practical, and Descriptive, of Hunting, Shooting, Fishing, Racing, and other Field Sports and Athletic Amusements of the present day. With upwards of 600 Woodcuts. A New Edition, thoroughly revised by Hahry Hieover, Epkemeba, and Mr. A. Graham; w ith numerous additional Illustrations. Svo. price oos.

Blair's Chronological and Historical Tiiblcs, from the C reatlou to the present Time; with Additions and Corrections from tlie moat authentic Writers; including the Computation of St. Paul, as counecting the Period from the Exode to the Temple. Under the revision of Sir Henry Ellis, K. H. New Edition, with corrections. Imperial Svo. price 31. 6rf.

Bloomfield. The Greek Testament: With copious P'nglish Notes, Critical, Philological, and P2spranatory. Especially formed for the use of advanced Students and Candidates for Holy Orders. By the Rev. S. T. BLoomrieLD, D. D. F. S. A. New Edition. 2 vols. Svo. with Map, price 2.

Dr. Bloomfield's Additional
Annotations on the above. Svo. price 15s.

Dr. Bloomfield's College School
Greek Test; iment, With brief English Notes, chiefly Philological and Explanatory. Seventh and cheaper Edition, with Map and Index. Fcp, Svo. price 75- 6rf.

Dr. Bloomfield's College and
School Lexicon to the Greek Testament. Ftp. Svo. price 10. 6d.

Bode. Ballads from Herodotus:
With an Introductory Poem. By tlie Rev, J. E. Bode, M A., late Student of Christ Church, I6mo. price 5.

A Treatise on the Steam Engine, in its Application to Mines, Mills, Steam Navigation, and Railways. By the Artisan Club. Edited by Joux Bourne, C. E. New Edition; with 30 Steel Plates, and 349 Wood Engravings. 4to. price 27.

Bourne. A Treatise on the
Screw Propeller: With various Suggestions of Improvement. By John Bourne, C. E. With-0 lar e Plates and numerous Vood-cuts. 4to. price 3Ss,

Bourne. A Catechism of the
Steam Engine, illustrative of the Scientific Principles upon which its Operation depends, and the Practical Details of its Structure, in its Applications to Minos, Mills, Steam Navigation, and Railways; with various Suggestions of Improvement. By John Bourne, C. E. New Edition. Fcp. Svo.6.

Brande. A Dictionary of Science, Literature, and Art; comprising the History, Description and Scientific Principles of every Brand) of Human Knowledge; with the Derivation and Definition of all the Terms in general use. Edited by W. T. Brande, F. S. S. L. and E.; assisted by Dr. J. Cauvin. Second Edition, revised; with Woodcuts. Svo. price GO.

Professor Brande's Lectures on
Organic Chemistry, as applied to Manufactures, including Dyeing, Bleaching, Calico-printing, Sugar"Manufacture, the Preservation of Wood, Tanning, etc. delivered before the Members of the Royal Institution in the Session of 1852. Arranged by permission from the Lecturer's Notes by J. ScofFERN, M. B. Fcp. Svo. Just ready.

Bull. The Maternal Management of Children in Health au"! Disease. By T. BulX,, M. D. New Edition, Fcap. Svo. price 5.

Dr. Bull's Hints to Mothers for the Mpnagement of their Health during the Period of Pregnancy and in the Lying-in Room: With "an Exposure of Popular Errors in connexion with those subjects, etc.; and Hints on Nursing. New Edition. Fcp. price 5.

PUBLISHED BY LONGMAN. BKOWN. and Co.

Bunsen- Christianity Man- liind; Their liej niininsjs and Prospects. Byc. C. O. BunseN, O. D., D C. L., D. l'h. Bc'iii ancwkditiuii,('nrrcctt'd, rem(Jtielled, and extended, of HippolitnS and his Age. 7 vols. 8vo. price 5. 5s.

This Second Editiou of the Hippolt-tui is composed of tlirce distinct works, which may be had separately! as follows:

Historical Section. Hippolytus and his Ag-e; or, the Beginnings and Prospects of Christianity. 2vols.8vo. price U. lus.

I. Hippolytus and the Teachers of the

Apostolictu Age; n. The Life of the Christians of the Apostolical Age.

Philological Section, 2. Outlines of the Philosophy of Universal History applied to Language and Religion, 2 vols. Svo. price U. V6s. '

Philosophical Section, 3. Analecta Ante-Nicaena., 3 vols. Svo. price 21. 2.?.

I. Ri; lir)uiib Literariw; IL Reliquire f anoiiicee; III. Rcliquiie Liturgicie: Cum Appcn-dicibus ad Tria Analectorum Vo-lumina.

Bunsen- Egypt's Place in Universal History: An Historical Investigation, in Five Books. By C. C. J. Bunsex, D. U., D. C. L., D. Ph. Translated from the German, by C. H. CotTRELL, Ksq. M. A. Vol. I., with many Illustrations. 8vo. price 28a.

, The second Volun: e is preparing for publication.

Burton- The History of Scotland, from the Revolution to the Kxtinction of the last Jacobite Insurrection (1689 1743.) By John Hill Burton. 2vo1s.8vo.

price 2G8.

Bishop Butler's General Atlas of Modern and Ancient Geot raphy; comprising Fifty-two full-coloured INlaps; with complete Indexes. New Edition, nearly all re-engraved, enlarged, and greatly improved; with Corrections from the most authentic Sources in both the Ancient and Modern Maps, many of which are entirely new. Royal 4to. price 245. half-bound.

The Modern Atlas, 28 full- c I I coloured Maps. Rl. Svo. I2.

beparately-p, Ancient Atlas 24 full- . Rl. Svo. 125.

- The Modern Atla I coloured Maps.! J The Ancient Atl coloured Maps. 1

Bishop Butler's Sketch of Modem and Ancient Geography. New Edition, carefully revised, with such Alterations introduced as continually progressive Discoveries and the latest Information have rendered necessary. Svo. price 9.?.

The Cabinet Gazetteer: A Popular Exposition ot all the Countries ot the World; their Government, Poptilation, Revenues, Commerce and Industries; Agricultural, Manufitctured, and Mineral Products; Religion, Laws, Manners, and Social State. By the Author of The Cabinet Lawyer. Fcap. Svo. price lu5.6rf. cloih; or 13ff. calf lettered.

The Cabinet Lawyer: A Popular Digest of the La "s of Kn land, Civil and Criminal; with a Dictionary of Law Terms, Maxims, Statutes, and Judicial Antiquities; Correct Tables of Assessed Taxes, Stamp Duties, Excise Licences, and Post-Horse Duties; Post-Office Regulations, and Prison Discipline. 16th Edition, comprising the Public Acts of the Session 1853. Fcap. Svo. price los. Gd.

Caird. English Agriculture in 185U and 1851; Its Condition and Prospects. By James Caird, Esq., of Baldoon, Agricultural Commissioner of The Times. The Second Edition. Svo. price 14.

Calvert The Wife's Manual5 or. Prayers, Thoughts, and Sonyi; s on Several Occasions of a Matron's Life. Ornamented from Designs by the Author in the style of

Queen Elizabeth's Prayer Book. By the Uev. William Calvert, Reclor of St, Autholin, and one of the Minor Canons of St, Paups. Crown Svo. 10. 6rf.

Carlisle (Lord). A Diary in

Turkish and tireek Waters. By the Right Hon. the Earl of Carlisle. Post Svo. Nearly ready.

Catlow. Popular Conchology5 or, the Shell Cabinet arranged according to the Modern System: With a detailed account of the Animals; and a complete Descriptive List of the Families and Genera of the Hecent and Fossil Shells. By Agneb Catlow. Second Edition, much improved; with 405 Woodcuts. Post Svo. price I4s.

Cecil. The Stud Parm or,

Hints on Breeding Horses for the Turf-the Chase, and the Road. By Cecil. Fcp. Svo. with Frontispiece, price os.

Cecil. Records of the Chase, and Memoirs of Celebrated Sportsmen; illustiating some of the Usages of Olden Times and comparing them with prevailing Customs: Together with an Introduction to most. of the Fashionable Hunting Countries; and Comments. Qy Cecil. With two Plates by B. Herring. Fcp. Svo. price Is. 6rf. half-bound.

Cecil- Stable Practice or Hints ou Traininjf for the Turf, the Chase, and the Road: With Observations ou Racing- and Huntintf, Wastini;, Race Riding, and Handicapping. By Cecil. Fcap. 8vo. with Plate, price 58, half-bound.

Chalybaeus's Historical Survey of Modern Speculative Pliilosophy, from Kant to Hegel. Translated from the German by Alfred Xulk. Post Svo. price 85. 6rf.

Peace, War, and Adventure 5

Being an Autobiographical Memoir of George Laval Chesterton, formerly of the Field-Train. Department of the Royal Artillery, subsequently a Captain in the Army of Columbia, and at present Governor of the House of Correction in Cold Bath Fields. 2 vols, post Svo. price I65.

Chevreul's Principles of Harmony and Contrast of Colours, and their Applications to the Arts: Including Painting, Interior Decoration, Tapestries, Carpets, Mosaics, Coloured Glazing, Paper-Staining, Calico Printing, Letterpress Printing, Map Colouring, Dress, Landscape and Flower Gardening, etc. Translated by Charles Martel; and illustrated with Diagrams etc. Crown Svo. price 125, 6d.

Clinton- The Autobiography and Literary Journal of the late Henry Fynes Clinton, Esq. M. A. Author of the Fasti Ilellettici, the Fasti Romania etc. Edited by the Rev. C. J. Fymes Clinton, M. A., Rector of Cromwell, Notts.

n the Press.

Conversations on Botany- New

Edition, improved; with 22 Plates. Fcp. Svo. price 6rf. j or with the Plates coloured, 125.

Conybeare and Howson. The

Life and Epistles of Saint Paul: Comprising a complete Biographj- of the Apostle, and a Translation of his Epistles inserted in Chronological order. By the Rev. W, J. Conybeare, M. A., and the Rev. J. S. Howsox, M. A. With 40 Steel Plates and 100. Woodcuts. 2 vols. 4to. price,"2. 85.

Dictionary of

Comprising General

Dr. Copland's

Practical Medicine

Pathology, the Nature and Treatment of Diseases, Morbid Structures, and the Disorders especially incidental to Climates, to Sex, and to the different Epochs of Life, vpith numerous approved Formulae of the Medicines recommended. Vols-Land II. Svo. price 3; and Parts X. to XVI. price 45.6. each.

The Children's Own Sunday-Book. By Miss Julia Corner. With Two Illustrations. Square fcp. Svo. price bs.

Cresy's Encyclopaedia of Civil

Engineering, Historical, Theoretical, and Practical, Illustrated by upwards of 3000 Woodcuts, explanatory of the Principles, Machinery, and Constructions which come under the Direction of the Civil Engineer. Svo. price 3. 13.6rf.

The Cricket-Pield 5 or, the Science and History of the Game of Cricket. By the Author of Principles ofscientijzc Batting. Second Edition; with Plates and Woodcuts, Fcp. Svo. 03. half-bound.

Lady Cust's Invalid's Book.

The Invalid's Own Book: A Collection of Recipes from various Books and various Countries. By the Honourable Lady Cdst. Fcp. Svo, price 3s. 6d.

The Rev. T. Dale's Domestic

Liturgy and Family Chaplain, in Two Parts: Thefirstpart beingchurch Services adapted for Domestic Use, with Prayers for every Day of the Week, selected exclusivelyfrom the Book of Common Prayer, Part II. Comprising an appropriate Sermon for every Sunday in the Year. 2d Edition. Post 4lo. 2I5. cloth; 3U. 6rf. calf; or 2.10a. morocco. c 1 f The Family Chaplain, 12,

P 5-1The Domestic Liturgy, 105.6.

Delabeche. The Geological Observer. By Sir Henry T- Delabeche, F. R. S. Director-General of the Geological Survey of the United Kingdom. New Edition; with numerous Woodcuts. 8ro. price I8s.

Delabeche- Report on the Geology of Cornwall, Devon, and West Somerset. By Sir Henry T. Delabeche, F. R. S. With Maps, Woodcuts, and 12 Plates, 8vo. price 14j.

De la Rive. A Treatise on Electricity, ill Theory and Prartice. By A. De la Rive, Professor in the Academy of Geneva. In Two Volumes, with numerous Wood Engravings. Vol. I. Svo. price ISs,

Discipline. By the Author of "Letters to My Unknown Frieuds," etc. Second Edition, enlarged. ISmo. price2s.6rf.

Eastlake. Materials for a History of Oil Painting. By Sir Charles Lock Eastlake, F. K. S., F. S. A., President of the Royal Academy. Svo. price 16.

The Eclipse of Faith? or, a

Visit to a Religious Sceptic. The Fifth and cheaper Edition. Fcap. Svo. price 5.

PUBLISHED BY LOxvGMAN, BROWN. AND Co.

A Defence of The Eclipse of

Faith, by its Author: Being- a Rejoinder to Professor Newman's Hepli. Second Edition, revised. Post 8vq. price 53. 6rf.

The Englishman's Greek Concordance of the New Testament: Being an attempt at a Verbal Connexion between the Greek and the Eny: lishtexts; including a Concordance to the Proper Names with Indexes Greek-English and English-Greek. New Edition, with a new Index. Royal 8vo. price 425.

The Englishman's Hebrew and

Chaldee Concordance of the Old Testament: Being an attempt at a Verbal Connexion between the Original and the English Translations: with Indexes, a List of the Proper Names and their Occurrences, etc. 2 vols, royal Svo. price 3. 13s. 6rf.; large paper, 4. 14. Grf.

Ephemera, A Handbook of

Angling; Teaching Fly Fishing, Trolling, Bottom Fishing, and Salmon Fishing; with the Natural History of River Fish, and the best Modes of Catching them. By Ephemera. Third and cheaper Edition, corrected and improved; with Woodcuts. Fop. Svo. price 5s.

Ephemera- The Book of the

Salmon: Comprisingthe Theory, Principles, and Practice of Kly-Fishing for Salmon; Lists of good Salmon Flies for every good River in the Empire; the Natural History of the Salmon, all its known Habits described, and the best way of artificially Breeding it explained. With numerous coloured Engravings of Salmon Flies and Salmon Fry. By Ephemera; assisted by Andrew Young, Fcp. Svo. wkh coloured Platefi, price 145.

W. Erskine, Esq- History of India under Baber and Humayun, the First Two Sovereigns of the House of Taimur. By William Erskine, Esq., Editor of ilf-moirs of the Emperor Baber 2 vols. Svo. price SX I2s.

Faraday (Professor). The Subject-Matter of Six Lectures on the Non-Metallic Elements, delivered before the Members of the Royal Institution in 1852, by Professor Faraday, D. C. L., F. R. S., etc. Arranged by permission from the Lecturer's Notes by J. Scofpekn, M. B. Fcp. Svo. price 5j. 6rf.

Norway in 1848 and 1849: containing Rambles among the Fjelds and Fjords of the Central and Western l)istricts; and including Remarks on its Political, Military, Ecclesiastical, and Social Organisation. By Thomas Forester, Esq.; and Lieutenant M. S. BidDulph, Royal Artillery. With Map, Woodcuts, and Plates. 8vo. price 18s.

Francis. Annals, Anecdotes, and Legends: A Chronicle of Life Assurance, ily John Francis, Author of The History of the Bank of England, etc. Post Svo. price 8j. 6d.

ruuom. The Marvels of Sci- ence and their Testimony to Holy Writ: A Popular System of the Sciences. By S. W. FulLOM, Esq. The Eighth and cheaper Editions with numerous Illustrations. Post Svo, price 5e.

The Poetical Works of Oliver

Goldsmith. Edited by Bolton Corxey, Esq. Illustrated by Wood Engravings, from Designs by Members of the j Uching Club. Square crown Svo. cloth, 21.; morocco

Gosse. A Natiiralist's Sojourn in Jamaica. By P. H. Gosse, Esq. With Plates. Post Svo. price 145.

Essays on Political and Social

Science. Contributed chiefly to the Edinburgh Review. By William R. Grko, 2 vols, Svo. price 24s.

Gurney.- Historical Sketches Illustrating some Memorable Events and Epochs, from a. d. 141)0 to a-d. 1546. By the Rev. John Hampden Gurney, M. A. Fcp. Svo. price 7s. 6d.

Gwilt. An Encyclopaedia of
Architecture, Historical, Theoretical, and Practical. By Joseph Gwilt. illustrated with mare than 1, U(I0 Engravings on Wood, from Designs by J. S. Gwilt- Third and cheaper Edition. Svo. price 42.

Sidney Hall's General Large
Library Atlas of Fifty-three Maps (size 20 in. by 16 in.), with the Divisions and Boundaries carefully coloured; and an Alphabetical Index of all the Names contained in the Maps. New Edition, corrected from the best and most recent Authorities; with the Railways laid down, and many entirely new Maps. Colombier 4to, price S. 5., half-russia.

Hamilton. Discussions in Philosophy and Literature, Education and University Reform. Chiefly from the Edinburgh Review; corrected, vindicated, enlarged, in Notes and Appendices. By Sir William IIamilton, Bart. Second Edition, with Additions, Svo. price 2l5.

Hare (Archdeacon) The Life of Luther, in Forty-eight Historical Engravings. By GnstAv Konio. With Explanations by Archdeacon Hare. Square crown Svo. Jn the press

Harrison. The Light of the
Forge; or. Counsels drawn from the Sick-Bed of K. M. By the Rev. William Harrison, M. A., Domestic Chaplain to H. R. H. the Duchess of Cambridge. With 2 Woodcuts, fcp. Svo. price 5j.

Harry Hieover. The Hunting- field. By Harry Hieover. With Two Plates, one representing The Right Sort; the other, The tf'rung Sort. Fcp. Svo. 5.

Harry Hieover. Practical
Horsemanship. By Harry Hieover. With 2 Plates, one reprtsentinir Going like Workmen; the other. Going like Muff). Fcp. Svo. 5. half-bound.

beinif a Guide to the Choice ot a norse lor use more than for show. By Harhy Hieover. Witli 2 Plates, one representing A pretty good sort for most purposes; the other, Kiiytlicr a bad sort for any purp Fcp. Svo. price 5. half-bound.

Harry Hieover. The Pocket and the Stud; or. Practical Hints on the Management of the Stable. By Harry Hieover. Second Edition; with Portrait. Fcp. Svo. price at. half-bound.

Harry Hieover. Stable Talk and Table Talli; or Spectacles for Young Sportsmen. By Harry Hieover. New Edition, 2 vols. Svo. with Portrait, 24s.

Haydn's Book ofdignities: containing Rolls of the Official Personages of the British Empire, Civil, Ecclesiastical, Judicial, Military, Naval, and IMunicipal, from the Earliest Periods to the Present Time: compiled chiefly from the Records of the Public Offices. Together with the Sovereigns of Europe, from the Foundation of their respective States; the Peerage and Nobility of Great Britain; and numerous other Lists. Being a New Edition, improved and continued, of Beatson's Political Index, By Joseph Haydn, Compiler of The hiettonari nf Dates, and other Works. Svo. price 5b. half-bound.

Haydon. The Life of Benjamin
Robert Haydon, Historical Painter, from his Autobioeraphv and Journals. Edited and compiled by Tom Taylor, M. A., of the Inner Temple, Esq.; late Fellow of Trinity College, Cambridge; and late Professor of the English Language and Literature in University College, London. Second Edition, with Additions and an Index. 3 vols, post Svo. price 3U. 6rf.

Sir John Herschel. Outlines of Astronomy. By Sir John F. W. Hebs-CBEL, Bart, etc. New Edition; with Platen and Wood Engravings. Svo. price 135.

Hill. Travels in Siberia. By
S. S. Hill. Author of Travels on the Shores of the Baltic. With a lar e coloured IVIap of European and Asiatic Russia. 2 vols, post Svo. price 2-l,

Hints on Etiquette and the
Usages of Society: S'ith a Glance at Bad Habits. New Edition, revised (with Additions) by a Ladyof Rank. Fcp. Svo. price Half-a-Crown.

Hole. Prize Essay on the History and Management of Literary, Scientific, and Mechanics! Institutions, and especially how far they may be developed and combined so as to promote the Moral Well-being and Industry of the Country. By James Hole. Svo. price oj.

Lord Holland's Memoirs.
Memoirs of the Whig Party during My Time. By Henry Richard Lord Holland- Edited by his Son, Henry Edward Lord Holland- Vols. I. and II. post Svo. price 9. 6d. each.

Lord Holland's Foreign Reminiscences. Edited by his Son, Henrv Edward Ijord Holland. Second Edition; with Facsimile. Post Svo. price 10. 6rf.

Holland. Chapters on Mental
Physiology. By Sir Henry Holland, Bart., F. R. S., Physician-Extraordinary to the Queen. Founded chiefly on Chapters con taiued in Medical Notes and Refiections, by the same Author. Svo. price 10. 6rf.

Hook. The Last Days of Our
Lord s Ministrv: A Course of Lectures on the principal Events of Passion Week. By Walter Farquhar Hook, D. D., Chaplain in Ordinary to the Queen. New Edition. Fcp. Svo. price 65.

Hooker and Arnott's British
Flora; Comprising the Phicnogamous or Flowering Plants, and the Ferns. The Sixth Edition, with Additions and Corrections, and numerous Figures, illustrative of the Umbelliferous Plants, the Composite Plants, the (irasses, and the Ferns. 12mo. with 12 Plates, price 14., with the Plates coloured, price 2U.

Sirw. J. Hooker'spopular Guide to the Royal Botanic Gardens of Kew. New Edition; with numerous Wood Engravings. 16mo. price Sixpence.

PUBLISHED BY LONGMAN, BROWN, and Co.

Home, An Introduction to the
Critical Study and Knowledge of the Holy Scriptures. By the Uev. Thomas Hartwell HobNB, B. t. New Kdition, revised and corrected; with numerous Maps, and Facsimiles of Biblical Manuscripts. 6 vols. 8vo. price 63s.

Home's Compendious Introduc- duction to the Study of the Bible. Being ail Abridgmeut of tlie Author's Irtrodurtion to the Criticfil Study and Knowledge of the Holy Scriptures. New Kdition; with Maps and other Engravings. 12mo. price 9s.

Howitt. (A. M-) An Art Stu- dent in Munich, By Anna Mary Howittj 2 vols, post Svo. price I4s.

Howitt. The Children's Year.

By Mary Howitt. U'ith Vout Illustrations,! engraved by John Absolon, from Originhl Designs by Anna Mary Uowitt. Square 16mo. price 5.

William Hewitt's Boy's Country Book. Being the real Life of a Country Boy, writ- ten by Himself: Exhibiting all the Amusements, Pleasures, and Pursuits of Children in the Country. New Edition; with 40 Woodcuts. Fcp. 8vo. price 65.

Howitt The Rural Life of England. By William IIowitT. New Edition, corrected and revised; with Woodcuts by Bewick and Williams. Medium Svo. 215.

Howitt,-Visits to Remarkable

Places; Old Halls, Battle-Fields, and Scenes illustrative of Striking Passages in English History and Poetry. By William Howitt. New Edition; with 40 Woodcuts. Medium Svo. 21.

Second Series, chiefly in the

Counties of Northumberland and Durham, with a Stroll along the Border. With upwards of 40 Woodcuts. Medium Svo. 2U.

Hudson's Plain Directions for

Making Wills in conformity with the Law: wirh a clear Exposition of the Law relating to the Distribution of Personal Estate in the case of Intestacy, two Forms of Wilis, and much useful Information. New and enlarged K. dition; including the provisions of the Wills Act Amendment Act. Fcp. Svo. price 25.6rf.

Hudson's Executor's Guide,

New and enlarged Edition; with the Addition of Directions for paying Succession Duties on Real Property under Wills and Intestacies, and a Table for finding tlie Values of Annuities and the Amount of Legacy and Succession Duty thereon. Fcp. Svo. price 6s.

Hulbert- The Gospel revealed to Job; or. Patriarchal Faith illustrated in Thirty Lectures on the princip l Passsagea of the Book of Job: With Explanatory, Illustrative, and Critical Notes. By the Rev. C. A. Hulbert, M. A., Svo. price I2s.

Humbley- Journal of a Cavalry

Officer: Including the memorable Sikh Campaign of 1845-6. By W. W. W. Humb-LEv, M. A., Captain, 9th Queen's Royal Lancers. With Plans and Map. Royalgvo price 21s.

Hlunboldt'S Aspects of Nature-Translated, with the Author's authority, by Mrs. Sabine. New Edition. i6mo. price 68.: or in 2 vols. 3. 6. each cloth; 25. Gd. each sewed.

Humboldt's Cosmos- Translated with the Author's authority, by Mrs. Sabine. Vols. 1. and II. 16mo, Half-a-Crown each, sewed; 3s. 6rf. each cloth: or in post Svo. 12s. Gd. each cloth. Vol. III. post Svo. 12. 6rf. cloth: or in 16rao. Part I. 28. 6rf. sewed, 35. 6rf. cloth; and Part II. 38. sewed, 4s. cluth.

Humphreys. Sentiments and

Similes of tshakspeare. With an elaborately illuminated border in the characteristic style of the Elizabethan Period, massive carved covers, and other Embellishments, designed and executed by H- N. Humphreys. Square, post Svo. price 2 s.

Hunt. Researches on Light in its Chemical Relations; Embracing a Consideration of all the Photographic Processes. By Robert Hvnt, F. R. S., Professor of Physics in the Metropolitan School of Science, Second Edition; with. Plate and Woodcuts. Svo. price 10. Grf,

Mrs- Jameson's Legends of the
Saints and Martyrs. Formiijg tlie First Series of Sacred and Legendary Art. Second Edition j with numerous' Woodcuts, and 16 Etchingsby the Author, Square crown Svo. price 28.

Mrs- Jameson's Legends of the
Monistic Orders, as represented in the Fine Arts. Forming the Second Series of Sacred and Legertdari Art. Second Edition, corrected and enlarged; with 11 Etchings by the Author, and 88 Woodcuts. Square crown Svo. price 28.

Mrs- Jameson's Leg: ends of the
Madonna, as represented in the Fine Arts. Forming the Third Series of Sacred and Letrendary Art. With 55 Drawings by the Author, and 152 Wood Engravings. Square crown Svo. price 28.

Jameson. A Commonplace Book of Thoughts, Memories, aud Fancies, Original and Selected. Part I. Ethics and Character; Part II. Literature and Art. By Mrs. Jameson. With Etchings and Wood Entrravings. Square crown Svo.

Just read!.

Lord Jeffrey's Contributions to the Edinbureh Review. A New Edition, complete in One Volume; with a Portrait engraved by Henry Robinson, and a Vignette View of Craigcrook, engraved by J. Cousen. Square crown 8vo. 2U. cloth; or 30a. calf.

, Also a LIBRARY EDITION, in 3 vols. Svo. price 42s.

Bishop Jeremy Taylor's Entire
Works: With his Life, by Bishop Hebeb. Revised and corrected by the Rev. Charles Paoe Eden, Fellow of Oriel College, Ox ford. Now complete in 10 vols. 8vo. price it. 58.

Jesse. Russia and the War.
By Captain Jesse (late Unattached), Author of Murray's Handbook for Hussia, etc. Crown 8vo. with Plan, price 2s. d.

Johnston. A New Dictionary of
Geography, Descriptive, Physical, Statistical, and Historical: Forming a complete General Gazetteer of the World. By Ale-T-ander Keith Johnston, F. R. S. E., F. R. G. S. F. G. S. In One Volume of 1,4411 pages; comprising nearly 50, OU0 Names of Places. 8vo. price 36s. cloth; or half, bound in russia,-ils.

Kemble. The Saxons in England:. History of the English Commonwealth till the period of the Norman Conquest. By John Mitchei.1, Kemble M. A., F. C. P. S., etc. 2 vols. Svo. price 28.

Kent. Aletheia 5 or, the Doom of JMythooJ y. With other Poems. By William Charles Mark Kent. Fcp. 8to. price 7s. 6rf,,

Kippis's Collection of Hymns and Psalms for Public and Private Worship. New Edition; including a New Supplement by the Rev. Edmdnd Kell, M. A. 18mo. price 4. cloth; or 4s. Grf. roan.

Kirby. The Life of the Rev. "Wii LiaM Kirby, M A., Rector of Barham Author of one of the Bridgewatertreatises, and Joint-. uthor of the Introduction tu Entomology. By the Rev. John Freeman. M. A. With Portrait, Vignette, and Facsimile, Svo. price 16s.

Kirby Spence's Introduction to Entomology; or. Elements of the Natural History of Insects: comprising an account of noxious and useful Insects, of their Metamorphoses, Food, Stratagems, Habitations, Societies, Motions, Noises, Hybernation, Instinct, etc. New Edition. 2 vols. 8vo. with Plates, price 31s. 6d.

The Lady Una and her Queen- dom; or. Reform at the Right End. By the Author of Home Trntha for Home Peace, etc. Fcp. Svo. price 7s.

Laing's (S.) Observations on the

Soci; il and Political State of Denmark and the Duchies of Sleswickand Holstcinin 1851: Being the Third Series of jxotes of a Tra' veller. Svo. price 12s.

Laing's (S.) Observations on the

Social and Political State of the European People in 1843 aud 1849: Being the Second Series of Notes of a Traveller. Svo. price 14s.

L. E. L. The Poetical Works of Letitia Elizabeth Landon. New Edition; with 2 Vitfnettesby Richard Doyle. 2 vols. 16mo. price 10a. cloth; morocco, l.

Dr. Latham on Diseases of the

Heart. Lectures on Subjects connected with Clinical Medicine: Jiseases of the Heart. By P. M. Latham, M. D., Physician Extraordinary to the Queeu. New EJiitioa-. 2 vols. l2mo. price 16.

Mrs. K. Lee's Elements of Natural History; or first Principles ofzoo-ioify: comprising the Principles of Classification, interspersed with amusintf and instructive Accounts of the most remarkable Animals. New Edition, enlarged; with numerous additional Woodcuts, f'cp. Svo. price "Js. 6rf.

Letters on Happiness, addressed to a Friend. By itie Author of Letters to My Uuknoion Friends, etc. Fcp, Svo. price 65.

Letters to my Unknown Friends

By a Lady, Author of Letters on Happiness, owti i and cheaper Edition. Fcp. Svo. price os.

Lindley. The Theory of Horticulture; Or, an Attempt to explain th principal Operations of Gardening upon Pliysiological Principles. By John Lindley, Ph O. F. R. S. New Edition, revised end improved; with Wood Enifravint s. Svo. n the press.

PUBLISHED BY LONGMAN, BROWN, AND Co.

LARDNER'S CABINET CYCLOPEDIA.

Of History, Biography, Literature, the Arts and Scienceb, Natural History, and Manufactures: A Series of Original Works by

SIR JOHN HERSCHEL, SIR JAMES MACKINTOSH, ROBERT SOUTHEY, SIR DAVID BREWSTER, THOMAS KEIGHTLEY, JOHN FORSTER,

SIR WALTER SCOTT, THOMAS MOORE, BISHOP THIRLWALL, THE REV. G, R. GLEIG, J. C. L. DE SISMONDI, JOHN PHILLIPS, F. R. S., G. S,

And other Emixent Writers.

Complete in 132 vols. Fcp. 8vo. with Vignette Titles, price, in cloth. Nineteen Guineas. The Works jeparately. In Sets or Series, price Three Shillings and Sixpence each Volume.

A List of the Works composing the CABINET CYCLOPieDIA: 1. Beil s History of Russia. 3 vols. 10s, Gd.

2. Bell'slivesofbritishpoets,2vols. 7.

3. Brewster's Optics,., 1vol. 3s. 6.

4. Cooley's Maritime and In- land Discovery. 3 vols. 10. 6rf.

5. Crowe's History of France, 3 vols. loa. firf.

6. De Morgan on Probabilities, I vol. 3s. Gd. J De Sismondi s History of the Italian Republics, I vol. Zs.6d.

8, De Sismoudi's Fall of the

Roman Empire., 2 vols. 7 9. Donuvan s Chemistry, 1vol. 8s. Gd.

10. Donovan's Domestic Eco- nomy. 2 vols. 7.

11. Dunham's Spain and Por- tugal. 5 vols. 7. 6rf.

12. Dunham's History of Den- mark, Sweden, and Norway. 3 vols. loj. Crf, 13. Dunham's History of Po- land. 1 vol. 3s. 6tf.

14. Dunham's. Germanic Em- pire. 3 vols. los. Gd.

15. Dunham's Europe during the Middle Ag es. 4 vols. lis.

16. Dunham's British Drama- tists.2 vols. 7 ' 17. Dunham's Lives of Early Writers of Great Britain, I vol. 3. 6rf.

18. Fergus's History of the

Uiiited States. 2 vols. 7 19. Fosbroke's Greek and Ro- man Antiquities. 2vols. Ts- 20. Forster's Lives of the

Statesmen of the Commonwealth. 5 vols. 17. 6rf.

21. Glei 's Lives of British

Military Commanders 3 vols, 10. 6d.

22. Grattan's History of the

Netherlands., I vol. 39.6.

23. Henslow's Botany., 1vol. Ss. Gd.

24. Hersehel'a Astronomy. 1 vol. 3. Gd.

25. Herschel's Disconrse on

Natural Philosophy. 1vol. 34.6.

26. History of Rome, 2vols. 7.

27. History of Switzerland. 1vol. Ss. Gd.

28. Houand s Manufactures in

Metal,. 3 vols. 10. Gd.

29. James's Lives of Foreign

Statesmen. 5 vols. 17a. 6d, 30. Kater and Lardner's Me- chanics. 1 vol, Zs. Gd.

31. Keightley s X Outlines of

History.1 vol. 3.6rf.

82, Lardner's Arithmetic. 1 vol, Ss. Gd.

83. Lardner's Geometry. 1 vol, 3. 6rf.

34. Lardner on Heat. 1 vol.

35. Lardner's Hydrostatics and Pneumatics.,. 1 vol, 36. Lardnerand Walker's Elec- tricity and Magnetism, 2 vols.
37. Mackintosh, Forster, and Cnurtenay's Lives of British Statesmen. 7'ols.
38. Mackintosh, Wallace, and Bell's History of England.,. 10 vols.
39. Montgomery and Shelley's Eminent Italian, Spanish, and Portuguese Authors,3 vols.
40. Moore's History of Ireland, 4 vols.
41. Nicolas's Chronology of History.1 vol, 42. Phillips' Treatise on Geo- logy. 2 vols.
43. Poweirshistory of Natural Philosophy. 1 vol.
44. Porter's Treatise on the Manufacture of Silk, 1 vol, 45. Porter's Manufacture of Porcelain and Glass. 1 vol.
46. Rescue's British Lawyers, 1 vol, 47. Scott's History of Scot- land.,.2 vols.
48. Shelley's Lives of Eminent French Authors. 2 vols.
49. Shuckard and Swainson's Insects. 1 vol.
50. Southey's Lives of British Admirals. 5 vols.
51. Stebbing's Church History, 2vols.
52. Stebbing's History of the Reformation. 2 vols.
53. Swainson's Discourse on Natural History. I vol.
54. Swainson's Natural His- tory and Classification of Animals.,1 vol.
55. Swainson's Habits and In stincts of Animals. I vol.
56. Swainson's Birds. 2 vols.
57. Swainson's Fish, Reptiles, etc. 2vol8.
58. Swainson's Quadrupeds, 1 vol, 59. Swainson's Shells and Shell-fish.1 vol, 60. Swainson's Auimalsin Me- nageries., 1 vol.
61. Swainson's Taxidermy and Biography of Zoologists 1 vol, 62. Thirlwall's History of Greece.,. 8vols, 3s.6rf. 35. fid.
24s. 6d.
35s.
10s. 6rf. I4rf.
3a. 6rf.
35,6f.

Dr. John Lindley's Introduction to Botany. New Edition, with Corrections and copious Additions; Six Plates and numerous Woodcuts. Svo. price 24.

Linwood- Anthologia Oxonien- sia; ive, Klorilcy ium e lusihus poeticis dive rsorum Oxoniensium (jriecis et Latinis decerptun Curante Gulielmo Linwooo, M. A. iedischristi Alummo. Svo. price 14.

Dr. Little on Deformities. On the Nature and Treatment of Deformities of the Human Frame. By W. J. Little, M. D., Physician to tlie Loiidou Hospital, etc. With 160 Woodcuts and Diagrams. Svo. price lo.

Litton. The Church of Christ, in its Idea, Attributes, and Ministry: With a particular Reference to the Controversy oil the Subject between Romanists and Protestants. By the Rev. Edward Arthur Litton, M. A., Vice-Principal of St. Edmund Hall, Oxford. Svo. price l- s.

Loch- A practical Legal Guide for Sailors and Mertliants durini W'ar: With Appendices containintj the Orders in Council and other Official Documents relating; to the present War. By Wit, i jam Adam Loch, of the Hon. Society of Liu-coin's Inu. Svo. price 9. 6rf.

Lorimer's (C.)Letters to a Young
Master Mariner on some Subjects connected with his Calling. New Edition. Fcp. Svo. price 5s. Gd.

Loudon's Self-Instruction for
Young Gardeners,. Foresters, Bailiff's, Land Stewards, and" Farmers; in Arithmetic, Book-keeping:, Geometry, Mensuration, Practicaltrigonometry, Mechanics, Land-Surveying, Levelling, Planning and Mappine, Architectural Drawing, andlsometrjcal Projection and Perspective. Svo. with Portrait, price 7. 6rf.

Loudon's Encyclopaedia of Gar- deniuif; comprising the Tiieory and Practice of Hoiticultnre, Floriculture, Arboriculture, and Landscape Gardening: Including all the latest improvements; with ma iy hundred Woodcuts. New Edition, corrected and improved by Mrs. Loudon. Svo. price 30ff.

Loudon's Encyclopaedia of Trees and Shrubs; or the Arboretuin et Fruticf-tum Britannicum abridged: Containing the Hardy Trees and Shrubs of Great Britain, Native and Foreign, Scientifically and Popularly Described: with their Propagation, Culture, and Uses in the Arts; and with Engravings of nearly all the Species. VVith about 2,00(1 Woodcuts. Svo. price 50.

Loudon's Encyclopaedia of Agriculture: comprising the Theory and Practice of the Valuation, Transfer, Laying-out, Improvement, and Management of Landed Property, and of the Cultivation and Economy of the Animal and Vegetable Productions of Agriculture. New Edition; with 1,100 Woodcuts. Svo. price 50.

Loudon's Encyclopaedia of
Plants, including all the Plaints which are now found in, or have been introduced into, Great Britain, t; iving their Natural History, accompanied by such descriptions, engraved Figures, and elementary details, as may enable a beginner, who is a mere English reader, to discover the name of every Plant which he may find in flower, and ac-(juire all the information respecting it which is useful and interesting. New Edition, corrected throughout and brought down to the year 1855, bymrs. LoudOX and George Don, Esq., F. L. S., etc. 8vo.

n the Spring:

Loudon's Encyclopaedia of Cottage, Farm, and Villa Architecture and Furniture: containing numerous Designs, from the Villa to the Cottage and the Farm, including Farm Houses, Farmeries, and other Agricultural Buildings; Country Inns, Pul)lic Houses, and Parochial Schools, with the requisite Fittings-up, Fixtures, and Furniture, and appropriate Offices, Gardens, and Garden Scenery. New Edition, edited by Mrs. Loudon; with 2,000 Woodcuts. Svo. price 63.

Loudon's Hortus Britannicus 5

Or, Catalogue of all the Plants indigenous to, cultivated in, or introduced into Britain. An entirely New Edition corrected throughout: With a Supplement, including all the New Plants, and a New General Index to the whole Work. Edited by Mrs. Loudon; assisted by W. H. Baxter and David Woosteu. Svo. price 315. 6rf. The Supplement separately, price H.

Mrs. Loudon's Amateur Gardener's Calendar; Being a Monthly Guide as to what should be avoided as well as what should be done in a Garden in each Month: with plain Rules low to do wliat is requisite. 16mo. with Woodcuts, 7 6.

Mrs. Loudon's Lady's Country

Companion; or. How to Knjoy a Country laig Rationally. Fourth Edition, with Plates and Wood Engravings. Fcp. Svo. price 08.

Low. A Treatise on the Domesticated Animals of the Britifih Islands: comprehending the Natural and Economical History of Species and Varieties; the Description of the Properties of external Form; and Observations on the Principles and Practice of Breeding. By L). Low, Esq., F. R. S. E. Svo. with Woodcuts, price 25.

PUBLISHED BY LONGMAN, BROWN, and Co.

Low's Elements of Practical

Atjriculture; cumprehenditig the Cultivation of Plants, the Husbandry of the Domestic Animals, and the Economy of the Farm. New Edition; with 20U Woodcuts, 8vo. 2U.

Macaulay. Speeches of the

Riuht Hon. T. B. Macaulay, MP. Corrected by Himself. 8vo. price 12s.

Macaulay. The History of England from the Accession of James II. by Thomas Babi. votox Macaulay, New Editiou. Vols. Land U. 8vo. price 32s.

Mr. Macaulay's Critical and

Historical Essays contributed to the Edinburgh Review. Four Editions, as follows:
1. Library Edition (the Seventh), in 3 vols. 8vo. price 365.
2. Complete in One Volume, with Por- trait and Vitrnette. Square crown Svo. price 21. cloth; or ios. calf.
3. Another Edition, in 3 vols. fcp. Svo.
price 21j.
4. People's Edition, in 2 vols, crown 8to. price 8s. cloth.

Macaulay. Lays of Ancient

Rome, Ivry, and the Armada. 13y Thomas Babinoton Macaulay. New Edition I6mo. price 4. 6rf. cloth; or los. W. bound in morocco.

Mr. Macaulay's Lays of Ancient

Rome. With numerous Illustrations, Original and from the Antique, drawn on Wood by George Scarf, jun. New Edition. Fcp. 4to. price 21s. boards; or 42s. bound in morocco.

Macdonald. Villa Verocchio; or the Youth of Leonardo da Vinci: A Tale. By the late Diana Louisa Macdonald. Fcp. Svo. price Gs.

Macintosh. A Military Tour in

European Turkey, the Crimea, and on th" Eastern Shores of the Black Sea: including Routes across the Balkan into Bulg. aria, and Excuri ions in the Turkish, Russian! and Persian Provinces of the Caucasian Range; with Strategical Observations on thj Probable Scene of the Operations of the Allied E-tpeditionary Force. By Major-Gen. A. F. Mackintosh, K. H., F. R. G. S., F. G. S., Commanding Her Majesty's Troops in the Ionian Islands. With Maps. 2 vols, post Svo. price 21s.

Sir James Mackintosh's History of Englnnd from the Earliest Times to the final Establishment of the Reformation. Library Edition, revised by the Author's Son. 2 vols. Svo. price 21s.

Mackintosh. Sir James Mackintosh's Miscellaneous Works: Including his Contributions to the Edinburgh Review. Complete in One Volume; with Portrait and Vignette. Square crown Svo. price 21s. cloth; or 30s. bound in calf.

, Also a NEW EDITION, in 3 vols. fcap. Svo. price 21s.

M'Culloch. A Dictionary,

Practical, Theoretical, and Historical, of Commerce and Commercial Navigation. Illustrated with Maps and Plans. By J. R. W'CulLOCH, Esq. New Edition; embrae ing a large mass of new and important In. formation in regard to the Trade, Commercial Law, and Navigation of this and other Countries. Svo. price 50s. cloth; half-russia, with flexible back, SSs.

M'Culloch. A Dictionary,

Geographical, Statistical, and Historical, of the various Countries, Places, and Principal Natural Objects in the World. By J. R. M'Culloch, Esq. Illustrated with Six large Maps. New Editiou, with a Supplement, comprising tlic Population of Great Britain from the Census of 1851. 2 vols. Svo. price 63s.

M'Culloch. An Account, Descriptive and Statistic: il of the British Empire; E. xhibiting its Extent, Physical Capacities, Population, Industry, and'Civil and Religious Institutions. By J. R. M'Culloch, Esq. Fourth Edition, revised; with an Appcndixoftables. 2vols.8vo. price42s.

Maitland. The Church in the

Catacombs: A Description of the Primitive Church of Rome, illustrated by its Sepulchral Remains. By the Rev. Charles Maitland. New Edition, with many VV'ood-cuts, Svo. price 14s.

Mrs. Marcet's Conversations on

Chemistry, in wliich tiie Elements of that Science are familiarly Explained and Illustrated by Experiments. New Edition, enlarged and improved. 2 vols. fcp. Svo. price 14s.

Mrs. Marcet's Conversations on

Natural Philosophy, in which the Elements of that Science are familiarly explained. New Edition, enlarged and corrected; with 23 Plates. Fcp. Svo. price I0. 6d.

Mrs- Marcet's Conversations on
Political Economy, in which the Elements of that Science are familiarly explained. New Edition. Fcp. 8vo. price . 6d.

Mrs. Marcet's Conversations on
Vegetable Physiology; comprehending the Elements of Botany, with their Application to Agiicuhore. New Edition; with Four Plates. Fcp. 8vo. price 98,

Mrs. Marcet's Conversations on
Land and Water. New Edition, revised and corrected; with a coloured Map, shewing the comparative Altitude of Mountains. Fcp. 8vo. price 5. Gd.

Martineau. Church History in
England: Being a Sketch of the History of the Church of England from the Earliest Times to the Period of the Reformation, By the Rev. Arthur Martineau M. A., late Fellow of Trinity College, Cambridge. 2mo. price 6s.

Maunder's Biographical Treasury; consisting of Memoirs, Sketches, and brief Notices of above 12,000 Eminent Persons of all Ages and Nations, from the Earliest Period of History. Eighth Edition, revised throughout, and brought down to the close of the year 1863. Fcp. 8vo. 10. cloth i bound in roan, 13. i calf, 125. 6d.

Maunder's Historical Treasury 5 comprising a General Introductory Outline of Universal History, Ancient and Modern, and a Series of separate Histories of every principal Nation. New Edition; revised throughout, and brought down to the Present Time. Fcp. 8vo. 10. cloihi roan, 12a.; cal,12.6rf.

Maunder's Scientific and Lite- raryj Treasury; A New and Popular En-cyclopredia of Science and the Belles-Lettres; including all Branches of Science, and every subject connected with Literature and Art, New Edition. Fcp. Svo orice 10s. cloth; bound in roan, 12s.; calf lettered, 12s. Gd,

Maunder's Treasury of Natural
History; Or, a Popular Dictionary of Animated Nature: In which the Zoological Characteristics that disting-uish the different Classes, Genera, and Species, are combined with a variety of interesting Information illustrative of the Animal Kingdom. W'itli 000 Woodcuts. New Edition; with 900 Woodctits. Fcp. Svo. price 10. cloth; roaoj 12.; calf, 12ji. Gd.

Maunder's Treasury of Knowledge, and Library of Reference. Comprising an English Dictionary and Grammar, an Universal Gazetteer, a Classical Dictionary, a Chronology, a Law Dictionary, a Synopsis of the Peerage, numerous useful Tables, etc. The Twentieth Edition revised and corrected: With some Additions. Fcp Svo. price 10s. cloth; bound in roan, 12s.; calf, 12. Gd.

Merivale. A History of th
Romans under the Empire. By the Rev. Charles Merivale, B. D., late Fellow of St. John's College, Cambridge. Vols. I. and II. Svo. price 2Ss.; and vol. III. completing the History to the Establishment of the Monarchy by Augustus, price 1-U,

Merivale. The Fall of the Roman Republic: A Short History of the last Century of the Commonwealth. 'By the Rev. Charlesmerivale, B. D., late Fellow of St. John's College, Cambridge. 12mo. price 7s. Gd.

Merivale. An Account of the

Life and Letters of Cicero. Translated from the German of Abeken; and Edited by the Rev. Charles Merivale, B. D, 12mo-price 9s. Gd.

Milner. The Baltic 5 Its Gates,

Shores, and Cities: With a Notice of the White Sea, etc. By the Rev. T- Milneb, W. A., F. R. G. S. Post Svo. Jtust ready.

Milner's History of the Church of Christ. With Additions by the late Rev. Isaac Milner, D. D., F R. S. A New Edition, revised, with additional Notes by the Rev. T. Gkantuam, B D. 4 vols-Svo. price 62.

Montgomery- Memoirs of the

Life and Writings of James Montgomery: Including Selections from his Correspondence and Conversations. By John Hol-LANi and James Everett, a the press.

Montgomery. Original Hymns for Public, Social, and Private Devotion. By James Montgomery. ISmo, ba. Gd,

James Montgomery's Poetical

Works: Collective Edition; with the Author's Autobiographical Prefaces, oomplete in One Volume; with Portrait and Vignette. Square crown Svo. price Os. Gd. cloth; morocco,21. Or in 4 vols. fcp. Svo. with Portrait, and seven Plates, price 205. cloth; morocco, 36.

PUBLISHED BY LONGMAN. BROWN, AND Co.

Moore. Man and his Motives.

By Geohoe Mooke, M-I Member of the Royal College of Physiciaus. Third and cheaper Edition, Fcp. Svo. price 6a.

Moore. The Power of the Soul over the Body, considered in relation to Health and Morals. By Georoe Moore, M. D., Member of the Royal Coueg e of Physicians, etc. Fifth and cheaper rf ton. Fcp. Svo. price 6s.

Moore. The Use of the Body in relation to the Blind. By George Moore, M. D., Member of the Royal College of Physicians, Third and cheaper Edition, Fcp, Svo. price 6.

Moore. Health, Disease, and

Remedy, familiarly and practically considered in a few of their Relations to the Blood. By George Moore, M. D, Post Svo. 7s, 6d,

Moore- Memoirs, Journal, and

Correspondence of Thomas Moore. Edited by the Ria: ht Hon. Lord John Russell, M. P. With Portraits and Vignette Illustrations. Vols. I. to VI. post Svo. 105, 6d. each. Vols. VH. and VIU. completing the work, are uearly ready,

Thomas Moore's Poetical Works-

Containing the Author's recent Introduction and Notes. Complete in One Volume; with a Portrait, and a View of Sloperton Cottage. Medium Svo. price 21s. cloth; morocco 425. Or in 10 vols. fcp. Svo. with Portrait, aud 19 Plates, price 355,

Moore. Songs, Ballads, and

Sacred Songs. BytHOMAs Moore, Author of Laua Rtiokh etc. First collected Edition, with Vignette by R. Doyle. 16mo. price oj. doth; 125. 6rf. bound iu morocco.

Moore's Irish Melodies. New

Edition, with the Autobiographical Preface from the Collective Editicm of Mr. Moore's Poetical Works, and a Vignette Title by D. Maclise, R. A. 16mo. price 55. cloth; 25. Qd, bound in morocco

Moore's Irish Melodies. Illustrated by U. Maclise, R. A. New and cheaper Edition; with 161 Designs, and the whole of the Letter-press engraved on Steel, by F. P. Becker, Super royal Svo. price 315. 6rf. boards; bound in morocco, 2. 125. 6rf.

, The Original Edition, in imperial Svo. price 63s. boards; morocco, d 4. 145. 6rf.; Proofs, s66. 65. boards, may still be had.

Moore's Lalla Rookh: An Oriental Romance. New Edition; with the Autobiographical Preface from the Collective Sedition of Mr. Moore's Poetical Works, and a Vignette Title by D. Maclise, R. A. 16mo. 5. cloth; Qt 2s."d, morocco.

Moore's Lalla Kookh: An Oriental Romance. With 13 highly-finished Steel Plates, from Designs by Corbould, Meadows, and Stephanoff. New Edition. Square crown Svo. 155. cloth; morocco, 2S5.

A few copies of the Original Edition, in royal Svo. price One Guinea, still remain.

Morton's Manual of Pharmacy for the Student of Veterinary Medicine: Containing the Substances employed at the Royal Veterinary College, with an attempt at their Classification; and the Pharmacopoeia of that Institution. Fifth Edition, Fcp. Svo, price IO5.

Moseley. The Mechanical Principles of Engineering and Architecture. By the Rev. H. Moselex-, M. A., F. R. S., Professor of Natural Philosophy and Astronomy in King's College, London. Svo. price 245.

Mure. A Critical History of the Language and Literature of Ancient Greece. By William INIure, M. P. of Caldwell, Vols. 1. to III. Svo. price 365. Voir IV. price 155.

Murray's Encyclopaedia of Creo- graphy: Comprisinga complete Description of the Earth: exhibiting its Relation to the Heavenly Bodies, its Physical Structure, the Natural History of each Country, and the Industry, Commerce, Political Institutions, and Civil and Social State of All Nations. Second Edition; with S2 Maps, and upwards of 1,000 other Woodcuts. Svo. price 6U5.

Neale- " Risen from the

Ranks;" Or, Conduct versus Caste, By the Rev. EnskinE Neale, M. A., Rector of Kirton, Suffolk, Fcap. Svo, price 65.

Neale. The Riches that bring no Sorrow. By the Rev. Erssiise Neale M. A, Fcp. Svo. price 65,

Neale. The Earthly Resting

Places of the Just. By the Rev. Erskine NEilE, M. A. Fcp. Svo. with Woodcuts,

Neale. The Closing Scene; or

Christianity and Infidelitr contrasted in the Last Hours of Remarkable Persons. By the Ret. Kbskixe Neale, M. A. New Edition. 2 vols. fcp. Sto. price 12.; or separately, 6a, each.

Ne-WTnan. Discourses addressed to Mixed Congregations. By John Henry Newman, Priest of theoratory of St. Philip Neri. Second Edition. 8vo, price 12.

Oldacre. The Last of the Old

Squires: A Sketch. By Cedric Oldacre, Esq., of Sax-Norraanbury, sometime of Christ Church, Oxou. Crown 8vo. 95. 6d.

Oldmixon. Gleanings from Piccadilly to Pera. By J. V. Oi. dmixon, Commander U. N. With Illustrations printed iu Colours. Postsvo. Jutt ready.

Opie (Mrs.) Memorials of the

Life of Amelia Opie, Selected and Arranged from her Letters, Diaries, and (, ther Manuscripts. By Cecilia Lucy Brightwell. Second Edition; with Portrait. 8vo. price loi. 6i.

Stray Leaves from an Arctic

Journal; or. Eighteen Months in the Polar Regions in search of Sir John Franklin's Expedition. Bv Lieut. S. Osborn, R. N., Commanding H. M. S. V. Pionfcr. With Map and 4 coloured Plates. Post 8vo. price 12s.

Owen Jones. riowers and their

Kindred Thoughts. A Series of Stanzas. By Mary Anne Bacon. With beautiful Illustrations of Flowers printeil in Colours by Owen Jones. Imperial 8vo. price 31s. 6d. elegantly bound in calf.

Owen. Lectures on the Comparative Anatomy and Pliysiology of the Invertebrate. nimals. By Richard Owen, F. R. S. Hunterian Professor in the Royal College of Surgeons. New Edition, corrected, 8yo. with Woodcuts, n the press.

Professor Owen's Lectures on the Comparntive Anatomy and Physiology of the Vertebrate Animals. With numerous Woodcuts. Vol. I. 8vo. price 14.

The Complete Works of Blaise

Pascal. Translated from the French, with Memoir, Introductions to the various Works, Editorial Notes, and Appendices. by George Pearce, Esq. 3 vols, post 8yo. with Portrait, 2.55. 6d.

Captain Peel's Travels in Nubia.

A Ride through the Nubian Desert. By Captain W. Peel, R. N. Post 8vo. with a Route Map, price 5s.

Pereira's Treatise on Pood and

Diet. With Observations on the Dietetical Regimen suited for Disordered States ot the Digestive Organs; and an Account of the Dietaries of some of the principal Metropolitan and other Establishments for Paupers, Lunatics, Criminals, Children, the Sick, etc. 8vo. 168.

Peschel's Elements of Physics.

Translated from the German, with Notes, by E. West. With Diagrams and Woodcuts. 3 vols. fcp. 8vo. price 21s.

Phillips. A Guide to Geology.

By John Phillips,. M. A. F. R. S. F. G. S., Deputy Reader in Geology in the University of Oxford. Fourth Kditiou, corrected to the Present Time; with 4 Plates. Fcp. 8vo. price.5s,

Phillips's Elementary Introduction to Mineralogy. A New Edition, with extensive Alterations and Additions, byh. J. Brooke, F. R. S., F. GS.; andw. H. Miller, M. A., F. G. S., Professor of Miueralogy in the University of Cambridge. With numerous Wood Engravings. Post 8vo. price ISs.

Phillips. Pigures and Descriptions of the Pala: ozoic Fossils of Cornwall, Devon, and West Somerset; observed in the course of the Ordnance Geological Survey of that District. By John IPhillips, M. A. etc. 8vo. with 60 Plates, price its.

Captain Portlock's Report on the Geology of the County of Londonderry, and of Parts of Tyrone and Fermanagh, examined and described under the Authority of the Master-General and Board of Ordnance. Svo. with 48 Plates, price 24s.

Power's Sketches in New Zealand, with Pen and Pencil. From a journal kept in that Country, from July 1846 to June 1848. With Plates and Woodcuts. Postsvo. 12.

Psychological Inquiries, in a
Series of Essays intended to illustrate the Influence of the Physical Organisation on the Mental Faculties. Fcp. Svo. price 5.

PUBLISHED BY LONGMAN, BROWN, and Co.

Pulman's Vade-Meciim of Ply-
Kisliiiiir for Trout; bciiij a complete Pr; ic-ticftl Treatise on that Branch ot the Art of Angling:; with plain and copious Instruc-tiodS for the Manufacture of Artificial Flies. Third Edition, with Woodcuts. Fcp. Svo. price 6.

Pycroft's Course of English
Heading, adapted to every Taste and Capacity; With Literary Anecdotes. New and cheaper Edition. Fcp. Svo. price 55.

Dr- Recce's Medical Guide-, for the use of the Clergy, Heads of Families, Schools, and Junior Medical Practitioners: Comprising a complete Modern Dispensatory, and a Practical Treatise on the distinguishing Symptoms, Causes, Prevention, Cure, and Palliation of the Diseases incident to the Human Frame. Seventeenth Edition, corrected and enlarged by the Author's Son, Dr. H. Reece, M. R. C. S. etc. Svo. price 125.

Rich's Illustrated Companion to the Latin Dictionary and Greek Lexicon: Forming a Glossary of all the Words representing Visible Objects connected with the Arts, Manufactures, and livery-day Life of the Ancients. With Woodcut Representations of nearly 2,000 Objects from the Antique. Post Svo. price 21j.

Sir J. Richardson's Journal of a Boat Voyage through Rupert's Land and the Arctic Sea, in Search ttf the Discovery Ships under Command of Sir John Franklin. With an Appendix on the Physical Geography of North America; a Map, Plates, and Woodcuts. 2 vols. Svo. price 31s. 6d.

Horsemanship 5 or, the Art of
Riding and Managing a Horse, adapted to the Guidance of Ladies and Gentlemen on the Road and in the Field: With Instructions for Breaking in Colts and Young Horses. By Captain Richardson, late of the 4th Light Dragoons. With o Line Engravings. Square crown 8vo, price I'is.

Riddle's Complete Latin-Eng- lish and English-Latin Dictionary, for the use of Colleges aud Schools. Ntio and cheaper Editiouf revised and corrected. 8V0.2U.
c. oi J' " "'? '- '" Dictionary, 7 Separately I l Latiu-Engli. hdictionar,15.

Riddle's Copious and Critical
Latin-English Lexicon, founded on the German-Latin Dictionaries of Dr. William Freund. New and cheaper Edition. Post 4to. price 31. fid.

Riddle's Diamond Latin-Eng- lish Dictionary: A (iuide to the Meaning, Quality, and right Accentuation of Latin Classical Words. Royal 32mo. price 4.

Rivers's Rose-Amateur's Guides containing ample Descriptions of all the fine leading varieties of Koses, regularly classed in their respective Families; their History and Mode of Culture. Fifth and cheappr Edition, much improved. Fcp. Svo. price 'ds. Gd.

Dr. E. Robinson's Greek and

English Lexicon of the Greek Testament. A New Edition, revised and in great part re-written. 3vo. price 18s.

Rogers- Essays selected from

Contributions to the Edinburgh Review By HEMiy KooeRb. 2 vols. 6vo. price24.

Dr- Roget's Thesaurus of English Words and Phrases classified and arranged so as to facilitate the Expression of" Ideas and assist in Literary Composition. New Edition, revised and enlarged. Rleilium Svo. price 14.

Rowton's Debater: A Series of complete Debates, Outlines of Debates, and Questions for Discussion; with ample references to the best Sources of Information on each particular Topic. New Edition. Fcp. Svo. price 6.

Letters of Rachael Lady Rus- sell. A New Edition, including several unpublished Letters. With Portrnits, Vignettes, and F'acsimile. 2 vols, post Svo price 15.

The Life of William Lord Rus- sell. By the Ritjht Hon. Lord John Rus-seLi,, M P. The Fourth Edition, complete in One Volume; with a Portrait engraved on Steei by S. Bellin. Post. Svo. price los 6rf.

St. John (the Hon. F-) Rambles in Search of Sport, in Germany, France, Italy, and Russia. By the Honourable Ferdinand St. John. With Four coloured Plates. Post Svo. price 9s. 6rf.

St. John (H-) The Indian Ar- chipelago; Its History and Present State. By lionaCE St, John. 2 vols, post Svo. price ila.

Mr. St. John's Work on Egypt.

Isis: An Eg-yptian Pilgrimagje. By James AcoustUs St. Johv. 2 vols, post 8vo. 21j?.

St. John (J. A.) There and

Back Ag! un in Search of Beauty. By J. A. St. John. 2 vols, post 8vo. 21.

The Saints our Example- By the Author of Letters, to my Unknown Friendst etc, Fcp. 8vo. price 78.

Schmitz. History of Greece, from the Earliest Times to the Taking of Corinth by the Romans, B. C. 146, mainly based upon Bishop Thirlwall's History of Greece. By Dr. Leonhabd Schmitz, F. R. S. E. Rector of the High School of Edinburgh. New Edition. 12mo. price 7 6f.

Sir Edward Seaward's Narrative of his Shipwreck, and consequent Discovery of certain Islands in the Caribbean Sea. Third Edition. 2 vols, post 8vo, 215. Au Abbidoment, in 16mo, price 2ff. 6rf.

The Sermon in the Mount.

Printed by C. Whittingham, uniformly with the Thumb JBi6e; boundandclasped. frlmo. price Eighteeupence,

The Sermon on the Mount.

Printed on Silver; with Picture Subjects, numerous Landscape and Illustrative Vignettes, and Illuminated Borders in Gold and Colours, designed by M. Lepelle du Bois-Gallais. Square ISmo. price in ornamental boards, One Guinea; or 31. 6(. bound in morocco.

Self-Denial the Preparation for

Easter. By the Author of Letters to my luikriown Friendsf etc, Fcp, 8vo. 25. 6rf.

Sewell. Amy Herbert. By a

Lady. Edited by the Rev. W. Sewell, B. D. Fellow and Tutor of Exeter College, Oxford. New Edition. Fcp. 8vo. price 6j.

Sewell. The Earl's Daughter-

By the Author of Amy'Herbert. Edited by the Rev, W. Sewell, B. D. 2 vols, fcp. 8vo.9.

Sewell- Gertrude: A Tale. By the Author of Amy Herbert, Edited by the Rev. VV. Sewell, B. D, New Edition. Fcp. Svo. price 6.

Sewell- Laneton Parsonage: A

Tale for Children, on the practical Use of a Portion of the Church Catechism. By the Author Amy Herbert. Edited by the Rev. W. Sewell, B. D. New Edition. 3 vols. fcp. 8vo. price 16.

Sewell. Margaret Percival. By the Author of Amy Herbert. Edited by the Rev. W. Sewell, B. D. New Edition. 2 vols. fcp. 8vo. price 12.

By the same Authorf

Katharine Ashton. New Edition. 2 vols. fcp. 8vo, price 12j.

The Experience of Life. New

Edition. Fcp. Svo- price 7s. 6rf.

Readings for a Month Preparatory to Confirmation: Compiled from the Works of Writers of the Early and of the English Church. Fcp. Svo. price 5. 6d.

Readings for Every Day in

Lent: Compiled from the Writings of Bisaop Jeremy Taylor. Fcp. Svo. 5;.

Sharp's New British Gazetteer, or Topographical Dictionary of the British Islands and Narrow Seas: Comprising concise Descriptions of about Sixty Thousand Places, Seats, Natural Features, and Oo-jects of Note, founded on the best Authorities; full Particulars of the Boundaries, Registered Electors, etc. of the Parliamentary Boroughs; with a reference under every name to the Sheet of the Ordnance Survey, as far as completed; and an Appendix, containing a General View of the Resources of the United Kingdom, a Short Chronology, and an Abstract of certain Results of the Census of 1351. 2 vola. Svo. price 2. 16.

The Family Shakspeare 5 in which nothing is added to the Original Text; but those Words and Expressions are omitted which cannot with propriety be read aloud. By T. Bowdler, Esq. F. R. S. New Edition, in volumes for the Pocket; with 36 Wood Engravings from Designs by Smirke, Howard, and other Artists. 6 vols. fcp. 8vo. price 30,

Also a Library Edition; in One Volume. Medium Svo. price 21.

Short Whist 5 Its Rise, Pro- gress, and Laws: With Observations to make any one a Vhist Player. Containing also the Laws of Piquet, Cassino, Ecarte, Cribbao; e, Backgammon. By Major A New Edition; to which are added. Precepts fortyros. By Mrs. B Fcp.8vo.3.

PUBLISHED BY LONGMAN, BROWN, and Co.

Sinclair- The Journey of Life.

By Catherine yinclAib, Autlmr of The Business of Life (2 vols. fcp. 8vo. price 10.) New Edition, corrected and enlarged, Fcp. Svo. price bs.

Sir Roger de Coverley. From

The Spectator. With Notes and Illuatra-tions by V. Henry Wills? and Twelve fine Wood Engravings, by John Thompson from Desig ns by Frederick Tayler. Crown 8vo. price 15, boards; or 27s. bound in morocco. A Cheap Edition, without Woodtuts, in 16mo. price One Shilling.

Smee's Elements of Electro-

Metallurgry, Third Edition, revised, corrected, and considerably enlarged; with Electrotypes and numerous Woodcuts. Post Svo, price 10a. 6rf.

Smith's Sacred Annals, Sacred

Annals: Vol. III. The Gentile Nations; or. The History and Religion of the Egyptians, Assyrians, Babylonians, Medes. Persians, Greeks, and Romans, collected from ancient authors and Holy Scripture, and including the recent discoveries iti Egyptian, Persian, and Assyrian Inscriptions: Forming a complete connection of Sacred and Profane History, and shewing the Fulfilment of Sacred Prophecy. By George Smith, F. A. S., etc. In Two Parts, crown 8vo. price 12a.

By the same Author,

Sacred Annals: Vol. I. The

Patriarchal Age; or. Researches into the History and Religion of Mankind, from thf Creation of the World to the Death ot Isaac. Crown Svo. price loj.

Sacred Annals: Vol. II. The

Hebrew People; or, The History and Religion of the Israelites, from the Origin of the Nation to the Time of Christ. In Two Parts, crown Svo. price 12a.

The Works of the Rev- Sydney

Smith; including his Contributions to the Edinburgh Review. Three Editions, as follows: 1. LibBART Editiox (the Fourth) t in 3 vols. Svo. with Portrait, price 36s.

3. Complete in One Volume, with Portrait and Vignette. Square crown Svo. price 2l. cloth; or 30s. calf, 3. A New Edition, in 3 vols. fcp. price21s.

The Rev. Sydney Smith's Ele- meiitarv Sketches of Moral Philosophy, delivered at the Royal Institution in the Years 1804, 1805, and 1806. Second Edition. Svo. price 12.

The Life and Correspondence of the late Robert Soulhey, Edited by his Son, the Rev. C. C. Soothey, M. A. Vicar of Ariileigh. With Portraits; and Landscape Illustrations. 6 vols, post Svo. 63.

Southey's Life of Wesley; and

Rise and Progress of Methodism. New Edition, with Notes and Additions, by the late Samuel Taylor Coleridge, Esq., and the late Alexander Knox, Esq. Edited by the Rev. C. C. SoutHEY, M-A, 2 vols. Svo, with 2 Portraits, price 2S.

Southey's Commonplace Books.

Comprising 1. Choice Passages: with Collections for the History of Manners and Literature in England; 2. Special Collections on various Historical and Theological Subjects; 3. Analytical Readings in various branches of Literature; and 4. Original Memoranda, Literary and Miscellaneous. Edited by the Rev.1. W. VVarteb, B. D. 4 vols, square crown Svo. price 3 183.

Each Commonplace Book, complete in it self, may be iiad separately as follows;
Fikstseries CHOICE PASSAGES. ISj.
2nd Series SPECIAL COLLECTIONS. ISj.
3rd Series-ANALYTICAL READINGS, 21s.
4th Series ORIGINAL MEMORANDA. 2Is.

Robert Southey'scomplete Poetical Works; containing all the Author's last Introductions and Notes. Complete in One Volume, with Portrait and Vignette. Me dium Svo. price 21. cloth; 42s. bound in morocco. Or in 10 vols. fcp. Svo. with Po trait and 19 Plates, price 3os,

Select Works of the British

Poets; from Chaucer to Lovelace, inclusive. With Biographical Sketches by the late llobERT SodTHEy, Medium Svo. 30s.

Southey's The Doctor etc. Complete in One Volume. Edited hy the Rev-J. W. Warteb B. D. With Portrait, Vignette, Bust, and coloured Plate. New Edition, Square crown Svo. price 215.

Sir James Stephen's Lectures on the History of France. Second Edition. 2 vols. Svo. price 24.

Sir James Stephen's Essays in

Ecclesiastical Bioeraphv; from the Edin burgh Review. Third Edition. 2 vols. Svo. price 24.

Stonehenge. The Greyhound:

Being a Treatise on the Art of Breeding, Hearing, and Training Greyhounds for Public Running; their Diseases and Treat-men: Containing also, Rules for the Mauageraent of Coursing Meetings, and for the Decision of Courses. By Stonehenoe, With numerous Portraits of Greyhounds, etc., engraved on Wood, and a Frontispiece engraved ou Steel. Square crown 8vo. price 21.

Stow. The Training System, the Moral Training School, and the Normal Seminary for preparing School Trainers and Governesses. By David Stow, Esq., Honorary Secretary to the Glasgow Normal Free Seminary. Tenth Edition'; with Plates and Woodcuts. Post 8vo. price 6.

Dr. Sutherland's Journal of a

Voyage iu Baffin's Bay and Barrow's Straits, in the Years ISoo and 1851, performed hy H. M. Ships Lady Franklin and Sophia under the command of Mr. William Penny, in search of the Missing-Crews of H. M. Ships JirekS and Terror. with Charts and Illustrations. 2 vols, post 8vo. price 28.

Tate. On the Strength of Materials; containingvarious orii,"inal and useful Kormulpe, specially applied to Tuhular Bridges, Wrought Iron and Cast Iron Beams, etc. By Thomas Tate, F. R. A. S. Svo. price 6. 6rf.

Taylor. Loyola: and Jesuitism in its Rudiments. By Isvac Taylok-Poet Svo. with a Medallion, price 10. 6rf.

Taylor.-Wesleyandmethodism.

By Is VAC Taylor. Post Svo. with a Portrait, price 10. Qd.

Theologia Germanica which setteth forth many fair lineaments of Divine Truth, and saith very lofty and lovely niings touching a Perfect Life. Trans lated by Susanna Winkworth: "With a Preface bv the Rev. Charles Kinosley; and a Letter by Chevalier Bunsen. Fcp. 8vo. price 6.

Thirl wall. The History of

Greece. By the Right Rev. the Lord Bishop of St. David's (the Rev. Connop Thirlwall). An improved Library Edition; with Maps. 8 vols. Svo. price A. 16.

Also, an Edition in 8 vols. fcp. Svo. with Vignette Titles, price 28.

Thomson (The Rev. W.) An Outline of the Liws of Thought: Being a Treatise on Pure and Applied Logic. By the Rev. W. Thomsox, M. A. Fellow and Tutor of Queen's College, Oxford. Third Edition, enlarged. Fcp. Spo. price 7. 6rf.

Thomson's Tables of Interest, at Three, Four, Four-and-a-half, and Five per Cent., from One Pound to Ten Thousand, and from 1 to 3(i5 Days, in a regular progression of Single Days; with Interest at all the above Rates, from One totwelve Months, and from One to Ten Years. Also, numerous other Tables of?"xchani; e8, Time, and Discounts. New Edition. 12mo. 8s.

Thomson's Seasons. Edited by

Bolton Cornty, Esq. Illustrated with Seventy-seven fine Wood Engravings from Designs by Members of the Etchingclub. Square crown Svo. price 21. cloth; or, 36. bound In morocco.

Thornton. Zohrab; or, a Mid- summer Day's Dream: And other Poems. By-wilLiaMT. TiioRNTON. Fcp. Svo.2.6rf.

Todd (Charles). A Series of

Tables of the Area and Circumference of Circles; the Solidity and Superficies of Spheres; the Area and Length of the Diagonal of Squares; and the Specific Gravity of Bodies, etc. By Charles Todd, Engineer. The Second Edition, improved iind extended. Post Svo. price 6h,

The Thumb Bible; or, Verbum

Sempitcrnum. By J. Taylor. Being an Epitome of the Old and New Testaments in English Verse. Reprinted from the Edition, of 1693, bound and clasped. In 64md. price Eighteenpence.

Townsend. The Lives of Twelve

Eminent Judges of the Last and of the Present Century. By W. C. Towsen0, Esq., M. A., Q. C. 2 vols. Svo. price 28.

Townsend. Modern State Trials, revised and illustrated with Esaajs and Notes. By W. C. Townsend, Esq., M. A. Q. C. 2 vols, Svo. price 3U.

Sharon Turner's Sacred History of the worid, attempted to be Philosophically considered, in a Series of Letters to a Son. New Edition, revised by the Author's Son, the Rev. S. Turner. 3 vols, post Svo. price 31. 6rf.

In course of Publication in Volumes at Hau-a-Crown, and in Parts price One Shilling each. Compriiing books of valuable information and acknowledged merit, in a form adapted for reading while Travelling, and also of a character that will render them worthy of preservation.

Vol. I. MACAULAY'S ESSAYS on WARREN HASTINGS and LORD CLIVE. 2 6 II. ESSAYS on PITT CHATHAM, RANKE GLADSTONE 2 6 III. LAING'S RESIDENCE in NORWAY 2 6 IV. PFEIFFER'S VOYAGE ROUND the WORLD 2 6
V. EOTHEN; or, TRACES of TRAVEL from the EAST 2 6
VI. MAC. ULAY'S ESSAYS on ADDISON, WALPOLE, and LORD BACON 2 6
VII. HUC'S TRAVELS IN TARTARY, etc 2 6
VIII. THOMAS HOLCROFT'S MEMOIRS 2 6 IX. WERNE'S AFRICAN WANDERINGS 2 6
X. Mrs. JAMESON'S SKETCHES in CANADA 2 6
Xr. JERRMANN'S PICTURES from ST. PETERSBURG 2 6
XII. The Rev. G. R. GLEIG'S LEIPSIC CAMPAIGN 2 6
XIII. HUGHES'S AUSTRALIAN COLONIES 2 6
XIV. SIR EDWARD SEAWARD'S NARRATIVE 2 6
XV. ALEXANDRE DUMAS' MEMOIRS of a MAITRE-D'ARMES 2 6
XVI. OUR COAL-FIELDS and OUR COAL PITS 2 6
XVII. M'CULLOCH'S LONDON; and GIRONIERE'S PHILIPPINES 2 6
XVHI. SIR ROGER DE COVERLEY; and SOUTHEY'S LOVE STORY 2 6
XIX. LORD CARLISLE'S LECTURES AND ADDRESSES j and, JEFFREY'S ESSAYS on SWIFT and RICHARDSON. "
XX. HOPE'S BIBLE in BRITTANY and CHASE in BRITTANY 2 6
XXI. THE ELECTRIC TELEGRAPH; and NATURAL HISTORY of CREATION 2 fi
XXII. MEMOlrof DUKE of WELLINGTON; and LIFE of MARSHAL TURENNE 2 6
XXIII. RANKE'S FERDINAND and MAXIMILIAN; and TURKEYl- and CHRISTENDOM
XXIV. BARROW'S CONTINENTAL TOUR; and FERGUSON'SI, SWISS MEN and SWISS MOUNTAINS J
XXV. SOUVESTRR'S ATTIC PHILOSOPHER in PARIS andl WORKING MAN'S CONFESSIONS '
XXVI. MACAULAY'S ESSAYS on LORD BYRON, and the COMIC DRAMAO,, TISTS; and his SPEECHES on PARLIAMENTARY REFORM J"
XXVII. SHIRLEY BROOKS'S RUSSIANS of the SOUTH; and.
Dit. KEMP'S INDICATIONS of INSTINCT "
XXVIII. LANMAN'S ADVENTURES in the WILDS of NORTH AMERICA 2 6
XXIX. De CUSTINES RUSSIA, Abridged 3 6
XXX. SELECTION'S from SYDNEY SMITH'S WRITINGS, Vol. 1 2 6
XXXI. BODENSTEDT and WAGNER'S SCHAMYL; and M'CULOLOCH'S RUSSIA and TURKEY
XXXII. LAING'S NOTES of a TRAVELLER, First Series 2 C
XXXIII. DURRIEU'S MOROCCO; and an ESSAY on MORMONISM 2 C
Sharon Turner's History of England duriug the Middle Ages: Comprising the Reigns from the Normau Conquest to the Accession of Henry VIII. Fifth Edition, revised by the Rev. S. Tcbneb. 4 vols. 8vo. price 50a.
Sharon Turner's History of the

Anglo-Saxons, from the Earliest Period to the Norman Conquest. The Seventh Edition, revised by the Rev. S. Turneb. 3 vols. 8vo. price 36s.

Dr. Turton'smanual ofthe Land and Freshwater Shells of the British Islands. New Edition with considerable Additions; by John Edward Gbvy. With Woodcuts, and 12 coloured Plates. Post 8vo. price los.

Dr. Ure's Dictionary of Arts,

Manufactures and Mines: Containing a clear Exposition of their Principles and Practice. The Fourth Edition, much enlarged and corrected throughout; with all the Information comprised in the Supplement of Recent Improvements brought down to the Present Time, and incorporated in the Dictionary. Most of the Articles being entirely re-written, and many New Articles now first added. With nearly 1,600 Woodcuts. 2 vols. Svo. price 60s.

Waterton. Essays on Natural

History, chiefly Ornithology. By C. Waterton, Esq. With an Autobiography of the Author and Views of Walton Mall. New and cheaper Edition, 2 vols. fcp. Svo. IDs. Separatelv: Vol. I. First Series), OS. 6(. Vol. U. (Second Series), 4s. 6rf.

Alaric Watts's Lyrics of the

Heart, and other Poems. With 41 highly-6nished Line Engravings, executed expressly for the work by the most eminent Painters and Engravers. Square crown Svo. price 31. 6rf. boards, or 45s. bound in morocco; Proof Impressions, 63s. boards.

Webster and Parkes's Ency- clopaediaof Domestic Economy; Comprising such subjects as are most immediately connected with Housekeeping; As, The Construction of Domestic Edifices, with the Modes of Warming, Ventilating, and Lighting them A Description of the vari ous Articles of Furniture, with the Nature of their Materials Duties of Servants, etc. New Edition; with nearly 1,000 Woodcuts, Svo. price 50s.

Wheeler. The Geography of

Herodotus Developed, Explained, and Illustrated from Modern Researches and Discoveries. By J. Taibots Wheeler, F. R. G S. Svo. with Maps and Plans.

Nearly ready.

Willich's Popular Tables for ascertaining the Value of Lifehold, Leasehold, and Church Property, Renewal Fines, etc. Third Edition, with additional Tables of Natural or Hyperbolic Logarithms, Trigonometry, Astronomy, Geography, etc. Post Svo. price 9s.

Lady Willoughby's Diary (1635 to 1663). Printed, ornamented, and bound in the style of the Period to which The Diary refers. New Edition; in Two Parts, Square fcp. Svo. price 8s. each, boards; or, bound in morocco, 18s. each.

Wilmot's Abridgment of Black- stone's Commentaries on the Laws of England, intended for the use of Young Persons, and comprised in a series of Letters from a Father to his Daughter. A New Edition, corrected and brought down to the Present Day, by Sir John E. Eabdley Wii-MOT, Bart., Barrister at-Law, Recorder of Warwick. 12mo. price 6s. 6rf.

Yonge. A New English-Greek

Lexicon: Containing all the Greek Words used by Writers of good Authority. By C. D. Yonoe,. B. A. Post 4to. price 21s.

Yonge's New Latin Gradus:

Containing every Word used by the Poets of good Authority. By Authority and for the Use of Eton, Westminster, Winchester, Harrow, Charterhouse, and Rugby Schools; King's College, London; and Marlborough College. Third Edition, carefully revised and corrected. Post Svo. price 9s.

Youatt. The Horse. By Wil-LiaM YODATT. With atrcatisc of Draught. A New Edition; with numerous Wood Engravings from Designs by William Harvey. (Messrs. Longman and Co."s Edition should be ordered). Svo. price 10s.

Youatt. The Dog. By William YouaTT. A New Edition; with numerous Engravings from Designs by William Harvey. Svo. 65.

Zvimpt's Larger Grammar of the Latin Language. Translated and adapted for the use of the English Students, by Dr. L. SchMitz, F. R. S. E., Rector of the High School of Edinburgh: With numerous Additions and Corrections by the Author and Translator. The Third Edition, thoroughly revised; with an Index, Svo. pricie 14a.

September, 1854.

London: Printed by M. Mason, Ivy Lane, Paternoster Kow.

THE LIBRARY

UNIVERSITY OF CALIEORNIA

Santa Barbara Goleta, California

THIS BOOK IS DUE ON THE LAST DATE STAMPED BELOW.

. ATTA. E FOE i0 i-8,"60(B2594s4)476

OUKO 9yjl 4 fl ESTLrysi:".

-Si' '-vr

Lightning Source UK Ltd.
Milton Keynes UK
UKOW050635111111

181873UK00003B/8/P

9 781152 627215